**THE
FADING
AMERICAN
NEWSPAPER**

GLOUCESTER, MASS.

PETER SMITH

1964

THE
FADING
AMERICAN
NEWSPAPER

BY CARL E. LINDSTROM

COPYRIGHT © 1960 BY CARL E. LINDSTROM
ALL RIGHTS RESERVED
PRINTED IN THE UNITED STATES OF AMERICA

REPRINTED 1964 BY PERMISSION OF DOUBLEDAY & COMPANY, INC.

CONTENTS

Introduction

THE MIGRATION OF JOURNALISM	7
1	
THE MIGRANT	13
2	
THE CLOCK	22
3	
ETHICS, THE PRESS, AND ITS PUBLIC	36
4	
THE EDITORIAL PAGE	58
5	
THE FORGOTTEN UNCOMMON MAN	69
6	
PRESS & STEAM ENGINE: $900	81
7	
CHAINS	87
8	
COLOR AND OTHER CUL-DE-SACS	108

9
MONOPOLY 114

10
JASON AND THE DRAGON'S TEETH 130

11
THE NEWS FUNCTION 142

12
"AS LOCAL AS THE TOWN PUMP" 153

13
REVIEWING VERSUS CRITICAL WRITING IN THE DAILY PRESS 166

14
THE NATURE OF CRITICISM 187

15
WORN-OUT TOOLS 199

16
SCIENCE AND JOURNALISM'S INQUIRIES 216

17
THE BEATS 228

18
PUBLIC RELATIONS 235

19
JOURNALISM AND THE ENGLISH LANGUAGE 245

20
THE RELIEF CORPS 251

Appendix I

A STUDY OF CONTENT 261

Appendix II

SYLLABUS FOR USE IN STUDY OF NEWSPAPER CONTENT 273

Appendix III

CODE OF ETHICS OR CANONS OF JOURNALISM 281

Index 285

INTRODUCTION:
THE MIGRATION
OF JOURNALISM

JOURNALISM IS A GOOD WORD. BUT once it was tossed into the snowdrift by newspaperdom and told not to darken the door again. It got around out in the world, prospered, kept excellent company, and developed new interests.

You can speak of a journalist today and refer to a man who never saw the inside of a daily newspaper office. The city room isn't big enough to enclose all of journalism. Even if the word and its true meaning had never existed it would now be necessary to coin an expression to cover the vast area embraced by the business of keeping people informed. The newspaper cannot have its unwanted child back; this robust offspring has migrated.

The daily press does not yet realize this. Its reactions continue to be what they were in the old era; habit thinking is strong. The hostility of publishers and editors to the report of the Hutchins Commission touched an old nerve and the reaction was reflexive.

The Commission was created to study the performance, functions, and responsibilities of the major mediums of mass communication, specifically newspapers, radio, motion pictures, magazines, and books — television not being a popular factor when the Commission began its studies early in the 1940's. It was instituted under a grant of funds from Time, Incorporated, and the Encyclopaedia Britannica, which were administered by the University of Chicago, whose Chancellor, Robert M. Hutchins, was chairman of the Commission.

The principal report appeared in the spring of 1947 but during the progress of the work the Commission sponsored and published no less than seven other works. The general report, entitled *A Free and Responsible Press*, was received irritably by the daily press, when it was noticed at all. The ground for complaint was that there was not on the Commission a single newspaper man — editor, writer, or publisher. Besides the chairman, who gave the Commission its name, the roster was: John M. Clark, professor of economics, Columbia University; John Dickinson, professor of law, University of Pennsylvania; William E. Hocking, professor of philosophy, Harvard University; Harold D. Lasswell, professor of law, Yale University; Archibald MacLeish, poet and former Assistant Secretary of State; Charles E. Merriam, professor of political science, University of Chicago; Reinhold Niebuhr, professor of ethics and philosophy of religion, Union Theological Seminary; Robert Redfield, professor of anthropology, University of Chicago; Beardsley Ruml, Chairman, Federal Reserve Bank of New York; Arthur M. Schlesinger, professor of history, Harvard University; George N. Shuster, President, Hunter College. There were four foreign advisers.

It is difficult to believe that the report's critics were deeply bothered by the absence of newspaper men, although that's what they said; they didn't really object to

Dr. Hutchins' advocacy of an endowed newspaper because they knew there was almost no chance of its coming about; their declaration that the Commission advocated government control was the best evidence that few if any of them read the report. The real reason they gagged on the finding was that it lumped radio, films, and all other mediums of communication under the heading of journalism. That made "journalism" almost a dirty word.

But for them only. Its use now is necessary to cover a territory of which the daily newspaper is only a part. "Press" no longer has special significance. Electronic and film transmission of news, even new printing methods, are leaving it behind and it is entirely possible in the not so remote future that it will go the way of the street car.

News has found fresh channels. There is the written word in periodicals, weekly and monthly; even books report with impact. News is vocalized in broadcasts and animated in films. As journalism migrates into new areas of communication, its practitioners, too, are on the move. The commerce in information flourishes and quickens its tempo, new skills are developed, and the major problem for the newspaper journalist is to keep his readers from migrating, too.

THE
FADING
AMERICAN
NEWSPAPER

1

THE MIGRANT

A MAN NO LONGER NEEDS TO READ A DAILY newspaper in order to be well-informed. Conversely, no single newspaper, with two or three brilliant exceptions, will bring an educated man anything like all the news he needs to know of his city, the nation, and the world.

This is a new condition of journalistic affairs for which the newspaper industry is answerable in its failure to respond intelligently to competitive communication mediums and in its willingness to let newspapers become a business and little more. Even as a business, the press has failed to do what every industry must do to survive — mobilize brains and money for research. The result of this neglect has been its capture in a cost spiral which threatens its freedom if not its very existence. It has resorted to merger and suspension to a degree which invites regulation as a utility. In its hunger for circulation it has sought status as a mass medium to the point where it is a hollow attempt to be all things to all men. It has scorned competition as an evil, and cultivated monopoly as a virtue. While claiming a holy mission with constitutional protection, it has left great vacuums of journalistic obligation into which competing mediums have moved with impunity and public acceptance. Today journalism is on the move at an ever-accelerating rate with the daily press showing no apparent concern. This indifference is in accord with its incapacity for relentless self-examination. In this vacant place self-delusion has built itself a nest.

The exceptional newspapers are so few and so weighted geographically as to be conspicuous to the point of irritation. John S. Knight, who is not only an astute publisher, but a perceptive and responsible editor, complained before a meeting of the American Society of Newspaper Editors: "I get a little weary of the proprietary attitude that is taken by a few editors on the eastern seaboard who tend to think that the rest of us are uninformed, illiterate people, who really care very little about what goes on!"

He was talking about the New York *Times,* which was under discussion, but since he pluralized the remark, he might have been thinking also of the New York *Herald Tribune,* the *Christian Science Monitor,* and the *Wall Street Journal.*

As a resident of Michigan, I had to wait for the New York *Times* in order to get the text of Eisenhower's address on the night of March 16, 1959. The President's speech on the Berlin situation called for a firm stand at the approaching Geneva summit meeting. It had been described in advance as one of the most important of his career. While there is but one morning newspaper in the entire state of Michigan, the Detroit *Free Press,* this paper did not publish the text of the president's address but ran instead only the digest of it by the Associated Press. It was the New York *Herald Tribune* that brought the first intelligible account of action by the House of Delegates of the American Bar Association looking toward revision of the Smith Act. The Associated Press account got widest use across the country but was so meager and ambiguous as to leave the impression that the lawyers had made an attack on the Supreme Court. Most newspapers also contented themselves with press association digests of the dramatic Lincoln tribute delivered by Carl Sandburg before an awed joint session of Congress on the twelfth of February. One turned to the New York *Times* for the full text. For the best and most detailed non-textual account of that historic event one had to look abroad to the *Manchester Guardian*.

But this is not a critique of exceptional newspapers; it is a commentary on the prevailing character of the American press.

Journalism is an expanding universe; at the same time, daily newspapers are rapidly shrinking in number and scope. Members of the Associated Press Managing Editors Association were undisturbed by the prediction of Sam Ragan, then Managing Editor of the Raleigh, North Carolina, *News & Observer*, that there would be fewer newspapers in the future, entirely content with his assurance that the survivors would thereby be better. Just as unquestioning were the ranks of the American Society of Newspaper Editors when the crystal ball of Norman Chandler, publisher of the Los Angeles *Times*, produced the same sinister reading for the big metropolitan newspapers — again with a better living standard promised for the hardy few. For this kind of reasoning both algebra and logic have answers in the back of the book, saying that perfection awaits the day when death and amalgam leave but one newspaper in America!

Publishers and editors who deplore the movement of journalism students into careers other than newspaper work might try to put themselves in the situation of the graduates, many of them married, some with master's degrees and children. What would such a man, after hearing leaders in the profession predict fewer and fewer newspapers, expect his wife to advise him when the time came to choose a job?

There is another condition against which we must assess the present and speculate about the future. Fifty years ago if a city of any size whatsoever found itself without a daily newspaper for even a few days there is no doubt that something like panic would quickly have developed in soil so fertile for the propagation of rumor.

We have in recent years had the spectacle of major cities without daily newspapers for periods as long as six months. There was inconvenience for the readers and the merchants lost money — but there was nothing like fear; and that was because citizens, by radio if by no other means, could still discern the broad outlines of what was going on. Newspaper people took to their hearts evidence that people *did* want newspapers because they were willing to pay premium prices for those from neighboring cities. Editors chose not to consider the uncomfortable likelihood that people were buying mostly familiar pabulum from these visiting journals — comics, crossword puzzles, astrologers, and other syndicated oracles. These seem to be worth the money one pays for the whole package. But the air waves are not to be underestimated. New York's Mayor Fiorello LaGuardia once resourcefully showed the way by reading cartoon continuities over the air, and radio has since done it again in emergencies. It is difficult for the broadcasters to take over such detailed news coverage as, for instance, obituaries, but in essence the citizenry is kept generally informed. They had, during strikes preventing newspaper publication, almost as much national and foreign news from radio as they get every day from the press.

This was all true before television. Now, visually, they may have in addition the spectacle of a queen's coronation, the election of a Pope, the fantastic mob scenes of national conventions, the occasionally sinister drama of Congressional investigations, and much besides. The President addresses us "live" and in full. The daily journals seldom print or consider as urgent news the text of a presidential message.

One reason is that the newspaper's have been filled up. During the past decade and a half, the cry in newspaper conclaves has been for more *interpretation*. It is not enough to print the facts; the press must tell what the facts mean. Why all this? Simply because the news weekly magazines made the discovery long ago, and in their own way filled a need. They flourished phenomenally and are so eminently successful today that several can prosper without visible hurt to each other. With at first glance little to distinguish them in approach, manner, or scope, they have found peaceful coexistence possible, while it is rapidly becoming impossible for two daily newspapers to live in the same territory.

If newspapers learned no lesson from the success of the news weeklies, other periodicals did. The *Saturday Evening Post*, which thirty years ago was distinguished for its fiction, has founded its present continued success upon solid journalism.

Curiously, journalism (the recorder of change) has feared change, as if it meant death. The greatest threat journalism ever faced was the invention of the printing press. Every town crier, every king's herald, every village gossip thought that he was out of a job. But the crying and the heralding and the gossiping went right on. Today in many New England towns and villages, the bulletin board still stands in front of the town hall and its use is still legally required for the posting of the call to meeting and the agenda. The gossip-monger has prospered, and often in print.

In modern history, journalism has been identified with the press, particularly the daily press. The printing mechanism has been embalmed in the Constitution's First Amendment, which protects the free dissemination of information. It takes no constitutional lawyer to construe the Bill of Rights as protecting the untrammeled safe passage of news reproduced by whatever means. Thus the word press has already taken on a metonymical sense: the part for the whole.

The printing press is on the way to obsolescence; yet journalism marches on. The daily newspaperman is not greatly concerned, except in his uneasy intuition that something is drifting away. This concern is not sufficient to inspire action in a vigorous enough fashion to enable him to continue reporting history while it is in ferment.

Both capital and labor have resisted invention: labor in the delusion that new processes create idle hands; capital through fear of competition. Newspaper capital, in pursuit of economic security, has in many instances gone to bed with and even married technology in the form of radio and television stations. These, however, have not been employed to advance in a new medium but to avoid the defection of advertising revenue. The opportunity to follow, grow with, and affect the flow of news through allied channels has been almost completely missed.

With periodical publications moving into journalism by taking a wider perspective on the arc of events, and with electronics in on the act, the time factor in the newspaper office has shrunk, robbing newspapers of what was once their most dramatic element — speed. Newspapers cannot be the first to tell anybody anything any more. Before picking up the paper the public already knows who was elected, who won the fight, which statesman is dead, what plane has fallen where and with how many casualties. The electronic mediums have communicated the news virtually instantaneously, often using the newspaper's facilities. How much of the news? As much as one person would tell another conversationally. Only the details remain to be told.

Whether newspapers should have availed themselves of a more deliberate tempo by not attempting to beat the deadline seems to be academic; they haven't done it. They have left much to the magazines. Untold stories lie around in a state of neglect for others to pick up at leisure. A story is a story anytime and will wait for the proper and the best telling.

The newsroom persists in the hopeless battle of the "scoop." The unbeatable air waves are always there first with their meager most; but first. The irony lies there — the press has been hoist on its own petard. The broadcasters have lit the fuse and blown up the newspaper's explosive before that paper could possibly be delivered. As electronic parasites, the verbal newsmen until recently have done little news-gathering. At first they had no reporters; but they are now doing more and more and have recruited news staffs. Once the announcer sat at a microphone with the newspaper just off the press before him and read it verbatim, hours before the journal landed on the householder's front porch. Now he reads canned or slightly rewritten takes from the wire services.

Has the daily press then done nothing to help itself?

It has rationalized problems rather than solved them. Besides the competition in communication, there has been the pressure of costs, the trend to selling refinements such as color printing, the paralysis of mobility due to traffic glut, and the loss, to other attractions, of the reader's time and attention.

Something has been done about all these challenges but the solutions have been partial, separate, and sporadic. Newspapers have only two major problems. One is to stay in journalism; the other to stay in business.

In this situation the rising dissatisfaction of the client is easily understood. At a time when newspapers are trying more than ever to please everybody, they are losing acceptance. At a time when journalistic ethics and a sense of responsibility are at a high mark, they are losing prestige and influence.

Publishers close their eyes to this new relationship with the public and, in the dark of their unwillingness to see, point a vague finger at circulation figures. They do not want to hear or see that population figures are rising at a much greater rate than circulation. To buy does not necessarily mean acceptance. A man may buy to see how his eight shares of A. T. and T. are doing and feel he gets his money's worth, while completely rejecting the rest of the paper, including the editorial page.

The battle has been a desultory rear-guard action. The publisher has found himself in the entertainment business, but left far behind; his slight research has tangled with color, a contest he cannot possibly win; he has surrendered the technological skirmish to labor.

Bravely he has retreated to the citadel of local news, a noble fortress which may save his life — yet awhile; but this at the cost of having made the American press the most parochial in the world, at a time when the United States is in a position of free world leadership. "There's no readership for foreign news," he will tell you, and he is right. Yet the editor might well be asked if that isn't his fault.

When the situation reaches the point where one looks to see whose fault it is, something disastrous has already happened. Perhaps it is not too late, but there is plain evidence that the subscriber is folding his tent for the purpose of stealing away.

The newspaper reader is about to become the displaced person of our day.

2

THE CLOCK

FEW FIGURES OF SPEECH CAN BE found which better dramatize the plight of the daily newspaper with respect to time than Poe's fantastic story *The Pit and the The Pendulum*. If you read it in early, impressionable years, its trauma persists through a lifetime: the scimitar-blade attached to a pendulum, oscillated by a clock mechanism and swinging ever nearer its victim, who is bound to the edge of a bottomless pit.

The newsman is caught by the cutting edge of creeping deadlines and lashed to the newsroom clock in the pit of circulation unlimited, a cavernous maw nearly filled with ads, gewgaws, divertissement, and fiction. The pit must be further filled with the issue of reporters' typewriters, with news "of the moment," or store-bought features.

The non-advertising content of a paper is called the news hole — ample enough usually, even at the short end of a 35–65 ratio to advertising. But most often there is too little genuine topsoil to fill the hole. It is a situation that calls for, but doesn't always get, "clean fill only."

The press, which once needed the newsroom clock, has

become its prisoner. This clock has no tick but hitches along silently, inexorably, and much faster than the clocks that other people go by. Its very silence is sinister. It is the cause of hypertension reporting, hypertension writing, and a tense and captious relationship between newspapers and their readers.

Even without the swinging scimitar, the news-room clock is crowding newspapers farther toward the narrow ledge of journalism to which they cling and into show business, circulation gimmicks, and advertisers' publicity.

The news-room clock is the master of all — and the master excuse. There is always the deadline; there is never time to do the job as well as it ought to be done. If there are typographical errors, misspelled names, or missing facts, it is always because the creation of the modern daily newspaper is a so-called "miracle" of speed, and the "wonder" of it all is that there are not more mistakes. Thus the press takes refuge behind old miracles and tired wonders. Every job must be done by the deadline, and the count-down mesmerizes reporters and editors alike.

The news-gathering day, especially for afternoon dailies, is eroding in four directions: first, news sources are now starting work ever later in the day — capitol, city hall, courts, banks, and business offices; second, there are problems of distribution, mainly the immobility of the automobile in traffic; third, there is the delusion that the paper must get to the reader's doorstep ever sooner — before the householders, big and little, turn the television switch; finally, the production job is increasingly complicated by obsolescent machinery and labor's intransigence.

It is not merely an illusion that other people's clocks run slower than the newsroom's. The working day is being shortened from both ends. The brief-case contingent in banks, insurance offices, and factories is rarely in desk position to be interviewed much before ten in the morning; civil servants arrive even later. There is a tendency to clip the day from the beginning; there seems to be prestige and importance to a late start in business. The extended lunch hour is becoming an American institution, and coffee breaks are not limited to the lower echelon. People are harder to reach than ever before; they like less and less to be disturbed at their homes by news-gatherers' inquiries. Some city managers have a rule against answering such queries; it isn't businesslike. But you could always reach the (political) mayor.

Even recognizing that traffic paralysis has shortened the news-gathering day and complicated the distribution job, to hold that the newspaper must arrive at the doorstep before the television set is turned on is to invite sheer frustration. It is surrender to admit that a news medium, providing some entertainment as well, cannot compete with an amusement medium which also provides some news. There is a dismal lack of competitive spirit in the assumption that television is *per se* more attractive than the newspaper; that the subscriber will look at his paper only when there is nothing to be seen on the screen.

Cost and production pressures, too, speed up the newsroom clock. The average newspaper, big and little, has been grossing revenues in record figures. Yet it must begin each new year faced with the necessity of grossing even more simply to stay in business. Papers must make more money because it costs more money to make more money; papers must get fatter because they must carry more fat to live. This means more pages, to be locked up sooner, with less spot news; the deadline must be moved forward because of the physical job of creating a larger paper.

Under this four-way abrasion, the news-room clock is moving four times as fast as ever before. Newspapers cannot turn back the clock, nor tell news sources when to come to work. They can't talk to a traffic jam.

The magazines have installed a slower clock. Their deadline may be just as inexorable, the production and distribution job may be even more of a problem in logistics but, in the relationship to instant news, time waits for them.

As an elementary step, newspapers could prepare themselves better. They could meet the story halfway. Most news casts its shadow in advance. The apparently "lucky breaks" that the big weeklies get are not entirely fortuitous. Their editors keep their eyes on the curve of the high fly and get under the ball.

Competitors have done much that newspaper editors with open minds might learn. The broadcasters have discovered things about people's interests; the news weeklies have demonstrated a new and readable style; the picture magazines show the power of photodrama. But the chief lesson taught by the competitors is that newspapers do have the time — must make the time, if they would excel. The news-room clock is a hallucination; the story will wait.

Denver was so full of reporters when President Eisenhower's heart attack became known that it was impossible to get a hotel room. They remained there for weeks faithfully transmitting the official bulletins and prognoses, as well as the business transacted by the President's aides and cabinet members. No news, in the ordinary sense of the word, was missed.

It was weeks later that Fletcher Knebel wrote for *Look* magazine an article of some seven thousand words detailing every minor incident. These included the movements and remarks of all and sundry connected with the President's entourage and medical staff — at what minute the President was seized, where his secretary was at the time, what Mrs. Eisenhower said and did, what the President had had for dinner, who said what to whom when. It was a deluge of trivia, in a way, but so gracefully and dramatically organized that the reader who began the article was bound to finish it.

Traditionally such space would have been allotted only to a presidential message on the state of the nation. At that time the President's illness *was* the state of the nation and every newspaper should have been willing to give it the space, had it anything like a reporter of Knebel's competence. This story waited for the telling.

Newspapers have thrown away their best opportunities by superficial reporting; by losing details in the rush, failing to follow up, and straining for a new lead; by asking too few questions at source and answering too few that the reader wants to ask. They are rushing through ripe wheatfields grabbing handfuls of grain — and leaving the big harvest for the gleaners.

Love of the aphorism may have conditioned the thinking of the men who run newspapers. General Nathan B. Forrest said in homely but trenchant language that the battle goes to him who "gets thar fustest with the mostest." Military history doesn't always agree with him. Napoleon defeated Blücher soundly but not completely. It remained only to follow up the little matter, and this job he gave to Grouchy so that he himself could be in a position to settle with Wellington. It was in the cards that Napoleon could do so because he seemed to have the means. Grouchy, however, ordinarily so able, but only able, moved indecisively. Then came the result — Waterloo.

The story will wait a long time for the right telling. The masterpiece of battle reporting of the Civil War waited until 1896, when Stephen Crane wrote the *Red Badge of Courage.* In 1898 Crane at Guantanamo wrote another news story:

> I heard somebody dying near me. He was dying hard. It took him a long time to die. He breathed as all noble machinery breathes when it is making its gallant strife against breaking, breaking. But he was going to break. He was going to break. It seemed to me, this breathing, the noise of a heroic pump which strives to subdue a mud which comes upon it in tons. The darkness was impenetrable. The man was lying in some depression within seven feet of me. Every wave, vibration, of his anguish beat upon my senses. He was long past groaning. There was only the bitter strife for air which pulsed out into the night in a clear penetrating whistle with intervals of terrible silence in which I held my own breath in the common unconscious aspiration to help. I thought this man would never die. I wanted him to die. Ultimately he died.
> At the moment the adjutant come bustling along erect amid the spitting bullets. I knew him by his voice.
> "Where's the doctor? There's some wounded men over there. Where's the doctor?"
> A man answered briskly: "Just died this minute, sir." It was as if he had said: "Just gone around the corner this minute, sir."

The story waited till 1900 to be told like that. It would have waited a hundred years.

The story of man's first powered flight in the heavier-than-air machine was offered to newspaper after newspaper, but all turned it down. Newsmen had covered Langley's failure when his machine plunged into the Potomac River but not one was present at the Wright's triumph. The story was first told in the Norfolk *Virginian Pilot*.

In the village of Mansfield, Connecticut, an eleven-year-old boy on a Saturday afternoon killed his brother with a rifle, and then proceeded to the farmhouse where he killed both his father and his mother — a collection of ugly, revolting facts waiting to be told intelligibly.

The boy starts down the road on his way to the sheriff to report what he has done, but the story hasn't broken yet because the boy turns around, goes back home, goes to bed, and sleeps through the night surrounded by a glut of incredible, stunning circumstances. The story is waiting. The next day at noon, while the church bells are ringing, the boy proceeds to a neighbor's house to recite in his own behalf a story he cannot comprehend.

The newsmen gather with the police. There are pictures and a flood of copy. These appear in the papers Monday morning and Monday evening and on subsequent days; that is the "follow-up." Every fact is related — all the five W's of who, what, why, where, when; all the details, gruesome and explanatory. The psychiatrists arrive and soon explain that the boy had been spanked by his father, which meant that he was discriminated against, and so he felt he was not wanted, hence . . .

But in the world are many spanked children who do not shoot their mothers. So perhaps the reader is not satisfied with the psychiatrists' explanation. Perhaps also the newspaper can find the whole story. But it will take time to dig it out and time to tell it.

In cities where there is more than one paper, whether competitive or under the same ownership, it is continually noted that people commenting on a story can seldom recall whether they have read it in one paper or the other. This can be frustrating to the reporter and to the city editor — bending their backs to get the news first to a customer who never remembers which paper won out in the scuffle. Experience encourages the belief that if one account is markedly superior, not necessarily in length but in quality, the reader is much more likely to remember in which paper he did read it.

Newspapers are quickly made, quickly read, quickly discarded. Time becomes a scanning eye that, no matter how searching and accurate, is focused only upon the flying moment. As newspaper life turns in its cycle, this eye, like the beam on the revolving telepicture drum, is just as blind to message circuits left behind as it is of those to come. Meaning appears only when the developing tank produces not outlines but the whole picture.

The time element is the adhesive with which the news writer connects the story. It need not be the only one. To lose control of it is to get tangled in the event. Writer and reader are confused. Under the formula, what happens last is told first and thus made to seem the most important.

Let us apply conventional news technique to the following hypothetical story:

A robber holds up a bank and after taking $20,000 speeds away in a car. He crashes into a tree. Seriously injured, he is taken to the hospital.

Most readers would probably think of this in chronological sequence. Except for the feeling of security that a criminal is under guard, the fact that the robber is in a hospital bed is, to the reader, a static, unexciting circumstance. The chase through the streets might step up his pulse a beat or two. The robbery would probably be his central interest, depending upon how big $20,000 looks to him, and it is this that he probably first tells his neighbor.

Not so the news formula. Time is often reversed in this fashion:

1. A robber is in the hospital.
2. He drove his car into a tree and was injured.
3. He robbed a bank of $20,000.

All these factors would, of course, be compressed into the first paragraph, and in expanding the story the sequence would be maintained, especially if an earlier newspaper first had the essential fact of the robbery. There must always be the new and most-recent angle, if only the temperature of the patient. The straining for immediacy, the just-now breathlessness, is often acute, and just as often disruptive of narrative cogency.

True, in digging for the ruins of ancient Troy, the archeologist found recent history in the topmost layer of centuries-old rubble; the record of what happened just before that in the second layer; and so on down. In the seventh layer Dr. Schliemann found the remains of the "topless towers of Ilium." History is not taught in reverse just because archaeologists have to dig it up that way. And they don't keep sifting the top layer.

The obsession for the new lead grows out of competitive pressure. No matter how complete an account has already been published, some fresh beginning must be found. Minutia will suffice; it need only be recent.

Radio and television have collapsed time values; television, through speaking and moving images, has frozen routine pictorial and printed communication in its tracks. What once was considered a high-speed reproducing process has become laborious; and distribution methods are now pedestrian. One-time skills have become old habits which now slow up the newspaper. Its job is still to hold the reader and it must find new ways if the old ones will not do.

Because the daily press is leaving stories half-told, other, slower mediums are finishing the job. The daily press never reported, for instance, more than a fraction of the story of the burning of the Bermuda liner *Morro Castle*. That remained for Thomas Gallagher, whose story was published by Rinehart & Company twenty-five years later. The *Morro Castle* story is only one of many losses, as the press goes on — intent upon trivial things that merely seem new.

Lyde Marland, widow of the former Governor Marland of Oklahoma who made a fortune of a hundred million dollars, disappeared six years ago. She is still missing. If newsmen are looking for her, or ever did, they lost a striking bit of journalism to John Kobler in the *Saturday Evening Post*.

Newspapers have rarely told completely the story of an airplane disaster. The facts are never known until the Civil Aeronautics Bureau has finished its investigation, which may take months or more than a year. When the report is made, however, parts of it are usually couched in plain, vivid English that would honor any reporter.

It took ten months to find out exactly what happened to an Italian Airlines DC–6B when it crashed at Idlewild on December 18, 1954. This job of journalism was to be found in the magazine *Aviation Week*, which carried the full text, "a yarn of lip-biting, squirming tension." Of the three wire services, one carried nothing at all on the report; a second serviced only a few local papers on Long Island; a third was satisfied to attribute the crash to "pilot fatigue."

Because there were survivors (though none of the crew

lived) and eyewitnesses, it was possible to obtain nonspeculative details. The report told of the liner's approach to the field in bad weather, of its being "laddered down" to landing position, not once or twice but three times, and still missing the approach. It circled the field for two hours before making the fourth attempt. In rain and fog even radar didn't succeed in getting the pilot to correct his drift. He was advised to maintain altitude but continued to descend. Orders were given sharply: "Your altitude is very, *very* low. Pull up!"

The angle of descent was increased momentarily and the controller thought the craft had begun a missed-approach procedure. The plane seemed to wobble. The passengers told of a sensation of an extremely sharp pullup; they had only fleeting glimpses of water and swamp area; gallery equipment spilled into the aisle.

The plane clipped a pier and took fire. The report was long and filled with technical terms but its official explicitness did not detract from a gripping narration.

The desegregation story is as thorny a challenge as the American press has ever faced. It is doubtful that with the best of intentions and efforts the job can be done to satisfy equally readers of both the northern and the southern press.

In the beginning, a few newspapers besides the metropolitan press sent their own reporters to the South. Since the Associated Press is a co-operative news-gathering organization and must rely chiefly on reports contributed by member papers, there was carping from both sides of the Mason-Dixon line. The New York *Times* characteristically dispatched a platoon of reporters to cover the entire South, and Grover Cleveland Hall of the Montgomery *Advertiser* appointed himself a one-man monitor of the northern press in its coverage of race incidents in its own back yard.

In the interest of objectively surveying press performance and gathering comprehensive news of the whole movement, the Southern School News Reporting Service was organized, with headquarters at Nashville, Tennessee. C. A. McKnight, at the time he was director of this service, said to the American Society of Newspaper Editors:

> 1. This is a bigger news story, and a more important news story than our treatment of it would indicate.
>
> 2. This story has received what I would call minimum coverage, and this minimum has all too often been unbalanced, and frequently distorted.

He made three other points:

> 1. It seems to me that many of our newspapers have done a fairly creditable job in reporting essential facts on developments in their immediate circulation areas, and to a lesser degree, within the borders of their states.
>
> 2. In my opinion, a good many newspapers, especially those within the region, have made a diligent effort to find space in their crowded pages for such wire stories as they happen to receive.
>
> 3. It is my impression that the editorial pages of the nation, by and large, have tried to argue convictions honestly and calmly, but that in too many instances the editorials on both sides of the issue reflect pre-established and over-simplified opinions more than they reflect current fact . . .

His observations were based on the daily clipping of fifty newspapers mainly but not exclusively published in seventeen southern and border states; and also on an extensive clipping service of news stories and editorials outside the South.

He went on:

> One of the built-in defects of our competitive newspapers and our competitive wire services . . . is the tendency to single out and to paramount the area of controversy, the area of conflict, the area of disagreement. It is a journalistic truism that "conflict is news," and that is simply an inversion of the old proverb that "no news is good news." Newspapers are written and edited by human beings, and it is in the nature of us that quiet, constructive and unspectacular developments do not stimulate the same quick interest that conflict, controversy and disagreement will create. But the net result of this tendency, insofar as the desegregation story is concerned, has been to create a doubly false impression in the minds of our readers.

This was in 1955, early in the desegregation movement. After that came Little Rock, which could not be said to have been reported with objectivity anywhere. Editorial comment in the northern press was appallingly self-righteous and uninformed.

In this story, as in many others, the excuse of the hurrying newsroom clock is of no validity. There is no time element in this vast movement; it will be going on for decades. But the daily press regularly loses interest because this crisis now has no deadline.

The press has made the clock a deadly enemy. This mesmerism is responsible for most newspaper costs, in terms of manpower, machinery, and communications. It is a habit that leaves its mark. Newspaper men think in terms of days and deadlines but events have no regard for either one or the other. It is an illusion that news is only *now*. Actually, many happenings that catch the headlines do not have their origin in a particular point of time.

The purists hold that it is incorrect to say that an event *transpires,* but that can be questioned. The landslide that crashed down the mountainside at 10:16 in the morning had its beginnings in the weeks, months, perhaps the years before, as erosion, moisture, and other factors prepared for a concert of circumstances. The railroad wreck had its origin in the careless inspection of a vital part a considerable time before the cars piled up and ten people were killed. Of a revolution, a romance, a medical discovery, or a great book, it can be said, without fighting the dictionary, that these things *transpire;* they do not occur. But somehow, like a collector impaling a butterfly, newspapers press the sharp point of time through the body of an event and then, what is the greater pity, too often go away and abandon the victim.

While there is little to be done about news while it is transpiring and before it happens, the press can certainly do more in covering the train of consequences that rides behind every news event. Beguiled by "nothing is so dead as yesterday's newspaper," they literally bury a story which seems to be all through happening but which has unfortunately not yet been told.

Perhaps the reader will have to wait a matter of weeks, but better tell the story late than not at all, or than sketchily and inaccurately. The good story *will wait* to be told. The author of the fourth gospel waited more than half a century before telling his story and then wrote it after three other reportorial geniuses had described substantially the same events.

That story, too, still goes on.

3

ETHICS,
THE PRESS,
AND ITS
PUBLIC

CHARACTERISTIC OF NEWSPAPERS, editors as well as publishers, is a pathological fear of criticism. This is the more astonishing since the press regards it as a duty to criticize everything and everybody — politicians, statesmen, artists, musicians, actors, authors, in fact anyone who offers services to the public — under the right of fair comment.

Certainly a degree of receptivity to criticism is an obligation of the warrant to criticize others, though the ratio is often as the beam is to the mote. The lack of capacity for self-criticism often condemns promising talents to mediocrity. The function of criticism is taken for granted by the press, and indeed that right resides in its protected freedom; but failure to exercise this freedom vigorously in relation to its own affairs mortgages its right to criticize others.

Is the press self-critical? There are those who think it is. Jenkin Lloyd Jones, editor of the Tulsa (Oklahoma) *Tribune* has written emphatically that newspaper editors are "great hair-shirt-wearers and hand-wringers." He declares that members of the American Society of Newspaper Editors, of which he is a former president, as well as members of the Associated Press Managing Editors Association and the National Conference of Editorial Writers, while often posing before the general public as infallible, shake off all smugness when they get together and "resemble groups of flagellantes whipping each other with thorns."

Why, then, have they not arrived at workable solutions to the problems that are making newspaper existence daily more precarious? Perhaps the fact that editors have pursued their self-examination behind closed convention doors has something to do with it.

Mr. Jones finds that the trouble with the newspaper business is that the editor is "perpetually being drowned in a sea of choice. There is only one way to make nails, four or five ways to bake a loaf of bread, and maybe 100 ways to stitch up a shirt. But there are a few hundred million ways to edit a 50–page newspaper."

Under the paralyzing influence of this "sea of choice" it appears that most editors have made very few choices and the result has been a country-wide array of mastheads crowning papers that bear a strikingly monotonous resemblance to each other.

The American Society of Newspaper Editors, has from time to time invited critical speakers to its conventions. It has winced under the thrusts, been stung and often had its head bloodied, but has been as willing to invite its critics to return as it has been unreconstructed by the assaults. This is not strange, because in the Society's membership are few owner-publishers who could do anything about suggested reforms, and an editor alone, no matter how invigorated by the steam chamber, goes back perforce to the same newspaper from which he had a holiday, checking the winter garment of repentance in Washington to await his return the following spring.

In one session a battery of no less than half a dozen critics fired their most devastating shots and escaped practically unscathed. In the early days of the Society, which was organized in 1922, Robert M. Hutchins delivered a keenly critical message, and when he was invited back again on the twenty-fifth anniversary of his first appearance, he gratefully responded with another dose of his withering urbanity. A. J. Liebling, author of "The Wayward Press," was heard; an American Newspaper Guild president was given his say; and Al Capp was allowed to defend his right to editorialize in comic strips.

The editors haven't liked it much, some not at all; but the Society has been willing to listen. It would be impossible to imagine the American Newspaper Publishers Association giving platform room to these speakers. The Associated Press Managing Editors Association has been chiefly concerned with the reports of its countless committees annually engaged in the so-called Continuing Study of all news moved on Associated Press wires and by mail, but in the decade or more of this survey the editors have learned to speak as Omar's pot did to the potter — "Gently, brother, gently pray!"

The A.S.N.E. represents the press at its best. It is a dedicated society; it sticks to its business pretty faithfully. It wastes less time on junkets than any other newspaper convention. It takes itself very seriously indeed. It is as undemocratic in the political business of electing directors and officers as any other professional society, but it means business. Its proceedings, faithfully recorded and printed since its inception, are a rich treasure, covering every phase of news and editorial problems.

The Society early in its history lost no time in drawing

up a code of ethics,* the essence of journalistic conscience and rectitude. The code emphasizes responsibility, fairness, and unselfish purpose; it stresses the need for absolute accuracy, not forgetting that headlines are often misleading. In the same breath with its defense of freedom of the press is maintained the right to discuss "whatever is not explicitly forbidden by law."

When the authors of these canons stoutly argued that a sharp demarcation should be made between news reports and expressions of opinion they probably did not foresee the vogue for "interpretive writing," nor the lengths to which it would go. In the solemn canon enjoining publication of news communications "from private sources without public notice of their source" they probably meant to make exceptions of "a high public official," a "departmental spokesman," and these other mysterious anonyms holding public jobs. (It might be far more important to insist upon the identity of such sources than it is of the spokesmen for capital or labor, without whose names it would be difficult if not impossible to substantiate "their claims to value as news."

Like many another excellent code it has no faults except the power of enforcement — acknowledged in the seventh canon. For this enforcement power it substitutes the "hope that deliberate pandering to vicious instincts will encounter public disapproval or yield to the influence of a preponderant professional condemnation."

It is not easy to find the reasons, in a day when most newspapers cleave fairly closely to such a set of principles, why criticism is more vocal and persistent than perhaps at any other time in American newspaper history. It is obvious that newspaper morality was in earlier times so far below present standards as to be beyond

* See Appendix III.

comparison. Certainly all will agree, again to quote Jenkin Lloyd Jones, upon good riddance to the "scurrilous days of 19th century journalism in which editors blistered each other, censored out the arguments of opposition party leaders, and pumped up circulation by outrageous hoaxes. Gone is the old Hearstian formula of the early 20th century, the gee-whiz journalism filled with sensation and little else."

Even worse, from the ethical standpoint, was the journalism of the pamphleteers in colonial America, the irresponsible partisanship of the press kept by Jefferson and Hamilton to fight their philosophical battle over the kind of government the new nation was to have. Or Civil War journalism, which couldn't even get the laconic nobility of the Gettysburg speech into print without the most wretched distortion.

Fewer people criticized the press in those eras. The public respected newsprint, though theirs was the respect of fear. They respected it enough to imprison editors and burn down their properties. Journalism was dangerous and powerful. Today it is neither. Almost no one is afraid of the press, nor is there any reason to be. There is no hesitancy about criticizing the press and the usual ground for criticism is failure in that public service to which the press has addressed itself; namely, the function of providing information — or perhaps, better said, the failure to vouchsafe to the reader his freedom to choose the kind of newspaper he wants.

The colonial American and his descendants had that freedom. They were unconcerned about unscrupulous partisanship. They reckoned that was the nature of journalism and they expected the press to act as it did. Rather, they *insisted* upon that kind of press. The reader no more wanted an objective, neutral newspaper that carried water on both shoulders than does the reader today. A man simply bought and read the newspaper that was unscrupulous and partisan in support of his own opinions. His neighbor of a different political persuasion shopped around until he found a paper equally unscrupulous and partisan in thinking as *he* did. Nobody criticized the press as a whole for its very nature.

It is, however, not for its ethical principles that the press today is being criticized. There is not enough room there for complaint. The lady's virtue is not in question. She has neither been accused of going to bed indiscreetly; nor is there complaint because she would not. She is, instead, amoral.

There is no evidence that the citizen of today has any higher appreciation of ethics, integrity, patriotism, or civic responsibility than did his eighteenth- or nineteenth-century forebears, simply because a newspaper society happens to have devised a code of deportment. It can be ventured that he will put up with just as much deviation from journalistic righteousness if his newspapers will give him the mental exercise or, to change the figure, the whetstone for his opinions that self-governing civilized man wants and needs.

The American citizen today, no matter how many papers he buys, will with difficulty find two opinions about: fluoridation of the water supply, parent-teachers' associations, the city manager plan as the highest form of local government, supermarkets and frozen foods, the rearing of children, and many other of the eternal verities of our times.

Along with these paradoxes — increased morality with the loss of influence, and the demand for objectivity which the reader really doesn't want — we have others. The more advertising a newspaper gets, the more independent it is. While the public increasingly carps at newspapers, more millions are sold than ever.

There has been no editorial compunction about deliberately misquoting and misrepresenting the critics. Denigration by the press of the Hutchins Commission's report was couched on the assumption that few people read it. They certainly were not encouraged to do so by newspaper comments. Significantly, the failure to read and digest this study was most conspicuous among editors and newspaper proprietors who did not hesitate to attack what they thought the report contained. The psychosis among editors and publishers, which bordered on a persecution mania, was evidenced in the very frequent references to "our enemies," "those who would destroy," "foes of the press," and the utterance of the word "critics" with a certain venom. Often they synthesized this name-calling under the withering term "the professors" to describe the Commission.

In the early days of American Society of Newspaper Editors, Paul Bellamy of the Cleveland *Plain Dealer*, as chairman and sole member of the Committee on Integrity of the Press, reported to the Society that two instances of criticism had been answered. The first was an article in *Harper's Magazine* entitled "Sell the Papers," by an anonymous writer, to the effect that newspaper ethics had gone by the board and that newspapers had subordinated everything to circulation. Bellamy protested. The editor of *Harper's,* Thomas B. Wells, in some astonishment that the article had caused offense, replied that "among newspaper men this article has aroused more commendation than condemnation."

The other instance cited by Bellamy was a series of articles in the *Outlook* by Don Seitz, long of the New York *World*. The chairman did not report just what it was in the articles that caused offense but he added: "This is not a case of ignorant criticism. The articles represent the settled opinion of a veteran newspaper man whose experience certainly has been as wide as that of any member of this Society."

Bellamy wanted the one-man committee to be discharged but the membership wouldn't have it. Apparently the membership's idea of an Integrity Committee was a kind of a fire department to put out sparks of criticism. In its salad days the Society seemed nevertheless to be mesmerized by its critics and on occasion took a deep breath and invited a bevy of articulate fault-finders to address it. That was in 1928 when, at the April convention, the speakers were Clarence Darrow, Dr. Joseph Collins of New York, Strickland Gillilan, and pastor Dr. Ralph W. Sockman. The clergyman let the editors off without too many bruises. So did Gillilan. Dr. Collins attacked what he regarded as the newspaper's obsession with crime and publicity. He told the editors that they had a wonderful opportunity to shape public opinion.

"Of course," he said, "no people that are standardized and conventionalized can be a thinking people, and that is the reason why the sort of syndicate stuff that is furnished by newspapers goes down with the readers. . . . Individuality in journalism has been replaced by stereotypy and humor, by horror and insipidity."

Darrow hit the hardest. He rambled on in his characteristic salty fashion. His sallies caused considerable laughter and took the sting out of much that he said. A newspaper was a purely commercial enterprise, he commented. Newspapers didn't really own themselves but probably would be even worse if they did. It was a question not of how many readers a paper could get but what kind of advertising it could get. Advertisers got the cleverest writers to pick the public's pockets by writing false and alluring statements to induce people to buy things they didn't need and couldn't afford. People said they didn't believe what they read in the papers but, he said, that was the trouble — they really did.

Darrow talked seriously of crime reporting and put the editors right on the difference between English justice and that of the United States. The talk was so frequently punctuated by laughter that nobody really got hurt.

Silas Bent, author and newspaperman, had gone after the editors with vigor and no punches pulled. His summary:

"I submit that you have become enslaved in your stereotyped patterns of news which are based solely on emotion and not at all on intelligence. . . . You have betrayed and deceived your public."

To take at their word some of its founding members, the Society was started in order to organize rebuttal against critics. The late Donald J. Sterling, a past president, once wrote: "The American Society of Newspaper Editors was conceived not in inspiration but in irritation." Caspar S. Yost, another founder, then editor of the St. Louis *Post-Dispatch,* asked why editors couldn't be collectively organized to combat attacks on the press. "Why doesn't someone take the initiative? Why," he went on, "don't I do it?"

By the time the Society got started, however, its constitution declared that the purpose was "improvement of Journalism" rather than a defense against critics. But it kept listening. When Hutchins was given a second hearing in 1955, the Society had organized a task force for rebuttal comprising Jonathan Daniels of the Raleigh *News & Observer,* Frank Eyerly of the Des Moines *Register and Tribune,* and William Steven of the Minneapolis *Star and Tribune,* and this team was privileged to see Hutchins' manuscript before he took the rostrum.

The society's publication, the *Bulletin,* recently asked for an estimate of the press by a man who, if it is an injustice to call him average, can at least be said to represent the view of many businessmen. Blake Wilson, described as college-educated, a church member, service club member, and reader of his local paper, the New York *Times,* and half a dozen magazines, wrote:

> Despite their pretensions, newspaper people display a curious lack of objectivity on the subject of freedom of information. Such failure would be forgivable in normal mortals, but not in a group whose swagger about the public's rights implies gifts of discernment greater than those of the public itself.
>
> This lapse occurs when a newspaperman, angered by someone's attempt to keep a matter out of the paper, fails to recognize that he, although resembling a human himself, demands to be the arbiter of what goes in the paper. To an outsider this can appear to be equally as dangerous as censorship at the news source. In fact, it may be considered more so, for public officials are more subject to the checks and balances of bureaucratic and electoral life than are editors. . . .
>
> Is a newspaperman better equipped than a given public official to decide what is to be published and what is not about the official's own specialty? Perhaps journalists will be shocked to discover that laymen can regard this as a moot question.
>
> That laymen can so regard it may be the result, paradoxically, of the newspaper fraternity's failure to express itself well.

It was to be expected that some of the most important criticism of the press should come from colleges and universities ("The professors") and with some justice as long as the press insists upon its role as educator. Certainly it should earn the title by listening first to what educators have to say about it. Many educators no longer read newspapers regularly, not out of prejudice, but simply because newspapers do not supply what the educator needs to know.

It was perhaps not without some justification that the second edition of the unabridged Webster's New International Dictionary defined the word *journalese* as follows:

> "English of a style featured by use of colloquialisms, superficiality of thought and reasoning, clever or sensational presentation of material, and evidences of haste in composition, considered characteristic of newspaper writing."

The word *journalistic* was defined as:

> "Characteristic of journalism or journalists; hence, of style, characterized by evidences of haste, superficiality of thought, inaccuracies of detail, colloquialisms, and sensationalism; journalese."

This irritated a good many newspapermen. The journalistic fraternity, Sigma Delta Chi, protested officially to the lexicographers of G. & C. Merriam Company. In the 1957 edition the definition of *"journalese"* is still unflattering, but *journalistic* is now defined with dignity as a result of this objection.

It will take more than such a revision, however, to alter the prevailing opinion among the academicians that newspapers are preoccupied with the more primitive aspects of current history. Many faculty advisers without hesitation advise students to shun journalism. A young student about to concentrate in the subject told me that her English instructor, when he learned of it, warned her that if she turned in papers written in the style of the journalism department, he would flunk her. (My reply was that if she turned in papers to me containing such words as "maximize," "objectify," "imaginal," "conceptualize," "schema," and "privatization," she would flunk my course.)

College professors (at least those surveyed at Michigan) are convinced that news writers are a group beaten down and compelled to write in journalistic style; that journalism suppresses creative talent; that the work brings beggar's pay; that circulation is the end aim of newspaper policy; that journalism is "the lowest form of writing"; that newspapers have lost whatever prestige they may have had; that radio and television are infinitely more influential; that the press merely confirms prejudices; that newspapers yield to infinite pressures from such organizations as the American Legion, Chambers of Commerce, and religious groups; that news is slanted by advertising interests; that newspapers have no regard for the right of privacy and are only superficially and selfishly concerned about freedom of the press.

Fortunately for newspapers they are not dependent upon the number of copies they deliver in dormitories and at professorial porches. Since, however, a good many students and faculty members are faithful readers of such comprehensive news mediums as the New York *Times* and the *Christian Science Monitor* their preferences might have some weight in trying to determine those values which make a newspaper acceptable. More and more, industry and business are working with the university.

The increasing willingness of editors and publishers to refer to their medium as a "business" calls for some reassessment of journalism's relationship to ethics. Any business, of course, involves a certain number of ethical principles, chiefly in a negative sense: one must not cheat the customer outright; there are certain things a business man must not do to his competitior. The manufacturer who goes into business to make money tells himself that he serves by altruistically filling a want.

So all of these negative aspects would apply to newspapers if we are to consider newspapering a business: don't cheat the readers or the advertisers; deal vigorously with competitors; and so on.

This does not seem quite enough. Newspapermen eagerly want to think of journalism as a profession in spite of the fact that there is no criterion for qualifying as a journalist, nor any code for continuing in the vocation. If it is indeed a profession, perhaps a more positive ethical factor enters the picture. And the fact that the press has constitutional protection gives it responsibilities beyond those of mere business.

There are certain things which newspapers feel called upon not to do. It is easy to think of these restraints as ethics. Reporters and editors do not break a confidence, or should not. But is this a matter of ethics? A newspaperman who breaks a confidence might as well change his occupation. He will no longer be trusted with the only commodity that gives him a livelihood — news — by sources that will immediately dry up if he betrays them. Keeping confidences involves as much selfish motivation as ethical. If the newsman seeks to justify a breach of confidence by arguing the public's right to all the news, he should never have accepted the confidence in the first place and ought to have dug up the news on his own from other sources.

Going to jail under a contempt finding cannot involve an ethical principle as long as the case is exploited by the victim and the newspaper involved to the aggrandizement of both. Aggrandizement is not the kind of soil in which ethics flourish.

Certainly, too, no analogy can be drawn between the confidences entrusted to doctor, lawyer, or clergyman and those entrusted to the reporter. The former professions have a pact of secrecy with their clients which is paramount; the reporter's client is the public, with whom he has a pact to tell all he finds out, within the limits of law and decency. He is bound to have no entangling alliances with confidential information.

We shall have to look further for what constitutes newspaper ethics.

Opportunities have, in too many instances, been missed by newspapers. The right of privacy is a natural right of man which also has, in certain of its aspects, constitutional protection. There is too little talk in newspaper circles of this right of privacy, although the private individual has a clear idea of what it is and how far it extends. This difference of viewpoint is a good deal like the attitude of the press toward the First Amendment. Journalism concerns itself only with that part of it which guarantees a free press. This is but a fraction of a fraction of the Bill of Rights, and the subjective clamoring of the press over its own right is hugely out of balance with the efforts it ought to be making over all civil rights.

The right of privacy is not completely ignored: A father arguing with his wife over the disciplining of their child got a bit noisy and neighbors sent for the police. At the back door, the policeman wanted to know what the trouble was, upon which the male parent declared: "None of your goddam business!" And so got his name on the police blotter. The local city editor read the brief item and tossed it into the wastebasket. His judgment was so compassionate as to have at least the color of ethics.

The press enjoys its privileged position on the theory that democratic government cannot exist without a free flow of information to the public. The Post Office Department classifies newspapers as an educational medium and on that basis justifies the second class mailing rate, a subsidy pure and simple. Not generally known is the fact that any weekly newspaper in the United States may be delivered entirely without postal charge within the county in which it is published. Here too the reasoning is that the newspaper is an educator.

Supplying information is of course educational. The power of information is the power of the press. Newspaper people are well aware of this, but that does not prevent them from cherishing other elected purposes. It has become almost axiomatic that one of the newspaper's functions is to entertain, but where this curious doctrine arose is far from clear. Another self-imposed duty is a fancied obligation to stay in business. Many a publisher seems to think this is paramount and, if he is merely the representative of the owner, perhaps it is important that he cleave to the notion devoutly. If, though, a newspaper is not serving its readers in the primary objective of keeping them informed, there is no really good reason why it *should* remain in business. Proprietors intent upon a new merger do not even stop for the question; and it is not unknown, once title has been acquired, for the new owner to so devitalize the purchased — but as yet unmerged — paper of its news content that justification for its suspension is easily argued. In fact, the intent of the purchaser can often be divined by the progressive emasculation of the newspaper doomed for the execution block. In cold business terms it does ensure for a community that the remaining paper will stay in business (the primary concern, after profits); but since the news obligation has already been demonstrated to be secondary the readers can be excused for harboring a modicum of cynicism. If the only independence a newspaper has grows out of its monopoly of advertising space, there is little virtue in its self-reliance. Its courage is merely a bank balance.

If the importance of staying in business is made a virtue over ethics, then there may be some reason for making the newspaper a midway of cheap entertainment. The comic strips may have their advocates; the puzzlers and the counselors some justification; but when a medium that purports to be educational deliberately purveys the black magic of astrologers, it forfeits the respect of all except the superstitious.

Journalism's relationship to ethics has always been a nervous one. The code of the American Society of Newspaper Editors is clearly upright and no one can quarrel with its noble tone. Yet the Society agonized through its early years mainly over the question whether the code should have "teeth" and be enforced. A breach of professional canon would, of course, cost doctor, lawyer, judge, or clergyman his fellowship and license to bar, bench, or cloth.

The Bill of Rights recognizes the right of the people to a free press. To the degree that this gives privileges to the press, it places upon it the obligation to supply a complete, untrammeled, uninterrupted flow of the news. If it provides anything less than all three, the press is not doing its duty.

It is dubious ethics to declare that a constitutional right

is a safeguard of the people and then to invoke it as a refuge for vested interest, be that vested interest even the press. Editors expound the philosophy that the "right to know" is the people's right, for they know this theory well. They preach it continually, but are mystified and disappointed that people do not seem to understand them.

The people are mystified because they *do* understand but cannot grasp the newspaper application of the principle.

During the recent newspaper strikes in London and New York, at least one or more newspapers were mechanically and contractually able to publish. These, too, suspended magnanimously, in order not to take advantage of their struck competitors. This generous gesture was, of course, a noble one but it was paid for with someone else's coin — the public's. It is easy to be big-hearted with what does not belong to you. In this instance, the sacrifice was the people's right to information. This is either the right of the people or of the press; it cannot be alternated for convenience. Ethics in the newspaper world has two adjustable handles and can quickly be made into an all-purpose tool.

Ethics is not a birthright. No man is obliged to have any sensibility about ethics at all. He can be a fairly decent citizen and have no real understanding of the word or what it means, except perhaps intuitively. It is a criterion, a self-adopted one, a measuring stick of one's own choosing. If the New York *Times* adopts the slogan "All the News That's Fit to Print" it incurs the obligation to measure itself by that yardstick. Inescapably so because, whether it does or does not, its clientele is bound to try on it the clothes of its own cutting.

It is for this reason that the press so often finds itself

the target of criticism. The press itself invokes the most idealistic of principles and makes a good deal of noise about them. But on the First Amendment, it invokes the free press section almost exclusively, and is sublimely indifferent or at best neutral when non-newspaper people's rights to free speech, assembly, and religion are in jeopardy.

Arthur Krock of the New York *Times* has commented satirically in the *Bulletin* of the American Society of Newspaper Editors on the speech-making proclivity of editors. He thinks they are neglecting their regular jobs, foregoing the obligation to edit "slurring adjectives and discrediting insinuations" from syndicated material, publishing cartoons in which public men who disagree with their editorial policy are depicted as "primitives, cowards and human embodiments of porcine greed," and refusing to correct plain errors of fact. "The freedom of the press is oddly distorted when newspaper management construes it as restraining its own freedom to edit out manifest abuses of the privilege. Or, if that is not the reason for this tolerance, the choice lies between negligence and crude commercialism."

Ethics gave the newly organized American Society of Newspaper Editors birth pangs that nearly proved fatal. The records of Society do not tell the whole story because more of the initial agonies occurred in the Board of Directors. But from 1925 onward various committees dragged the bones from the closet, assembled the skeleton for all to see, and then reconsigned it to the closet in the sacred name of freedom of the press.

The story was that a member of the Society had misused his newspaper in a way that seemed a clear violation of the newly adopted code. The Board of Directors voted his expulsion but he was to have a hearing.

At this hearing, the accused was represented by counsel and made it clear that, if expelled, he would sue individually and personally all members of the Board. The directors also consulted counsel, who found that under their loosely written constitution they had no right to expel anybody and were, indeed, sitting ducks for a lawsuit. Hence, no expulsion. The issue was resolved by the resignation of the accused member, and not only the Board, but the entire membership of the Society were now righteously smarting. At this point the discussion began.

In succeeding conventions what to do about ethics became a major topic. It was pretty well agreed that the Society's constitution needed repair, and amendments were offered. It was argued logically enough that a code of ethics was useless without enforcement power.

The opposition, as is so often the case when newspaper dilemmas arise, reached for the free press issue and declared that any enforceable code was tantamount to censorship. The hottest fight of all came in the convention of 1931.

Tom Wallace, of the Louisville *Times*, declared:

> I believe that this Society will perish through disintegration if we don't do something to show that we have a reason for existence. If we come here to spend three days listening to Sunday School lectures, curtain lectures, college professors' talks, and don't show we are actually trying to do anything about anything, then I think we had better quit and I think eventually as a body we will quit.

During the presidency of Walter M. Harrison, of the Oklahoma City *Oklahoman*, a move was made to amend the constitution, empowering the Board to examine complaints of "disgraceful conduct" and "to censure, suspend or expel the offending member." The amendment was drawn up by John W. Davis, who was then counsel for the Associated Press, and it was presented to the convention by Willis J. Abbot of the *Christian Science Monitor*. Previously an exploratory mail ballot had been taken to which only twenty-eight members had responded, twenty-one favoring the amendment. Abbot argued that if the amendment were not adopted "this association stands absolutely without any legal power whatsoever to discipline any member . . . however execrable, however heinous his offense against the code of journalism we have adopted . . ."

This is about what Abbot had been saying at every convention for the previous five years. The opposition followed in general the tenor of reasons given by M. V. Atwood, then associate editor of the Gannett Newspapers, who voiced five points:

> 1. Such a rule might easily be applied so that it became an infringement upon free speech. 2. What constitutes "ethical conduct" is too intangible to make conformity to it a serviceable yardstick for the measurement of a man's fitness to be in newspaper work. For example, it's my belief that one of the greatest newspapers in the country persistently violates Section 5 of our Canons having to do with impartiality in news reports. I would not vote for the expulsion of the editor of this paper. I do not believe the editor unethical, for reasons not necessary to be detailed here. 3. The modern newspaper is too complex an institution to make it possible to hold the editor responsible for all the practices in its conduct which some might term unethical. 4.

The setting of a rigid rule of this kind is not in harmony with the growing opposition to creeds in religion and statutes regulating personal conduct. "The letter deadeneth, the spirit maketh alive." 5. Nothing in the operation of a similar rule by physicians and lawyers would lead us to believe that our proposed rule would be so applied as to be either effective or just.

Finally some of the members got thoroughly tired of the talk. Paul Bellamy felt that the way to get rid of the issue was to vote the amendment:

I am a somewhat recent convert to it. For four or five years after its first introduction I opposed it. . . . For myself I am sick and tired of having come down here eight years and preached ethics until I was black in the face and then run away from the only concrete method or form in which an ethical problem was really put right up to us.

On April 22, 1932, according to the *Proceedings* of the Society, President Fred Fuller Shedd, presiding, said:

"All those in favor of the adoption of this amendment as a part of our constitution will signify by rising. Contrary minded. It is a unanimous vote, thank God!" (Applause)

And so the enforcement of ethics was pretty well allowed to rest, in the American Society of Newspaper Editors.

One wonders how the case of Samuel Bowles might have turned out if his dilemma had been cited to the Society's code and court. A cub reporter in the old days did such a good job with an obituary that the grateful survivors gave him a dollar. His conscience bothered him for several days and finally he confessed to Samuel Bowles, who pondered the weighty question for some time and resolved it:

"Young man," Bowles said, "you may give *me* the dollar."

4

THE

EDITORIAL

PAGE

THE PRESENTATION OF OPINION, AS we think of what appears on the editorial page, fulfills the second function of the newspaper: to influence and to guide. This is a process that calls into play the subjective reactions of one writer to a set of circumstances surrounding events.

Such opinion is the product of emotional and intellectual reactions born of inspiration, fear, resolution, combativeness (perhaps a reaction to the warlike posture of a potential enemy), civic projects footless or imaginative, analysis of a puzzling combination of events, or whatever personal foibles the editorial writer cares to expound. We still need opinion. But what is it?

A person loses weight, becomes mentally depressed, feels certain ill-defined and unnatural sensations in parts of his body. Fear, a purely subjective state of mind, enters, but as yet there is nothing that can be termed an event. Our subject consults a physician who, after a professional exploration, declares that his patient is the victim of a growth. That is his opinion and it is news — bad news. After further tests he declares that the growth is not malignant. That is his professional opinion and his opinion is news — good news, or at least news which mitigates fear.

News in this case begins the moment the physician voices his opinion, and it is news only because of his professional competence. It is this element of competence which divides his judgment from the judgments of his patient's friends and relatives, all of whom have neither expert knowledge nor disciplined experience and whose beliefs consequently can have no value as news, private or public.

Thus informed opinion, in its character as tidings, establishes its legitimacy with news and the newspaper. But opinion cannot be merely a composite of diverse motives and impressions. Opinions are emotionally arrived at and jealously embraced. In its present character, the editorial page strives to make a beachhead on neutral ground. There is no neutral ground. Opinion, to be respected, must be firm, thoughtful, unmistakable. You cannot, however, be everybody's friend by being nobody's unchallengeable friend.

The editorial page itself is the vermiform appendix of the American newspaper, of no known use, its potential for trouble slight and easily contained. Originally the editorial page was the *raison d'être* of the newspaper. A sheet was founded or bought because a man had something to say on his own account and he said it, the news and advertisements being incidental.

But the page is torpid now and there is grave doubt that it can or should ever be revived in a press bent on mass appeal. To attempt being all things to all people is to be nothing much to anybody. Opinion must stand up and be recognized if it is to be heard at all. Not to know what a man thinks is to conclude fairly that he hasn't thought.

There are too many things that the editorial page is not allowed to think about. There does not appear to be in the United States a newspaper willing to be recognized as an opponent of war. Newspapers are in favor of peace because it is a comforting word; they are not willing to make it an absolute. Peace that is treasurable only until war interrupts it is not peace at all but merely an editorial.

One searches hopefully for editorial pages that are willing to say that mitigation of the cold war requires that one must have a beachhead, however narrow, of confidence that the Soviet Union can be trusted to keep its word. It is only on such a slender rim of trust that understanding can be enlarged. There are editors who recognize the fact, but there are scarcely any who write it. There are probably editors who know that an economy largely supported by munitions manufacture and a nation whose principal export is weapons of war is in an unsound condition, but they are not willing to tap that grisly foundation, however lightly and tentatively.

Editorial pages are extremely important, but sometimes a point is better illustrated by the trivial and hodiernal. Can any person of ordinary sensitivity accept the defacement of the countryside by garish advertising signs? Editorial writers, who are sensitive human beings, probably resent billboards as much as anybody, and there may be some who have honestly expatiated in type against this vandalism, but such pieces are hard to find. The cynical will promptly reply that one couldn't expect newspapers that live by advertising to inveigh against a business in which it enjoys such a large share.

Even among those editors who believe, as Francis Pharcellus Church did, that there is a Santa Claus, and who on Christmas Eve take from the reference shelf the office

Bible and reprint the Gospel according to St. Luke, there are few who write editorials against the commercialization of Christmas. An editor may gag at holy carols as sung in department stores, but he keeps his feelings to himself in the knowledge that there is a sort of pocketbook anesthesia in those sacred strains — music which, with its present promiscuous uses, may come to be barred in church because of commercial connotations.

No doubt the intelligent editorial writer has rebelled at the poisonous din of power lawnmowers which tear the summer silences to shreds, but he will grind his teeth and write an editorial instead in praise of an insurance company's annual statement. Its balance sheet has already appeared in a full-page advertisement and the same statistics have been printed in the financial columns. But because an insurance company advertises once a year, that full page will also rate an editorial written by a man who can't even balance his own checkbook.

The editorial page is dying by self-immolation. When house room was voluntarily given to the by-line columnist it marked the beginning of the end. If you have no opinions of your own, or can't express them, buy them. The supposition that one can balance off various opinions against each other or purchase gift-wrapped views contrasting with the policy of the paper (if it has a policy) is a delusion, because most of the columnists are nearly as reactionary or as timid as the press itself. The columnists are distributed by syndicates and these are businesses too. It doesn't pay a syndicate to sign up a writer who cannot garner at least fifty papers. To ask if there are fifty liberal newspapers in the country is to stumble upon the number at which Abraham began his bargaining with the Lord for the righteous souls in Sodom.

What was left of the lifeblood of the editorial page has been sucked out by the news department. This took place about the time that newspapers awoke to the success of the news weeklies. The first diagnosis was that the magazines were not merely reporting deadpan news, but were making events mean something. Out of this profound discovery Interpretive Writing was born. The phrase was a new one; it sounded good; it was grist for the mills of oratory.

"Down with the bitch-goddess Objectivity!" declaimed David Patten, managing editor of the Providence *Journal* and *Bulletin* at an Associated Press convention.

Others before and after preached "creative reporting," "explanatory writing," "backgrounding," "digging below the surface of the news." Under whatever name, interpretive writing was supposed, without having an opinion, to suggest what the news might mean. Soon there was nothing left for the editorial page to explain. Broadcasting commentators, too, were explaining, persuading, convincing, pontificating, or whatever else it was that editorial pages had ever done.

The distinction between news reporting and opinion writing (under the name of interpretation), is so hazy that a man can sit at a typewriter in New York or Washington and pretend to tell what is going on in Russia or the Orient. This is not difficult to do, especially with so many newsworthy parts of the world shrouded in a censorship which makes it impossible to determine whether or not the interpreter is on solid ground. There is no great hazard involved if an "interpreter" of the news declares that three hundred thousand Chinese will starve to death next winter, that the waters of the Yenisei have become hopelessly contaminated by nuclear wastes, or that grocery stores in Kiev no longer honor trading stamps. There is no one to call the turn on him, and this kind of interpretive writing, if based on guesswork, is worse than mere opinion writing because it has not the virtue either of responsibility or conscience.

Insofar as the plea for interpretive writing (explanatory is a better adjective) is in response to a reader need, it can be granted enthusiastically. However, the current remedy ignores the cause. The reader does not understand the news as reported because he has not been given sufficient information. Puzzling facts can be explained only by more facts. The added facts make clear what previously was obscure. The discussion — and it is a hopeful sign that there has been room not only for plural opinions but for a host of definitions — significantly has not been limited to the word interpretation, but also to synonyms — for the news behind the news. Nothing could better illustrate the fact that the issue arose because the customer had been given short weight on the commodity he came to buy — news. He may not be satisfied with the premium — opinion.

I do not know of any obscure or enigmatic or complicated situation in the news that cannot be explained by more facts. Facts — historical, circumstantial, biographical, statistical, reflective — can usually throw sufficient light on spontaneous news events as to make them fairly intelligible. If this be interpretive writing, well and good, but the moment opinion and speculation enter, then the writer is poaching on the editorial page. Such poaching is the modern trend — more than a trend, it has been going on so long as to have bled the editorial page white. Its readership has declined as well as its influence.

Significantly, it was within fairly recent times that the National Conference of Editorial Writers was organized. With the rise of the columnist and broadcasting commentator and with the encouragement of news-column interpretation, such a group was needed. The editorial writers knew that something was happening — already had happened — that threatened their reason for being. Faithfully they meet once a year, publish their organ the *Masthead,* and in justice to their zeal it must be acknowledged that they foregather in a working convention and go home replenished with fervor and idealism. It is observable, however, that much of their discussion and much of the topical matter in their publication is concerned with typographical and other mechanical devices for inviting readership to the page rather than with attracting and confirming readers by courageous, thoughtful exhortations on challenging and thorny subjects.

It was only a few years ago that Jenkin Lloyd Jones, the articulate and spunky editor of the Tulsa *Tribune,* coined the word "Afghanistanism" to describe with deadly effect the reluctance of editorial writers to tackle difficult questions on the home ground but instead, armored and beplumed, to ride into the lists over issues that wrack faraway places and peoples.

To explain what the reader wants to understand presupposes the knowledge of what he is thinking about. The editorial writer is to assume that the reader is thinking about what he (the editorial writer) believes he (the reader) ought to be thinking about. This is most often not the case at all. To sharpen the point one has only to look at the topics about which readers choose to write letters to the editor. These are seldom Afghanistan.

The news department is equally guilty. There are fashions in news coverage, based chiefly upon ideas of what the public ought to be thinking about. When the Russian Sputnik suddenly vaulted into space, it was quickly realized that the Russians had done first what the United States had been trying to do. Conclusions were swift and about as accurate as most shooting from the hip, which meets its mark only in the movies. The national faults were (1) the science lag; (2) education.

The science lag was also a problem from the newspaper standpoint. We all said: Newspapers must have science-trained reporters. The order was quite a large one. In more than forty years of watching gifted people pass in and out of a newsroom, I've seen almost every kind of talent available. These included a reporter who made a hobby of repairing and restoring scrapped reed organs; jazz piano players, tobacco farmers, coin collectors, water-colorists, oil painters, gourmets, miniature railway operators, sports car drivers, skin divers, Latinists, moose hunters, and clergymen. But I have never hired or had a chance to fire a reporter who knew anything about science. There is something about science and the journalistic urge that is almost antithetical. If a body has the urge to write, he somehow just doesn't hanker to inhabit the chemistry or physics laboratories. Yet the need was suddenly to create a corps of scientific reporters. The success or lack of it will be seen in other parts of this study which suggest the difficulty of finding good reporters of any kind. It is the news fashion that here concerns us. The reasoning was that science reporting is necessary because that is what people are thinking about — a conclusion arrived at because that was what people *ought* to be thinking about.

Nothing could be further from fact. People are not and have not been thinking about science. It is assumed that people are interested in the atomic age and the hazard of nuclear warfare, but it would be hard to find anything more remote from their deepest concern. They may start nervously at an automobile backfiring, but it's a false start. One has to look no further than at the sublime indifference of the populace to Civil Defense. Such national unanimity is rare: an apparent accord that civil defense is something you don't talk about or think about. If additional proof were needed one has only to point to the circumstance that the great majority of American citizens believe firmly that the atomic tests have completely dislocated nature's weather apparatus. This is our common thought about science, and our reporters are not likely to disabuse us. The public may even be right.

There is a science reporter whose pre-eminence is not questioned in newspaper circles. He was early in the field and he writes with great authority and acceptance. His work was under discussion one day in a group of scientists and their estimates of his competence were at a surprising discount. A question about him brought the answer: "The trouble with him is that he tells us what we ought to find and what conclusions we ought to arrive at."

Public interest in science extends about as far as that of freshmen who are under the impression that with a bachelor of science degree it is easy to get a better-paying job. The science-consciousness of the rest of the populace is limited to a pretty well-founded conviction that the space cowboys would do well to leave the moon to Buck Rogers.

The other fashion in news reporting and editorial writing was the discovery of education. All editors now know that education is important, that the field has been neglected, and that the public is interested. Again this is merely a convenient theory. Public interest in education goes about as far as the Parent-Teacher Association. It is in effect a cheering section for whatever doctrine the educators are cultivating and wish to sell to parents.

But the big news story happened a long time ago. During a period of thirty years, the misnamed "progressive" education movement took hold in schools with varying degrees of strength. Parents talked about it occasionally in the awed and cowed way that people have when they are not quite sure what is going on and have no way of finding out — as with atomic tests and the weather. The progressive movement crested and subsided, and all during this critical period newspapers in general never took it upon themselves to go into the classroom and find out what was going on. They all had an education beat, but it was the reporter's duty to attend Board of Education meetings, when they were open to the public, visit the superintendent's office occasionally, and pick up the luncheon menus once a week for publication. The only thing that parents knew about what the young were being fed was what they had to eat.

That story is not yet over. But people are no longer talking quite as much about the affairs of the grade schoolroom. Their concern now is what college their offspring will attend and how they will ever get him or her inside the gate. The college area of the education field is now the one ripe for reporting and so are the high schools, in their new role as "prep" school.

So those who raise the ethical question of whether a newspaper should give the public what it wants are wasting their energies. Few newspapers are in danger of doing that. Most of their mistakes arise from the fact that they are giving the readers too much of what the editors mistakenly think the people ought to have.

This is as much an editorial-page problem as it is the news department's. Editorial writers are serious people. They work hard. To turn out even one competent editorial a day is difficult work, and few of them get off that easily.

They keep themselves fairly well informed. They know about the hazard of ivory tower pallor, and talk and write eloquently about the need of getting out among people, but few of them have the chance because of the pressure under which they are supposed to get inspiration.

There is no question but that these men are thoughtful, even scholarly fellows. One wonders why there are so few women editorial writers. Perhaps it is in recollection of that earlier day when readers got mad over something that appeared on the editorial page and came in with a bull whip or a pistol.

Today there are no editorial page editors who deserve to be horse-whipped.

Maybe that's what is the matter.

5

THE FORGOTTEN UNCOMMON MAN

> A nation cannot consist solely of the common people; it needs an eminent minority. It is like a live body which consists not only of muscle but also of nerve ganglia and a cerebral center.
>
> **ORTEGA Y GASSET**

IN THE EARLY SUMMER OF 1910, Halley's Comet became visible to the naked eye. In those halcyon days this phenomenon had such a violent impact upon life and mores that even a soda fountain confection came to be known as a "Halley's Comet Special." That great space wanderer, incidentally, will return to us in precisely 76.2 years from the date of its last appearance — that is, in the summer of 1986.

This is an arbitrary but convenient arc of time for the assessment of changes in journalism, because the bloody and dislocating yardsticks of war, which transformed technology, and economic cataclysm, which revolutionized people's relationship to government, had less effect on the American newspaper than did the intellectual socialization of man — hints of which were appearing even before 1914. The half century has witnessed an erosion of freedoms that could not but affect the reader's mind, and yet the reader's mind has changed less rapidly than the daily newspaper's level of address to it. The newspaper's responsibility for this change has been at least tendential and maybe even determinative.

Most conspicuously eroded is the freedom of choice as to newspapers. In the first place, more than a thousand dailies have disappeared since 1910. Second, newspaper publication, now primarily a business, has grown to such a size that in most communities it is in the upper half among employers, both as to number of workers and size of payroll. This, as with any business, has necessitated a depersonalization, and in newspapers an attempt to arrive at an appeal so broad as to the lowest common denominator of readership. Size has fostered monopoly, which in turn fosters stereotype. Third, with the end of the era of personal publishing, when the sharply-focused images of Greeley, the Bennetts, Dana, the Pulitzers, Hearst, and McCormick were imprinted across the face of journalism, newspapers assumed a neutral, across-the-counter perspective which can be described only by the ambiguous and shopworn term objectivity. These factors served to produce a blandness in the press, infertile for vigorous thought and action. Instead of providing leadership, newspapers sought out and cultivated the common man in order to follow him in the march toward mediocrity.

Mass production is the inevitable recourse of the monopolizing newspaper and it began to manifest all the characteristics of products so produced: absence of appeal to special tastes, elimination of everything that is not, as the phrase goes, standard equipment. The address must be aimed as close as possible to the base of the social cone, for the maximum readership; and of necessity, by reason of rising costs, for the maximum revenue. Thus the press gave itself no choice but to abandon the uncommon man.

The mass mind goes with mass production. Even in so highly competitive an industry as automobile manufacture, where each mammoth producer must offer a great variety of models covering nearly every step in the price range lest he lose sales in an unprotected fifty-dollar bracket, the buyer has virtually no choice as to car-length, decoration, horsepower, and non-manual detail. Manufacturers will produce a gearshift car, but the buyer must order and wait — for he is uncommon. There is no escape from the monotony of automation. The one-way street, the traffic light, food packaging, clothing styles, plastics — one could name thousands of other examples — are dripping away upon the once so firm freedom of choice.

An inevitable concomitant of mass production is the survey technique. It is the divining rod that spells out what is average. It is a levelizer that rivals death itself. Modern business cannot do without it. The survey operator hunts out the average man, sketches his profile, and the manufacturer then fills in his very features, clothes him, decrees what he shall eat, what manner of house he shall live in, how he shall rear his children and establish his life expectancy to create actuarial tables. The survey will provide him through a lifetime not with what products he may want but what it is convenient and profitable for the manufacturer to make in great quantities; what it is convenient and profitable for the chain retailer to permit the customer to help himself to from the shelves whose contents are completely predetermined. The customer who once was always right is now assumed to be without any will whatsoever — except to pick a brand — and somewhat of a nuisance besides.

The newspaper editor steers his course by the survey chart. The syndicate salesman, unasked, will provide him with the precise standing of every comic strip on his page broken down, if he wants it that way, geographically and by sex and age group. The editor will make his own shallow surveys and rarely passes up an election season without a local straw vote either by postcard or by the enquiring reporter on a street corner. Not yet content, he will buy every pollster and survey available for his territory. The publisher and the advertising manager employ their own solicitors to ring doorbells and to sit down with the housewife to inquire how many "traffic stops" her eyes made in scanning the paper left on her doorstep. The professional survey institutes are the masters of a nation's opinion and their chief concern is to crystallize that opinion in manipulative shape.

The time has gone by when an editor was supposed to sit quietly in his cubicle and prayerfully ask himself: "What manner of paper shall I create?"

The only evil of mass production to which the newspaper product is not heir is the induced decay of obsolescence. This is due merely to the circumstance that the newspaper itself is so quickly out of date. So instead of renewing its own market by obsolescence it expands itself artifically by creating new customers in its established image.

The objective of the market survey is less — "What want of yours can we satisfy?" than — "How do you like the product we have prepared for you? It happens to be what is convenient and profitable for us to make and sell."

The newspaper did not create the circumstances in whose stream it has willingly drifted. It is a socialistic current, despite a dominant allergy in America to the word itself. The individual mind has been adjusted — yes, even regimented. Even the two-party system has been levelized and reduced to indistinguishably common denominators. Government has drifted further away from the people, whose control of it has greatly diminished. Culture — the arts, education, the amenities of life — have spread over a broader social base than ever before, but not so as to increase taste and discrimination. In drama, music, books, the public wants the same things, desperately and at the same time — but briefly. The ten top plays, the hit parade of Tin Pan Alley, the Fifty Pieces of symphony (in Virgil Thomson's phrase), the book clubs, and the week's best seller. Even recreation has its status sport: he who golfed, who skied, now must own a boat of whatever size.

In the face of this kind of socialism, the American press has done nothing for itself or anyone else except to protest violently against bureaucracy in the form of rapidly closing doors in government. In this, of course, newspapers have a vested interest in spite of their clamorous declarations that the free press is the people's constitutional guarantee, a truth which everyone perceives except the people themselves, who in this as in other respects seem to think the same thing at the same time. The common man has elected himself to an overlordship of complacency.

In this era of merger and monopoly the local newspaper has withdrawn further and further into the community it has elected to serve, not with the thought of providing a variety of services but to bend the community will to acceptance of its product. This has produced an acute parochialism. The homely dictum that a newspaper should be "as local as the town pump" was invented in a day when the United States did not wear the mantle of world leadership, a responsibility of which it will soon be free if the press (among others) continues to foster such short-sighted mental isolationism.

The formula of localizing has not bred special newspapers. There is little to distinguish one from the other. Again this is merely a circumstance, for it is not only the journals that look more and more like each other. Drop a man blindfolded into the middle of St. Louis, Columbus, Minneapolis, Houston, or almost any American city; let him open his eyes, and it is doubtful if he could tell you where he was. The architecture of office and factory buildings is stereotyped, even to the strained modernity of the newest ones. The neon signs, traffic controls, the store fronts, and all the other appurtenances of urban life are monotonously identical. Even the plazas of downtown redevelopment are taking on a uniform gloss. In all this pattern the look of the newspaper is only slightly more varied than that apotheosis of uniformity, the expressway.

Even the newspaper features chosen for variety — comics, columnists, departments of advice and deportment, puzzles — conspire to defeat differentiation for they appear endlessly from coast to coast. Because so large a proportion of non-advertising space is devoted to such entertainment it is easy to think there was more news in the papers of 1910. Probably there was not, but it depends upon what sort of yardstick is used to measure news. Recreation, household and social interests, health, education, and the arts are pursued with regimented zeal, and these topics do provide readership. If reading matter about gardening, boating, hunting, fishing, decoration, music, games, bird-watching, backgammon, and stamp collecting can be classified as news, well and good. However, none of this content is calculated to make subscribers better-informed citizens of the world.

In cultivating the common man and total circulation, the community has demanded its price of the newspaper. The press, it has discovered, is a great, friendly, shaggy pet that wants to play. It will not bite, as once was feared; it doesn't mind being ridden about nor having its tail pulled. As a member of the community household it can be used! And so it is.

The editor belongs to the luncheon clubs as do the advertising solicitors and counting house personnel; the publisher is on the hospital board and on bank and industrial directorates. All can be trusted to keep the community atmosphere sweet and clean, even to the point of looking the other way when it is necessary to sweep a little unpleasant dirt under the rug — nothing important, of course.

Then it comes time for the civic campaigns: fund appeals to fight every disease in the calendar, charity drives, college endowments, and the whole roster of good-doing and general betterment. The newspaper, of course, is a heavy contributor, as it should be. A bank president is asked to be grand marshal of the whole effort and is assured he will have no work to do — it is only the use of his name that is wanted. His captains and lieutenants are recruited with the same assurances. They all know better, but they and the chief have been through this before and they know what the bounty is, as thoroughly as though they had received written promises.

Their pictures will appear in the paper, individually and in groups!

These have all been published before, everyone knows what the boys look like, but this is a new campaign. The newspaper expects to provide generously of its space to promote the drive and to encourage people to open up their pocketbooks by printing human interest stories on the great need for this noble money. That is neither begrudged nor disputed. But the newspaper which has given its own money, and more space than it can afford, does not owe the marshal and his captains and lieutenants anything. This the great, shaggy, friendly dog has to put up with, but he asked for it when he joined the family circle.

This is a far different role from that of the press whose personnel from top to bottom used to brag that they had no friends nor wanted any. To join a club or a society was to be beholden. It blunted the lance of the crusader. The crusading newspaper is not a money-maker, and this discovery profoundly changed journalism. There seems to be some sort of community housekeeping pride that resents the uncovering of scandal and corruption whether petty or not. This cannot happen in our fair city, it is reasoned, in much the same spirit that a bank will absorb good-sized defalcations rather than face the publicity of prosecution.

The press today stands in a limited utilitarian relationship to the community. It isn't news to publish the starting time of the feature picture at the movie theater; the church member ought to know what time the Sunday morning services begin; but the reader wants to check the schedules in the paper. Radio and television as competing mediums have their means of publicizing their calendar of attractions, but again the reader wants his newspaper checkpoint. Many publishers definitely construe this not as news but as advertising and charge space rates for it.

Information can be both. News of the market-place has always commanded the highest reader attention, especially among women who, as is well known, make most of the family purchases. But the traffic in this information bears a heavy toll and advertising rates are fixed accordingly. It has been said that a newspaper without advertising is not acceptable and, while experiments are not conclusive, this is not hard to believe. Be that as it may, this great need for news of the market moves the newspaper ever nearer to the function of public utility. By its cultivation of the common man, whose needs in transportation, light, fuel, and communication are watched over by government commissions, the press has put itself in a somewhat more vulnerable position than it occupied before.

The news and editorial rooms stand in a passive relationship to the market-place. If the product is ready-mixed, frozen, dehydrated, or pulverized, food editors dilate upon all of these magical qualities without raising the question of flavor. Technology has played a comic bit of irony. A few generations ago, the American farmer was required by one means or another to preserve foodstuffs in quantity because a single snowstorm might cut him off from the provision store for weeks on end. He had his barrel of sugar, his barrel of flour, his sides of ham and bacon in the smokehouse, his fruits and vegetables in the underground bins. He and his family could live all winter if necessary without going to the store. By groundhog day he knew that he ought to have about half of his provender left. But today, when no one is more than three minutes away from the supermarket, the householder freezes down quantities of food sufficient to provision an army. Surely the second ice age is upon us. Whatever happened to taste?

This is the era of good will. Its sun began to rise about the time personal journalism ended. In those days there were no guessing games, no beauty contests, no youth derbies; no community sings nor any of the manifold events called "promotions in the interest of public service" — as though these were public services more important than providing readers with the news.

Government — local, state, and national — moves further from people's control, not as the result of a dark plot to deprive the people of their democratic rights but simply because the country has become so populous and the machinery of government so complicated that of necessity much must be done by directive and by bureaucratic authority. The New England town meeting, which was the essence of democratic self-rule, is all but obsolete, because its machinery is too complicated for completely democratic operation. Most of the citizens are quite content to hire a town manager and leave in his executive hands a host of decisions which once were settled by popular vote. Our officials sit behind closed doors.

Newspaper societies are in fever heat most of the time about this and properly so. It is a valiant rear-guard action. Like it or not, every year that goes by will see more and more decisions made in executive offices. Modern government is frustrating to news gatherers. There is in Washington a greater concentration of reporters than in any other city in the world and yet it would be impossible for them to explore every governmental nook and cranny. That means handouts, and though editors may chafe, they could not do without them. The mimeograph machine runs off handout "news" from behind the closed doors.

Election coverage runs to the same impersonal patterns. Newspapers are obsessed with the question of who is going to win; it is a great guessing game. The press feels some sort of obligation to tell the news in advance of its happening. True, the reader wants to know who's the likely winner; but it is really more important that he be familiar with the party platform. It's hard to find in many papers.

Newspapers have followed the common man in assuming a passive relationship to society. The concern of the newspaper should be more than just to report the styles, the manners, the tastes, the deportment, and the caprices of mankind. Its function is instead to help establish real criteria of taste and style; to establish manners; to encourage and keep alive the civic conscience; to create a climate favorable to cultural life and unhealthy for epidemic philistinism. The common man is to be respected. Let them even exalt him, but editors should not accept him as their leader when it is he who needs leadership. This is to follow the common will on its commonest level.

Journalism's forgotten leader is Uncommon Man and this is the result of a high fever for unlimited circulation.

The Old Country Editor of whom Henry Beetle Hough wrote used to go from Martha's Vineyard to Boston "to solicit advertising" and generally made the most of the city's hospitality. Once he returned home, particularly set up by two days among the fleshpots and the wine ewers of the city, and retired all aglow to his sanctum. In due time he emerged with a sheet of paper and called to his grandnephew.

"Here, Sampson, set this in italic!"

Wrote Hough: "The boy read the words: *We print today 8,960 copies of the Vineyard Gazette. We ask for no patronage. We have all we want!* "The circulation was never anything like that figure except in the happy fancy of the Old Editor."

So the newspaper has changed; it is still changing but not encouragingly. Its gestures toward improvement are weak. Perhaps once again it will be more concerned with *content* than with the circulation figure and the rate card, knowing that one follows the other in that order. Perhaps it will be demanding of recruits — in education, apprenticeship, and regimen — so that only men of dedicated fiber will be hired. But these men must fill jobs for which only the few are chosen. They must be, in short, uncommon themselves.

There could be a return, not of the power of the press, but of the influence of the press. Then the newspaper would be written and edited for individual men, not averages. Perhaps if the newspaper world can straighten itself, the world everybody lives in can once more become so peaceful, idyllic, and millennial that when Halley's Comet once more sweeps its tail across our terrestrial face, the American newspaper will again find that visitation the biggest news of the day.

6

PRESS &

STEAM

ENGINE:

$900

"I TALKED FAST TO THREE MEN. ONE was Governor Morrell, at the State House. I got $1000 out of him. Another was Major Hood, the local aspirant for governor. I got $1000 out of him. The other was the estate of Old Senator Plum, who was a very good friend of mine. His wife and family hated the Major. I thought they would be good for another thousand. And I bought the *Gazette*.

"We had a cylinder press with a water motor, three, four or perhaps five cases of type, two stoves and that was all. I was a good enough printer to know that after the glamor and the glory of the transaction was over, that I had bought about $750 worth of actual physical assets and something like $2250 worth of good will. The good will consisted of a subscription list of 485 which I counted at the end of the press while the boys were folding the first papers."

That was how William Allen White came to own the Emporia *Gazette*. You had to own a paper in those days to write: "What's the matter with Kansas?" It was a violent, emotional, name-calling editorial and White later somewhat regretfully recognized it as such, but better to regret than never to have written it. The same with the unsparing editorial he wrote on the death of Frank Munsey, about which he afterwards felt a little apologetic. Again better to regret it than not to write it. Probably neither one would have been published, even in those days, by the Kansas City *Star*, where White worked before he got married and became a newspaper owner.

Today owners, publishers, and editors have nothing to regret and cannot afford the luxury of venture.

Willie O. Burr, owner of the Hartford *Times*, used to recall how he as a boy sat behind the barred doors of the office with his father Alfred E. Burr, who had a rifle across his knees while the sheriff kept vigil on the doorstep. Physically, by a hooting mob, and economically the paper was threatened with ruin, but the sturdy hearts behind it felt that the *Times* could afford to oppose the Civil War and drew down the name "Copperhead sheet" for their courage.

The paper opposed Lincoln and, when the travel-stained President was met at the railroad station with cheering citizens and a cornet band, the *Times* reporter wrote about his "dirty shirt." Time came when there were regrets about that.

In the 1880's the *Times* paid $10,000 for the first rotary press in Connecticut; in 1924 a fourteen-unit press cost it $400,000; in 1959 the cost of a new one exceeded a million dollars. But the price of mistakes has gone up even more rapidly, so is it any wonder that no one in the newspaper business is taking any chances? Consequently there cannot today be anything the matter with Kansas.

In those days anybody could start a newspaper and almost anybody did. Daniel C. Birdsall, for instance.

The year was 1883, and there were three evening newspapers and one morning paper in Hartford. Judge Birdsall decided to start a fifth. He was a massive man but short; his girth was enormous and he had a huge head set almost neckless on the broadest of shoulders. Birdsall strutted, the soul of dignity, and had piercing black eyes which were said to be unfriendly and eternally speculative. Where he acquired the title of Judge was uncertain, but prior to his arrival in Hartford he had a law office on Broadway.

Birdsall started the Hartford *Telegram* in a second-floor office on Asylum Street, the narrow, crooked thoroughfare that leads from Main Street to the railroad station, and for this he paid $25 a month rent. For $20 a month he rented a composing and press room a block away on the corner where Trumbull Street crosses Asylum. These rooms were mechanically equipped at a cost of $1600. He got a press and a steam engine for $900. A news wire and telegraph operator cost $25 a week.

Thus a competitive newspaper could start from scratch at a capital outlay of less than $10,000. Birdsall had precisely $9500 to get going, of which $8000 was his own and the rest borrowed. The transportation on Asylum Street in those days was a horse car line to serve the bluebloods on Asylum Hill, but the printing process hadn't changed much. Still, over on Main Street the *Times* already had its rotary.

Birdsall began with 5000 copies run off a hand-fed press in the gray of morning. Of these some 2000 only were bought. From that point on the figures existed mostly in the judge's imagination. At one time he claimed a circulation of 11,000, far more than those of either the long-established Hartford *Courant* or the *Times*.

When the time came that the new proprietor realized he would have to do something besides dream, the circulation had fallen below 1000. The total daily income of the paper was not over $15. And this is what he did: he got advertising — after his own fashion.

The opera house, for instance, not only did not advertise but even refused the new publisher a free pass.

As well-behaved and circumspect a city as Hartford was in those days, there still were those who liked a drop of grog in a teacup Sunday afternoons, or to spin the wheel or hold a poker hand. Most people knew, but nobody mentioned these things in the interest of community peace and quiet. Everybody also knew that the rendezvous was a cellar café in the opera house — everybody, including Birdsall. It was no trouble at all for him to get the names of frequenters. He wrote the story himself, but used no names except those of the opera-house owner and his father. The guest list would be saved for the next day's issue.

The press ran till noon that day, but the promised follow-up did not appear. What did appear was a large space advertisement paid for by the opera house. He went after the local skating rink in the same fashion, but drew down upon his head a $10,000 libel suit that resulted in a hung jury. Judge Birdsall had had enough and quit town. The paper endured for another two years.

Colonel Edward M. Graves, assistant adjutant general on the Governor's staff, borrowed a few hundred dollars and kept it going. He took more modest quarters, dropped the wire service, and did what he could with local news and boiler plate at $2.50 a page. Salaries were paid only occasionally.

The time came when Graves couldn't attract any more capital and asked for a receiver. Who should show up but old Judge Birdsall, who bid $500 for the paper. The receiver asked him to raise his own bid, which he did, to $1000, and got the *Telegram* back free of debt.

He restored the wire service, hired a few men, and threw out the boiler plate. Everything went along pretty well until the campaign of 1888. Birdsall was through with little shakedowns; he was loaded for bear, or something bigger — elephants. The Republican party.

The story was that the Connecticut delegation to the Chicago convention had been provided with something unusual in the way of entertainment. Someone had put up money to subsidize the delegation at the most palatial house of prostitution in the city and also had provided cabs to operate from the Palmer House to the doorstep of Carrie Watson's establishment.

Birdsall didn't use innuendoes in his scoop; he used affidavits from cab drivers and the proprietress herself. There was excruciating civic embarrassment and, for the most part, silence. Joseph R. Hawley's Republican Hartford *Courant* was silent; so was Alfred Burr's Democratic Hartford *Times*. The head of the delegation to Chicago was silent — everybody, in fact, except the newsboys hawking the *Telegram,* who did quite well for themselves and Judge Birdsall.

Then the judge made a mistake. In an editorial he wrote that the bill in Chicago was paid by the insurance company of which Morgan G. Bulkeley was the head.

Bulkeley had been mayor of Hartford and became Governor of Connecticut by leverage that gave him the appellation of the "crowbar governor." His opponent in the campaign had several thousand more votes but not a majority over all candidates. Bulkeley considered himself elected and, although the door of the governor's office was locked, he returned to the Capitol with a crowbar and let himself in.

This was not the type of man to take much from Birdsall, especially when the name of the Aetna Life Insurance Company was involved. The very day the editorial was published presumptuous deputy sheriffs appeared at the *Telegram* office and carted off press, steam engine, type, and all other equipment. Nothing was said about courts, injunctions, or legal action of any kind.

All this apparatus was understood to be stored in the basement of the insurance company. No one knew for sure because still nobody said much about it except behind the hand, and as for getting the news out, this was before the day of the freedom of information committees and the Civil Liberties Union.

Birdsall threatened to put out a flyer the next day but he was reminded that Wethersfield prison was only three miles away, and he left town.

The paper was taken over by Frank Grogan, a well-established citizen who, by giving assurance that Birdsall would never again reappear on the scene, got back press and equipment and resumed publication. Grogan died in 1891, the same year as that of Birdsall's death. From 1891 until 1906 the *Telegram* was run by Grogan's widow. It had never made much money for anyone, but no one had lost much on it either.

Quite apart from rising newspaper costs (one reason for this anecdote), Birdsall's kind of journalism could not exist today, but then neither could the rape of any kind of sheet whatsoever be brought off in America any longer.

Money is an important part of the story. When Lord Northcliffe was told of a man who had just bought a newspaper and began by cutting down costs, he said the new owner might just as well sell the paper again.

"Why?" Northcliffe was asked.

"Because successful newspaper publishing is a business of reckless expenditure."

7

CHAINS

MEN WHO OWN MORE THAN ONE newspaper today are meticulous and emphatic in the distinction they avow between the "chain" and the "group." Explicitly, this means that each paper in the group runs its own affairs independently and that the local publisher or editor is answerable, within reasonable limits, for policy. The implied distinction, sometimes voiced, is that the owner does not buy papers for aggrandizement or power, but to cut costs. No doubt some have been able to convince themselves to a degree. That William Randolph Hearst used his chain for power there can be no doubt. Frank E. Gannett's refusal to let any of his papers accept liquor advertising was unselfish, altruistic, and benevolent but it was nevertheless, and continues to be, use of power.

The distinction becomes foggy, though the result may be perceptible in some of its outlines.

Gannett was an idealist. He was a tall man of friendly appearance. His mouth was small, his jowls conspicuous, and his countenance benign. His most violent expletive was "My goodness!" He was a teetotaller and I never saw him smoke. When at a gala anniversary clambake at Hartford Times Tower atop Talcott Mountain, Frank E. Tripp, his right-hand man, paid hair-rumpling tribute to him in a speech by saying, "I've been doing all his drinking for him for forty-five years!" Gannett broke down and wept.

Hypersensitive, he was watched over by a special providence that thwarted his political ambitions. The slings and arrows of the hustings and of public office might have killed him.

His policies exemplified the contention that chain ownership cuts costs. The Hartford *Times* was a crying example of wasteful, unbusinesslike operation until he bought it. It had stumbled its way into great profits at a time when it was nearly impossible not to make money. Gannett took over just before the start of the depression. Where the former owners had at Christmas time surreptitiously slipped selected department heads a fifty-dollar bill each under the table, Gannett instituted profit-sharing for all employees. Hospitalization and a pension plan came later, although at a time when these benefits were fairly general.

Gannett thoroughly believed that his local autonomy was genuine. At meetings of Gannett executives in Rochester, which they referred to as the "cathedral town," Gannett would often squirm over the independence issue. He never missed saying, in one connection or another: "Sometimes I think we go to extremes about this local autonomy business ——" Then after a pause he would shake his head dubiously and resume, "But that has always been my policy and we'll stick to it."

At 10:30 in the morning Tuesday, January 30, 1928, Albert I. Prince, city editor of the Hartford *Times*, emerged from the office of Editor Clifton L. Sherman. He walked more quickly than was his custom but held his head slightly to one side as his custom was. His round face was red; it was usually pink.

He pulled up in the middle of the city room and addressed himself to no one in particular, as though in a loud, hurt soliloquy. His voice shook:

"The paper has been sold."

Nobody said anything for quite a while; all were struck silent, groping for a place to begin to think. The paper was making money — lots of it. Nobody in the city room knew how much, but the paper had been getting fatter and fatter and news space was being squeezed down proportionately. There was no sensible reason for selling out. Well, perhaps one . . .

The five men who owned the *Times* were squabbling among themselves like a flock of elderlies in a fraternal poorhouse. When they weren't squabbling, they weren't speaking. There were more cabals and axis-lines than would have been thought possible in a five-man set-up. If the astonishment was in any sense mitigated, it was because the management friction was common knowledge from the eaves to the press pit.

"Sold down the river!" murmured Fred Latimer, chief editorial writer, who had wandered grimly out of his cubbyhole and who was the first to show any curiosity about who the purchaser was.

Somebody by the name of Gannett.

Leslie Young, who came from Lewiston, said there was a Maine publisher by that name. Speculation then began about why a Maine Yankee would want to buy a newspaper in Connecticut. A copy boy who had just been to the dictionary said that a gannet was a tolipalmate sea bird akin to the fen duck. Presently the handout copy

89

for the news announcement came out to the news desk and disclosed that it wasn't the Maine bird but another Gannett, who owned some rapidly concatenating newspapers in New York State. That was the first time anyone in the city room had ever heard of Frank E. Gannett.

In a matter of days, Tripp was talking to the assembled staff. After some homespun wisecracks Tripp said nobody was going to lose his job. The magnanimity fell a bit flat because, on a paper that was laying a hatful of golden eggs every day, nobody had ever given much thought to such a possibility. Then Tripp issued, with a no-fooling seriousness, a command that he meant to be remembered.

Nobody, he declared, must ever use the word "chain" in regard to Gannett newspaper properties. The word must not appear in the paper. It must not be voiced. If outsiders were so indiscreet or ignorant as to utter it they must immediately be apprised that in referring to Gannett newspapers the word was Group. It must be explained, as he was then explaining, that the cardinal principle of Mr. Gannett in operating his papers was Local Autonomy. Each publisher and each editor was to make his own decisions, shape his own policies. The Hartford *Times* was an independent Democratic newspaper and Mr. Gannett, a Republican, had no intention of changing that or dictating what candidate, in any election, was to be supported or what party policies were to be followed.

The sale jolted Hartford. The idea of absentee ownership was much resented. The Asylum Hill aristocrats subscribed only to the *Courant,* "the oldest paper in continuous publication in the United States." The *Times* was something of an upstart, even a nouveau riche because it had left the *Courant* behind in both circulation and pelf. Yet, out of that curious loyalty that is extended to the ugly, the misshapen, the stepchild, the maverick, and the upstart, the *Times* was tolerated even by the bluestockings because it was at least a local upstart.

There was also a somewhat less altruistic reason for shock. The money to buy the *Times,* even at the price of $5,500,000, could have been raised in Hartford ten times over by nightfall. Within minutes of the posting of window bulletins about the sale, local brokers were on the wire. They were told that Hemphill Noyes were selling $3,000,000 in six percent debentures and were offering $2,000,000 in preferred stock. Of the latter 200,000 shares were offered in London. One broker who made a dash for New York got about a million dollars' worth of these wanted shares to sell.

As far as the *Times* was concerned it was a cash deal — $5,500,000 across the counter was what Gannett paid for "lock, stock, and barrel." That was the phrase Editor Sherman used in telling it to his managing editor. There were exactly one thousand shares which brought a price of $5500 each. Included was a cash surplus in the banks of $600,000.

Realizing almost immediately that he had a public relations problem on his hands, Gannett persuaded Sherman to stay on as editor for at least a time; also Francis S. Murphy, who was business manager. Sherman had been associated with Hartford journalism for some forty years, much of that time as managing editor of the Hartford *Courant*. His acquaintance was extremely large and if anyone could improve public relations for the Gannett-owned *Times* he could.

His first stipulation to put Gannett's "local autonomy" to the test. He wished Gannett success and would serve him as well as he was able considering the absences he expected to take from the paper. He was to have complete independence as far as day-to-day duties were concerned and he was to be free to spend his time as he pleased. If this was not satisfactory, the matter could be settled then and there.

With that he warned Gannett that the fight ahead was against the idea of "foreign" ownership and chain ownership, both circumstances resented by advertisers as well as readers. The office force didn't like the idea either and not only would morale have to be maintained but it must be built up. Contact with the actual owner would be infrequent, he stipulated, and there couldn't, of course, be the sympathetic bonds between owner and personnel that had previously existed. Nobody in Hartford was going to keep step to music played in Rochester. Having made that clear, Sherman reminded Gannett of the great circulation gains under his own ten-year leadership. He then made some changes in the news announcement that Gannett had written in order to give himself and his associates full credit and to spell out the fact that the same editorial management would have control of the paper's policy in the future as it had in the past.

He was almost brutal in twisting the barb that the Gannett Newspapers had made a fine acquisition in taking over the *Times* but that association with the Gannett chain didn't help the *Times* either in Hartford or Connecticut; that if the public got the idea that policies were Gannett-directed it would be disastrous. He would be answerable for a policy that not only gave local management control, but acknowledged their control of the paper.

Sherman felt that the *Times* would be stronger as an independent Democratic, rather than straight independent, paper. There were some traditions Gannett probably didn't know about: that the *Times* had been independent enough to fight the established Church and the Federalists; that its great editor, A. E. Burr, had had enough political spunk to reject an offer to become part owner of the *Courant* if he would turn Whig and join the Congregational church; that the *Times* bolted Bryan three times.

Sherman, during the two years that he remained, did pretty well as he pleased. Gannett made suggestions, but if Sherman didn't like them he said so and usually had his way. There were differences of opinion about content of the financial pages, but Sherman was in a position to say he was more thoroughly informed on Hartford financial life than Gannett could ever hope to be.

When Gannett sought to foist upon the *Times* a financial service that Tripp had recommended, Sherman would have none of it. It looked too much like a stock promotion scheme to him. This was in 1929. Gannett withdrew his recommendation. Sherman refused to set financial tables in smaller type, such as that used in Rochester, on the ground that it was chiefly older people who were interested in stock and bond tables and their eyesight was likely to be poor. Gannett probably lost that tilt because he mentioned the anathematic name of Rochester. Any suggestion that bore the phrase as-we-do-it-in-Rochester faced sudden death, no matter how good.

The following year a large offering of Gannett preferred stock was made and all the employees were expected to ring doorbells and find buyers for it. They had no choice in the matter. Without consulting them, stock salesmen's licenses had been obtained for each and all. Gannett asked Sherman why he had not bought any of it and Sherman said he didn't expect to remain long anyway. That was in August; in December he retired.

The Gannett principle of "local autonomy" was fairly well known and it may have had some effect in appeasing public resentment over the intrusion of a chain operation. It is to be doubted, though, that Sherman did much evangelizing for the new ownership because he found the idea odious and did not believe that management from a distance of 350 miles could possibly know the character, foibles, and temperament of a New England community where the aura of Thomas Hooker still prevailed.

In 1928 Asylum Hill was running the town. Its temper can be illustrated by the incident of Wadsworth's barn. Col. Jeremiah Wadsworth was a friend of George Washington, who was entertained at the Wadsworth house at least once. The house stood on Main Street and was torn down after the Civil War to make way for the Aetna Life Insurance Company building. The barn, however, remained standing until a decade ago. It was in dilapidated condition and full of termites. The fear was that termites might cross the street and infest the new art Museum, Avery Memorial. The barn must go.

Hartford being the city it is, there arose immediately a dedicated little group in the Hill section that couldn't put up with such sacrilege and started a movement to save the barn. A reporter with a satirical turn of mind, doubtless recalling Oliver Wendell Holmes' rescue of *Old Ironsides,* began one of his stories this way:

"Tear down the Wadsworth barn? Do you realize that George Washington's horse might have slept there!"

Hartford doesn't take things like that lightly. The little group seized upon that bit of rhetoric and made a slogan of Washington's horse. The barn was dismantled, timber by timber, and, doubtless including the termites, was raised again at Lebanon, Connecticut, where it may be seen today.

In this city then, and others, the Gannett Newspaper Corporation believed it could harmoniously own a newspaper property without creating the consciousness that upstate New York was the seat of authority and counsel for places as remote and disparate as Danville, Illinois; Plainfield, New Jersey; and, for a time, Brooklyn, New York.

Even with his protestations of a complete hands-off policy, Gannett could not refrain entirely from interfering. The *Times,* in his opinion, seemed to have been *against* too many things. It ought to be *for* more things. He cited the dikes, the Main Street widening, and the policies of the Metropolitan District (water) Commission. He was so little informed about the newspaper's stand on these questions that Sherman (while still on the job) was in a position to refute him and point out that the *Times* had taken a positive and favorable stand on all of them.

This era of sweetness and light had, as a matter of fact, begun nearly a decade before. In the years prior to 1920, the managing editor had been Captain Roland F. Andrews, a swashbuckling, hard-hitting newspaper man who not only fancied himself created in the Richard Harding Davis tradition — he actually looked like Davis. The captain earned the nickname "Bull" and he liked it; he was a crusader who didn't care upon whose toes he trod. The list of his exploits is a long one, but suffice it that the staff idolized him and never worked harder nor loved the calling more than they did under Andrews.

Then Sherman quarreled with Charles Hopkins Clark of the Hartford *Courant,* where he was then employed, over the League of Nations issue and resigned. Everett Willson, who then was making decisions for the *Times* and for the owner, Willie O. Burr, who never decided anything, immediately offered Sherman the managing editorship of the *Times.* "Bull" Andrews was assigned to an editorial writer's desk. He soon left to become managing editor of the Worcester *Telegram*.

Willson was all for community peace and quiet and in Sherman he thought he had his man. Sherman wasn't afraid of any kind of a story, and he met trouble when it came his way but he didn't go around looking for it as Andrews did. Sherman must have smiled when Gannett thought the *Times* was against too many things. He had gotten his job on the opposite premise.

When Gannett got into trouble, Sherman met that head on too. The Rochester magnate had been indiscreet enough to borrow a million dollars or more from the International Paper Company, of which he was a good customer. International had also gone into the hydroelectric power business and this the United States Senate didn't like because it smelled of a controlled press, an objection which seems a bit ironical today when newspapers are worrying about government control.

A Senate investigating committee summoned Gannett and there was quite a bit of news copy about it. Gannett borrowed money elsewhere on short notice and paid off International, but meanwhile Sherman made the Gannett investigation the lead story on page one of the *Times*. This was smart if his purpose was to convince Hartford of the "local autonomy" policy, but the copy editors who faithfully showed Sherman the news play in advance could detect a modicum of relish as he approved each headline.

During the next decade or so there was evidence of some pixie satisfaction in the *Times* office in seeming to "kick Rochester in the teeth." The issues didn't amount to much and Rochester can never be said to have lost anything except occasionally its patience.

In 1940 Gannett got the presidential bee and spent hugely to get the Republican nomination at the Philadelphia convention. Earlier there had been a group consultation. While nobody thought that Gannett was of a temperament to withstand the bruises of political roughhouse, he was told that he could naturally count on the support of his papers.

However, the delegate from Hartford reminded Gannett of the independent Democratic tradition of his Hartford paper. It couldn't go along with Roosevelt for the third term, but if anyone other than Roosevelt were nominated on the Democratic ticket, that nominee would get the *Times'* support even if Gannett won the Republican nomination. There was, of course, as little likelihood of Roosevelt *not* being named as there was of the lightning striking Gannett rather than Willkie.

When an editorial page editor wanted to go to the San Francisco peace conference, he made, and was confirmed in, his travel and hotel reservations only to be ordered from headquarters to cancel and stay home.

When Francis S. Murphy retired as editor and publisher in 1953 the last vestiges of local decision-making disappeared. The telephone bills between Rochester and Hartford skyrocketed. Semi-annual meetings were cut down to one a year, that being sufficient to get meanings across. Protocol was carefully outlined as to who should talk to whom at general headquarters.

Earlier there had been no group buying of features. Headquarters could have made a better deal by buying for all the score of papers, but at that time editors were allowed to make their own purchases. The first breach in this policy came when a telepicture circuit set up by Acme and later taken over by United Press, one satisfactory to the Gannett member papers, was cancelled for the principal reason that the Associated Press undercut the United Press price very substantially. None of the papers had any choice but to go along.

The *Times* had independently made a most favorable deal for the mailed feature service of NEA (Newspaper Enterprise Association). A very low figure was agreed upon because the *Times* was able to make only limited use of the service, added to the fact that it could hardly be considered exclusive since competitors seven and ten miles away already had it. Because of continued limited use this bargain figure was subsequently reduced by another one third.

When Rochester found out about this there was a violent protest about what was actually an excellent locally made bargain! The two Headquarters papers were paying four times as much. This would never do: pay more or cancel. The executive editor cancelled. When, a month later, he went to Europe, a contract was signed in his absence for a group deal with NEA under which the *Times* was required to pay two and a half times as much as it had paid before. This undoubtedly resulted in a saving to other newspapers of the group and perhaps to the group as a whole, but it was a deep and unprecedented bite out of local autonomy.

When Gannett was taken ill in 1955 and lay in critical condition for two years before his death in 1957, the lines began to be more tightly drawn.

As managing editor, I had made many addresses before national and regional newspaper conventions and at more than a dozen universities as well as at innumerable local meetings. Within newspaper circles these were sometimes critical of professional practices; in public gatherings I tried to keep them inspirational.

In late 1957 I was called to the publisher's office and

it was made clear that he had heard from Rochester. The result of this conference was my cancellation of a scheduled speech before the American Association for the Advancement of Science in Indianapolis, of my reservation for the Associated Press Managing Editors' convention in New Orleans, and of a scheduled lecture at the University of Michigan.

The year before I had given a lecture at the University of Michigan. After it was delivered, although my permission had already been granted for publication in the *Michigan Journalist,* the order came peremptorily that certain references be stricken out, thus impairing the literal accuracy of a paper over which Rochester, of course, had no control. It was felt that my lecture should have concerned itself with Gannett idealism, or with a discussion of the fact that when Gannett bought the Hartford *Times* at the height of the boom he was (in the language of the Rochester complaint) "charged a fancy price rented at usurious rates by kindly New Englanders." The reference may have been to the financing under which staff members were required to sell Gannett preferred. Actually some reporters made a fairly good thing of commissions for selling the stock to news sources, especially to those sources to whom a favorable press was important.

The censoring of the Michigan lecture made me feel that it would be wise to check with headquarters when in January, 1957, I was asked to write an article for the *Atlantic Monthly* on mass communications. Grave doubts were expressed and I was advised against the project on the surmise that the magazine was counting on me to do "an inside job of cracking the safe" and that I should "avoid falling into the trap."

In 1956 William H. Heath, then editor of the Haverhill

(Massachusetts) *Gazette,* and I organized the New England Society of Newspaper Editors. The principal reason was that the chief existing group required Associated Press membership; topically it was limited to AP affairs. Heath's was a United Press paper. We wanted an organization that could address itself to all the problems of journalism. I also hoped that we could include weekly newspaper editors. There are many outstanding ones in New England.

Toward this end a publication was needed and the Board of Governors of the new organization authorized me to launch a quarterly to be called *The American Editor.* As its editor I wrote all the editorials for the magazine, including the following, which appeared in the April, 1958, issue:

> It is one of the heartbreaks of American journalism today that while some of the best metropolitan papers are having a struggle to keep their heads above water, many small city dailies seem to prosper on mis- mal- and nonfeasance in their obligations to the community.
>
> If the smaller paper is alone in a not-too-large city, with competition reasonably distant, it can operate about as it chooses and still make money for somebody. It can suppress news, slant news, fail to cover news, fill the pages with boiler-plate and second-rate features, omit Democratic news and glamorize Republican affairs (though instances of the reverse would be hard to find.)
>
> There are metropolitan dailies of unimpeachable integrity, with brainy news executives, sound editorial policies which are faced with declining revenues and circulation no matter how they struggle. And struggle they do: changing format, intro-

ducing new areas of coverage, re-examining possibly dated techniques and inventing new ones.

Can it be that the climate is healthier for second-rate papers than for first-rate ones, depending upon geography?

The result was astonishing. Tripp, chairman of the board of Gannett Newspapers, while in New York for the convention of the American Newspaper Publishers Association, read an account of the editorial in *Editor & Publisher*. He wrote a letter to the editor of that weekly magazine, which circulates among newspaper people the country over. His letter read:

EDITORIAL DEPLORED

By giving this space, will you please assist in contradicting and deploring a story on page 101 of *E&P* for April 19th?

It was a quotation from *American Editor*, a new quarterly publication:

An editorial wherein the very backbone of the American press was misrepresented, insulted and libeled — the country's so-called "small newspapers" designated as "flourishing second-rate papers" — of all places to come from — New England, the cradle of the American free press.

Since I do not know how to sneak in back doors (since Prohibition) I wish to make this request for your space clear at the outset.

The *American Editor* is published in Hartford, Conn., by the New England Society of Newspaper Editors. Its editor is also an editor of the Hartford *Times*. I am president of the Hartford Times Company.

My aim is to disassociate the Hartford *Times*, its publishers and owners from any connection or agreement with the editorial, in toto, or any single reference to "small newspapers" contained therein.

I have never read an article in any publication, purporting to represent any segment of the newspaper press, that showed so little understanding of our Fourth Estate and what makes it click; such complete disregard and hatred for its grass roots, from which it grew; or which could better feed the fires of those who would destroy us.

If it had been signed by our arch-critic Harold Ickes (who died repentant) it would have been understood.

From an important section of our craft it is appalling and most regrettable. Here is one "damn Yankee" — and his newspapers — who deny, abhor and resent its absurd and vicious content.

Subsequent issues of *Editor & Publisher* carried vigorous replies by David Brickman, then president of the New England Society of Newspaper Editors, A. E. Rowse of the Boston *Globe,* and others.

Soon a letter followed from Rochester saying that the time had come to stop writing and talking as I had or else retire from the *Times*.

As soon as it was possible for me to divest myself of many involvements I retired from the *Times* and went to the University of Michigan's Department of Journalism in January, 1959, as a visiting professor. In April I was appointed to a permanent professorship.

The owner of a newspaper, which is a property, has a right to run any kind of newspaper he chooses, within the limits of law and decency. It is certain that he will run it his way whether he owns one or twenty.

In 1947 Arthur Hays Sulzberger, publisher of the New

York *Times,* said to the American Society of Newspaper Editors:

> Personally, I am not in favor of chain newspapers. I believe that newspapers should be leaders in the community but, at the same time, hold that the thinking that precedes that leadership should be "home grown."
>
> I had good evidence of the difficulties inherent in duplicate ownership in the 1940 campaign. Mr. Ochs' heirs control the *Times* in Chattanooga as well as the *Times* in New York. However there is no connection between the two newspapers other than that the Chattanooga *Times* now buys the New York *Times* service. We determined in New York after a good deal of wrestling with the angels, to support Wendell Willkie for the presidency. In Chattanooga the editor and his assistants wished to support Mr. Roosevelt. Those of us in New York who swung toward Willkie were normally voters in the Democratic column. There is no telling that we might not have wished to stay in it had we lived in Chattanooga, but we didn't and, as the responsible parties for policy of both newspapers, we couldn't support a Republican in the North and a Democrat in the South.
>
> I realize that there are those who would argue that the judgment of the editor and his associate in Chattanooga should have prevailed, and that true editorial independence would permit no other course. My answer is that such a solution turns a newspaper into another business in which ownership is concerned solely with profits. I have a different conception. The man who has the final responsibility of keeping a newspaper running must do more than stoke the boiler. He has to steer as

well and in most cases he can do so without in anyway lessening the sense of responsibility of the crew.

We solved our particular situation by giving the editor and his assistant in Chattanooga six months' leave of absence with pay. We announced the fact and the reasons in the columns of the affected paper — and both newspapers supported Willkie. Personally, I didn't like the solution, but it was the one which rang truest in my ears and I like it better than anything short of not owning newspapers in two communities.

In the boom and bust days of April, 1929, Frank Knox, who then was riding two horses as publisher of an independent newspaper and as manager of the Hearst chain, told the American Society of Newspaper Editors that he could not have had a better time (Hoover was in the White House) to discuss the question: "Is the Chain a Menace to American Journalism?" Because, he said,

> this nation is presided over by one whose life has been devoted to the very things that are aimed at by newspaper combinations — greater efficiency, increased production with less waste, a higher grade of product, giving people more of what they want and should have at less cost, speeding the wheels of commerce — in short, helping to make this country, day by day and year by year, a better and happier place to live.

He didn't like the word journalism; you seldom heard it outside of college. If one meant the journalism of earlier days, when editors went at each other hammer and tongs in the morning and drank mint juleps or shot at each other in the afternoon, then chains were indeed a menace.

If one meant by journalism anything that was not businesslike, efficient, and in keeping with the demand of the present day the answer was still, yes — chains were a menace. But one might as well ask, he said, if express trains and automobiles were a menace to transportation.

The development of chain newspapers was as necessary, Knox felt, and as inevitable as that of chain stores, chain hotels, great railroad systems, branch banks, big factories, and other great combinations. One might as well argue against the law of gravitation. Then there was the advertiser: If there were in a city three newspapers appealing to three different income classes — the man with one automobile, the man with two, and the man with three (!) — he must advertise in all three. This was economic waste. He had discovered that, to reach all customers and consumers, he must find newspapers that appealed to all classes.

"The advertisers' demands must be met and, as in meeting the demands of the reader, there was but one answer, the group newspaper, because no individual newspaper could carry this burden alone."

He thought that the chain newspaper tended to draw the nation closer together, to do away with sectionalism, to make the United States more truly than ever the *United* States. Chain operation was good, he knew, because newspapering was a business and nothing more was to be expected of it than efficiency.

In those days reasoning was simple and ingenuous. Knox was ahead of his times only in that he glimpsed the day when it would be necessary to admit that newspaper-making was merely a business. That day is here but the rationalizing is subtler.

The three Ridder brothers and their eight sons own newspapers in seven cities from New York to California.

Bernard H. Ridder, president of the St. Paul *Dispatch* and *Pioneer Press,* acknowledges that communities differ in character and needs and argues therefore that local editors have complete independence as to policy and procedure because Long Beach, Duluth, and New York occupy different places in the philosophical spectrum between liberalism and conservatism.

But do economies justify group ownership? No doubt Woolworth managers have local autonomy to adapt their stock to the foibles of the community — button hooks or paperbacks, washboards or transistor tubes — but sooner or later the community will have to adapt itself to what Woolworth has to sell. This might be called a form of education.

The means of communication and directive in a chain ownership may vary from autocratic rule to the mildest suggestion, but those editors who declare that they have been given a free hand are either deluding themselves or else they are smart enough to know what the boss wants without being told.

At a meeting of British and American editors in London in 1955 there was a free and frank exchange of professional notes. Donald Tyerman, then editor of the *The Times* of London, spoke at some length on editorial independence and ended by saying: "The publisher of the London *Times* doesn't know what I'm going to say in my leader until he reads the paper."

Blanche Hixon Smith, editor of the Meriden (Connecticut) *Record* and *Journal,* of which her husband is publisher and owner, commented that a publisher didn't dictate in so many words, but it stood to reason that the owner of the paper was going to get the kind of editorial page he wanted or else he was going to get a new editor.

Advertisers do not, of course, influence news departments, because a well-run news department knows what the advertisers won't stand for.

As to chain ownership, one insoluble problem is the distinction in character between cities. A single owner or editor can, if he is diligent, succeed in attuning himself to a community. He must do so if he is to be successful and if he is to serve the news needs of the city understandingly.

But to presume to own many newspapers in widely scattered and differentiated cities is perforce to adopt a pattern sufficiently neutral and nondescript to somehow suit all of them. This is the policy of the average; these communities cannot be averaged, but the publisher will reckon they can be and then see to it that they become so according to his own lights.

8

COLOR AND OTHER CUL-DE-SACS

WHATEVER SAVINGS CHAIN OWNERship may have effected, the fact must be faced that too little research has been done to change materially the complicated problem of producing a newspaper. About the only difference between the press of forty years ago, costing some $30,000 per unit, and the press of today, at about four times the price, is the ability to print run-of-the-paper color. (It was possible to print so-called "spot color" with the old press.)

But even the most modern newspaper press is already obsolescent when its product is compared with the results of competing mediums. Run-of-the-paper color printing is probably the greatest technical delusion to which American daily journalism has subjected itself in recent history. It can be likened only to the diversionary adventure stumbled upon at the turn of the century, *The Yellow Kid,* a comic strip, and after him the deluge of comic continuities: *Happy Hooligan, The Katzenjammer Kids, Maude the Mule, Buster Brown.* This was the point at which journals of communication decided that entertainment was an inherent function.

Color printing in the daily press was an anachronism before it started. Its heyday was the color comic of the Sunday press. In 1960 it is scarcely an also-ran. It is still poorly registered, albeit somewhat better than in the 1900's; the color combinations are for the most part in the poorest of taste; color pictures of food are something to make the gorge rise.

The housewife can go to the chain store and for the same price she pays in many instances for her daily paper she can acquire a slick-paper magazine in which the color printing is excellent. The food pictures actually make the mouth water. There are delicate nuances in the most subtle pastels.

It is a great mistake to embark upon competition in which you cannot possibly win, unless the issue is liberty, patriotism, or moral principles. None of these are factors involved in the economic competition between newspapers. The result of competing in color makes the daily press a ridiculously weak loser in the inevitable comparison. Primitive common sense should teach that color printing in the dailies can be nothing but an absurdity as long as they are compelled to use the only kind of paper and ink they can afford. On that count alone the newspaper press of today is out of date.

At the moment some advertisers are paying for color, but it is a grave question whether they will continue to do so. Newspapers see an increase in revenue and after a time a profit, but they have not reckoned the loss of the housewife's good will when she discovers that these primitive yellows and reds and greens rub off on her dress, as the blacks have always done. She must wash her hands after handling the paper, and it is a question whether her resentment points itself against the newspaper or the advertisers. Neither seems to have weighed this question.

Meanwhile Ossa costs are piled on Pelion costs and newspapers are disappearing at a rate which alarms those who have no capacity for self-delusion. Since cost is the crux of the newspaper problem it is an uncalculated risk to embark upon so costly an adventure as color in the supposition that the advertiser will carry the load. It would be a more reasonable speculation that the reader might pay considerably more if he could get more of the product the paper putatively sells — news.

Five years is plenty of time for a delusion to make considerable headway, but in 1955 not a few editors were still skeptical about color. A poll taken by the *Bulletin* of the American Society of Newspaper Editors found some of them grateful when they could get good results in black and white; one was disappointed with experiments and content to leave color to the advertisers; another "couldn't afford it." Other comments were: "pretty terrible," "a necessity for the modern newspaper," "here to stay," "enthusiastic," "far from attractive," "messy."

George B. Williams of the Geneva (New York) *Times* wrote: "I think we ought to pay editors and reporters better and forget color."

"Color is an eye-arrester," wrote W. Earl Hall of the Mason City (Iowa) *Gazette,* "but the same can be said of buck teeth or bow legs."

Newspaper publishers are so thoroughly oriented to the prospect and importance of advertising revenue that they are apt to become dislocated when a competitive medium discovers a new gimmick. Magazines employ color; television too. Therefore, newspapers must get into color.

The handicaps of the dailies with color are newsprint, the high speed press, and ink. There are limits — and the limits seem to have been reached — to how far these materials and equipment can go in reproducing black and white images, to say nothing of color images. The magazines begin with superior paper and at that point the contest is about over. So the lesson for the newspaper is: don't compete or invest in an area which is not the basic one of news dissemination.

It is always flattering to lively minds to think that they are at the head of the procession. These are likely to seize upon what is new *because* it is new and gamble on its future. Sometimes refinements in any apparatus are sufficiently satisfying to conceal the need for a new apparatus. The linotype machine and the press are basic and interdependent, just as the stereotyping process is the basic bridge between them. To replace the typesetter by a totally new apparatus — which is already in sight — will eliminate the stereotyping process and require a revolutionary approach to the press.

It has been the enthusiasm for and the satisfaction with improvements in these out-of-date machines that has postponed the long-overdue revolution in the entire newspaper manufacturing process.

For some, any new gadget has fascination. A sort of mesmerism prevents them from dropping the experiment which fails to prove itself. That, for a time, was the attitude toward facsimile, a transmitting apparatus which could be placed in the home and, runnning by electric transmission, automatically unroll a complete newspaper in scroll form on the subscriber's floor by breakfast time. It was a promising thing, born, as so many inventions are, out of war. The armed forces use it to transmit orders, maps, photos, and much else, proving it a usable communications medium. As experience accumulated it was apparent that in relationship to newspapers it was at best a new system of delivery — which the press does not particularly need, if the traffic problem (everybody's problem), can be solved.

Now it can be definitely stated that the newspaper industry is through with facsimile. It too was a cul-de-sac. Virtually all of the newspapers that had been experimenting with it have given it up.

Leading in this study was Lee Hills, co-author of the book *Facsimile,* when he was managing editor of the Miami *Herald.* He now says: "I don't know of any development which would indicate that facsimile newspapers would replace standard newspapers as presently produced. Our feeling at that time was that we had carried on the pioneer work long enough to learn what we could get from it and that there was no immediate prospect, because of the high cost of handmade receivers, of putting it on an economic basis."

He is wise who recognizes the result of the experiment and is prepared to abandon it when the time comes. It is my feeling that the same sort of discovery regarding color will soon be made.

Even a gadget that is successful in itself needs to be looked to for its consequences. Such a device is the teletypesetter — a machine which by electrical impulses transforms news matter into type by remote control. From a single point it can set identical type in an unlimited number of newspaper offices the country over simultaneously. This is practical, efficient, and in fairly general operation. The result calls, however, for serious attention because it also stereotypes the language of every line of telegraph news in the country, telling every story in identical words — including typographical errors. What could be better than this mechanical marvel — the apogee of uniformity and regimented news presentation? It is a valuable agent in cutting costs and labor, but it should not be misused and its effects should be carefully weighed.

As long as newspapers are written and printed there will be certain fundamentals that cannot be replaced or short-circuited. These are reporting, writing, and editing. Where journalism is visual or aural these elements can be modified, but if the newspaper is to continue as a medium to be read there must be trained observers to write it, people who know how to put words together and supervisors skilled in presentation. Gadgetry must aid, not interfere with, these crafts.

9

MONOPOLY

EVEN SO DISTINGUISHED AN APOLOgist for monopoly newspapers as Paul Block, Jr., editor of the Toledo *Blade,* concedes that

> Americans instinctively oppose monopoly. The very word conjures up horrendous images and thought. Monopolists are frequently arbitrary, if not downright criminal. These antagonisms have largely been overcome by some utilities through intelligent public relations. Newspapers, trying to avoid the problem, haven't directed their public relations programs specifically to this point, contenting themselves to emphasize their public service, their features, or the magnitude of their circulation.

As applied to newspapers, readers know what monopoly is and they don't like it. Masking it behind names such as "non-competitive newspapers" or telling them monopoly offers a better product doesn't change their minds. Further, where there are two newspapers in the same city under the same ownership, it is difficult to convince subscribers that there is genuine competition or freedom of reader choice.

Walter Adams and Horace M. Gray cover the subject in their book *Monopoly in America:*

> Monopoly . . . is an abomination in a free society. It can come into existence only by the destruction of economic freedom; it can perpetuate itself only by the continued suppression of economic freedom. Thus, by the necessities of its own being, monopoly is the antithesis of competition. But monopoly, in order to preserve itself, can do more than merely destroy the free market and restrict competition; it can, transcending the narrow confines of the market-place, reach out to suppress both social and political freedom.
>
> [They add] Even if a monopolist were personally disposed to . . . assume the role of a benevolent steward he could not, for he must exercise his economic power continuously and effectively lest it slip from his grasp. The imperative of survival is so compelling that one who wields monopoly power has no personal choice in the matter; he must either act like a monopolist or cease to be one.

The first observable effect of monopoly operation is a radical redefinition of what makes news. What was once grist for the mill is reclassified as chaff. (Some of the chaff may be dull, but it is basic.) Engagement items and weddings are culled for only the "best" names; wedding reports first strip the attendants of their gala raiment, then the bride's mother is similarly disrobed, and in the redefinition only the bride herself retains newsworthy nuptial finery. Obituaries are limited to those who have won either class or distinction and the rest may pay for their linage, poetry and all, or go to the graves without notice. Similar selection is applied to the parents for birth notices. Thus the southern female who was taught that a lady has her name in the newspapers only three times — when she is born, when she is married and upon death — may miss the only sanctions left to her if she lives in a monopoly town and is not a friend of the editor. Real estate transfers, city and town assessors' lists, and the names of high school graduates are similarly redefined out of the monopoly press. The size of the community has something to do with these arbitrary classifications, but when competition for news still exists, newspapers in fairly large cities still publish this journalistic routine, dull as much of it is, because this kind of data was always considered basic local information.

True the cry in recent years has been for brighter, more interesting papers; they circulate better. But much that is dull is still news and if a paper were to publish only what is dramatic, absorbing, and eye-fetching it could no longer be considered a medium of comprehensive information. A journal is a record.

The dictum that competition breeds sensationalism is only half true, as some of the best competitive papers have proved. Competition does, however, encourage wasted space on matters of extremely limited public interest. If competitive papers are out to get advertising accounts, they are likely to devote unconscionable spreads in pictures and reading matter to the furniture dealers' grand ball or a solid page of newsphotos to Main Street merchants gamboling at softball, horse-shoe pitching, or other diversions at the annual outing in the barbecue dell.

By the same token all letters to the editor are printed, with rare exceptions, and particularly during political campaigns when, because of their volume, they are likely to run over onto news pages.

Conscience in competition or monopoly has some flexibility. When feeling runs high on such hot issues as birth control or the parochial use of public school buses, the letters will be put in cold storage and published some weeks later when temperatures have subsided. This device has also been resorted to when drama or music critics are being taken over the hurdles by indignant readers.

Competitive newspapers can be wanting in courage but that does not justify cowardice in the monopoly newspaper, which need have less fear that spinelessness will be discovered.

Speaking of the 7686 newspapers in Soviet Russia, E. A. Lazebnik, deputy director of propaganda for the Party's Central Committee in the Ukraine said: "If one were to conceal the names of the newspapers, it would be impossible to tell which is which." This could in truth be said of more than a thousand newspapers in America.

Paul Block has said that "newspapers, as they have become more responsible and more independent, inevitably have come to resemble each other more and more."

Uniformity is not the sin of newspapers alone. The music business has produced uniformity in types of concerts given and stereotyped program material; in the consolidation of all the concert agencies into two giant corporations; in the centralization of musical activity in New York; and in the "tie-in package" by which series ticket buyers must hear second- and third-rate performers in order to hear the artists they are eager for. The publishing business has its book clubs, the theater has its Shuberts (or perhaps it should be stated the other way around), and the movies — at least until they got into serious trouble — made of uniformity and mediocrity a stock in trade.

It is unsettling to observe that though it is easily possible to talk about the average newspaper, you cannot talk about the average reader. In newspaper content the peaks above the average are not very high and the dips below the norm are not so deep as to be scandalous. Newspapers are steering a pretty straight and level course. This should not be disturbing except that the steady course also points in the direction of what is stereotypical, massively common, and undiscriminating as to taste, intelligence, social needs, and civic responsibility.

It isn't difficult because any editor and many amateurs know what the average newspaper should contain: a national wire service to fill the non-local columns as well as the wastebaskets; recipes on Thursday afternoon and Friday morning because food advertisers expect them; one of the new advice-to-the-lovelorn columns which seem to be read for their piquancy and sarcastic morality; sports; comics; decoration; travel; baby care. Every editor knows that good reporters are a convenience when handout material is running low; that anything but a mild editorial page would be risky business.

What really makes it impossible to start a newspaper is that the public has all the average newspapers it wants and needs and isn't going to buy any more of them. In fact, since the tempo of consolidation and monopoly is ever quickening, the prospect is that the public will buy fewer and fewer dead-level papers. Total circulation is gaining, to be sure, but so is population — at an even quicker pace.

Nor do all non-competitive newspapers serve their communities inadequately. The manner in which the single-ownership *Register* and *Tribune* serve not only Des Moines but the state of Iowa is distinguished. Oddly, or perhaps not so oddly, since they are both Cowles papers, the *Star* and *Tribune* do a similar but not identical job for Minneapolis and its larger environs, with sturdy competition as near as the crossing of the river to St. Paul. Thus monopoly serves if it will; competition serves if it will. There is only the matter of conscience, an attribute over which there is not likely soon to be a monopoly.

It is also worth noting that where monopoly is associated with enterprise and imagination, as in Des Moines and Minneapolis, there exists also the will and incentive for research and experimentation, both of which are usually the liveliest where there is vigorous competition.

The monopoly situation in Toledo was the basis of Paul Block's discussion in the Niemann Reports. (Incidentally, his brother William Block is publisher of the competitive Pittsburgh *Post-Gazette*). He wrote that forthright discussion of the trend toward single ownership could "help the public better understand the benefits that single ownership offers readers. I can illustrate the fact that this trend is the best hope to improve the quality of journalism and reduce abuses which flourish in all but the largest of cities, where newspapers can compete for different groups of readers instead of trying to be all things to all people."

He dismisses the notion that newspaper consolidation

results from efforts to accumulate wealth or power. He feels that rising cost is only one of the factors behind the trend; another is the waning of the two-party press and the American people's "lack of interest in political doctrine." With other defenders of single ownership he holds that competition means sensationalism, while monopoly papers can take their time for better writing and accuracy; also that the city editor of a "one voice" paper must print news that competition would reject, just as its editorial page editor will publish all letters to the editor, short of blasphemy, pornography, or sedition, while the competitive editor can be choosey. He acknowledges that the Toledo *Blade* edits political news during election campaigns "with a ruler partly in deference to the political prejudices of readers, partly to protect the *Blade* from that type of post-election survey which implies that a newspaper was grossly unfair because the speeches of one party's candidate received more space than those of another."

It cannot be denied that there are good non-competitive newspapers but to declare that competition creates reckless sensationalism, as cause and effect, assumes that there are no other planes on which competition can operate.

Among newspaper people, two things learned, as at a mother's knee, are the dictum that advertisers do not influence the newsroom and that there is no economic waste in advertising.

Let us see where the advertiser comes in with regard to monopoly. In a competitive city of, say, three newspapers, the local advertiser is likely to divide his budget, though in uneven assignments. That, for one thing, gives him bargaining power apart from sales return. He can al-lot a little less or a little more to space in one paper or another, depending on how each of the papers is behaving itself with regard to the advertiser's interests. If he leaves out one entirely there is at least one disaffected organ in town. For some advertisers such a risk is scarcely tolerable, although it is not to be supposed that most merchants deliberately buy immunity if they get nothing else for their money. If one of the papers absorbs the laggard among the three, his advertising budget is still split only two ways, but he is now spending less and getting more for his money because it is paying to cover the whole field, he thinks. Let us now suppose that the two remaining papers were to merge. The saving is potentially substantial; there should be still more money for the merchant's other purposes: commercials, renovation, profits.

The moral is: There is some reason for the merchant to like monopoly. He welcomes it, though tacitly. Even if it is accepted that advertisers do not affect policy, it is nevertheless fairly obvious that in the long run they get what they want.

It is the custom to suggest a variety of reasons to explain an ambiguous phenomenon, especially when the explainers are not quite satisfied with any one answer. That is the case with the ground swell toward monopoly in the newspaper world. That the answers are contradictory is of no account. If monopoly produced better newspapers per se that might be ample moral justification. It cannot be proven. If monopoly were born out of irreducible costs and profitlessness, that might be sufficient. It cannot be proven. If monopoly brought about freedom from sensation — but the next murder trial involving a doctor will disprove that.

None of these reasons is completely convincing. Were candor to prevail, the pressure of the advertiser would probably prove a factor more potent than any of the three others. The honesty of publishers would be more apparent if they were to explain their policies where they own a morning and an afternoon paper in the same city. In some places one of the papers is strong and vigorous and wealthy; the other is deliberately kept in a moribund state merely to hold down the spot against competition. No money is spent on the lightweight paper; its staff is a corporal's guard; there is no dynamism in the circulation department; neither *esprit de corps* nor pride in any department. The paper is merely garrisoned. At any time the publisher can revitalize the second paper but he knows he has little fear of an interloping competitor as long as the nominal masthead appears.

The claim that the two staffs compete is hollow. What self-respecting newspaperman could reconcile himself to working on a garrison newspaper, if he had anywhere else to go? Or, what ambitious journalism graduate could be happy helping to hold down a neglected fort against the remote possibility of a new competitor?

Publishers who try to justify monopoly fail to recognize a rule of selling — the customer who has a choice buys more. It is doubtful whether customers in metropolitan New York, Los Angeles, San Francisco, who can choose from among seven to fifteen different papers, local and big city, buy fewer papers than those who can buy only one. There is also doubt that if half of the papers were merged or suspended the survivors' circulation would increase by the same amount. There are dramatic instances to the contrary.

It is an advertising fallacy to look at the circulation figure alone when buying daily newspaper space. In the race for circulation much wasted space is sold. Does the newspaper publisher ever ask himself or tell his advertisers what kind of circulation he has? It is a quantitative deal, pure and simple, and he hasn't the slightest idea who is reading his paper until he has established a character for the paper that is something besides "all things to all people." Then he has something to sell. If, on the other hand, he levels all human creatures, he will find that the average man has no needs and has no money to spend. Advertising is wasted on this imaginary creature. We are rich man, poor man, beggar man, thief — or somebody else.

In a competitive situation, then, let the "thinking man's" paper forget about the great unwashed and fix an advertising rate to suit the merchant who wants to sell products to the thinking, washing man. Let the sensation-monger go for a different kind of advertising, if he can find out what people who like sensation spend their money for. The merchant must ask himself, "Whose dollar can I get?"; the publisher, "Whose dollar can I get for him?"

Why create the average paper when there is no average merchant or average product? Only the dollar is average, but it is in the hands of people whose wants and needs are different. There are innumerable ways in which to compete for it. If one paper runs to sex and crime, its competition can be better written, cover wider fields, provide better services or stronger editorial pages. A paper with a high standard of coverage and criticism in the field of culture is a better advertising medium for many merchants who would be wasting their money in a cheap journal.

Sumner H. Slichter, economist, has said that America is the most competitive country in the world and the result has been great rivalry in products and processes. "Sometimes," he writes, "the new product virtually drives the old one out of use, as electric lighting has done to gas or kerosene lighting, and as the automobile has done to the horse and buggy. More often, however, the new product or service forces improvement in the old product."

Newspaper research has been negligible and the need for it has been overlooked because of stubborn refusal to recognize true competition. Publishers and owners declare steadfastly that radio and television do not hurt the press but increase readership. It is the failure to see and appreciate the new medium that leads to the driving out of the old of which Professor Slichter speaks. So we have monopoly to the extent that there are left only thirteen states with competitive newspapers; Michigan has only one morning daily.

The customer's wants must be respected. Again Professor Slichter:

> Sometimes the preferences of the public seem to reflect poor judgment, but sellers have learned that there is no appeal from these preferences and that the seller who ignores them or attempts to persuade the public to accept a better-considered set of preferences is headed for trouble. A few years ago Childs Restaurant chain had a disastrous experience attempting to persuade customers to accept a diet that the president of the company considered good.

The tidal wave toward newspaper mediocrity through monopoly is so strong that anyone attempting to breast it is not only conspicuous but is stamped as one of the enemies of the press that publishers and editors are forever seeing under the bed. The worst crime of these enemies seems to be that they are enemies of standard practice.

William Loeb, president and publisher of the Manchester (New Hampshire) *Union-Leader* is one of these. He is not a member of the American Newspaper Publishers Association, which in itself makes him a sort of maverick. As a monopolist he runs the only ten-cent paper in New England. It is not too much to say that some publishers hate him. And not only publishers, he admits:

> One thing OUR readers can say is that they may hate us but they have never been bored. I suppose one of the troubles is that newspapers are owned by duller and duller people who, in turn, hire duller and duller people to run them. . . . Here at our paper we are always raising hell about something . . .
>
> While we have strong editorial opinions, we give our readers free play with theirs. We run more letters to the editor, I am sure, than any other newspaper in the nation. We give up our entire editorial page each Tuesday to our readers and frequently run two or three more full pages of letters during the week, as well as those which we ordinarily run on the editorial page each day.
>
> Beyond the matter of libel, we place no restrictions on our letter writers. Several years ago one of them wrote in on some subject or other on which he was considerably irritated with us, as you can gather from the ending of his letter, which was about as follows:
>
> "And in conclusion, Mr. Loeb, I hope they skin

you alive and nail your hide to a bridge across the Connecticut River, where the rubber-neck tourists will REALLY have something to gawk at."

We ran his letter in full, including his delightful ending.

On another occasion one of our readers began his letter as follows: "Dear Mr Loeb: You are a moron — withal a diabolically *clever* moron!" We ran that too.

One of these days they are going to make papers so dull that people will stop reading them, and that will be THAT.

By the way, we have been hammering the hell out of these out-sized automobiles for a great many years. Interestingly enough, we haven't suffered any lack of advertising, either.

This is monopolist Loeb who can and does run his own kind of newspaper.

Publishers and owners, while they strain to find a virtue in monopoly, pretend to regret the loss of papers through consolidation or suspension. They are all vigorous defenders of free enterprise.

Yet they close ranks reflexively when monopoly is threatened. A curious case in point was at Haverhill, Massachusetts, a one-newspaper town until the *Gazette* had a strike. In a predominantly union town this was a serious matter because carriers were dissuaded by parents from delivering the paper, and advertisers, too, felt the pressure of labor. The *Gazette* lost both circulation and advertising disastrously. Part of this was attributable to sore toes stepped on by William Heath, outspoken editor of the paper, who is a model of Yankee bluntness and independence.

At this juncture Loeb of Manchester, just across the New Hampshire line, entered the picture. He came down into Haverhill and started a newspaper. In any gritty situation where a lone newspaper has accumulated a store of ill-feeling and resentment the newcomer has encouraging success at first. It is impossible to do business of any kind without a certain amount of disgruntlement and dissatisfaction; the more, of course, where labor hostility and a strike have acidulated community emotion.

Loeb got advertising and he got circulation. Since this was a new venture there was *esprit de corps,* while the staff of the heretofore non-competitive paper was scarcely geared to the kind of war that Loeb brought to Haverhill.

What is of interest here is that a large group of New England publishers united and contributed a capital fund to support the *Gazette.* In simplest terms they took their stand behind monopoly and against competition. The fear was that Loeb or someone else could come in and menace the status quo anywhere in New England.

Loeb's version of the Haverhill episode is this:

> I was just about to buy the opposition when this group of 32, consisting of newspapers and people associated WITH newspapers, operating under the grandiose name of Newspapers of New England, Inc., took over the Haverhill *Gazette* and have been proceeding to try to put me in my place since last December.
>
> Of course IF these individuals can get away with this, then no one can ever start a competing newspaper anywhere in the United States.
>
> For instance, let us visualize a growing and rapidly developing city in California with an established daily paper. Some professional people, business people, and possibly some labor people

and others, decided that, while they have nothing special against the present paper, the city would be better off with two papers, so they start a paper. They have good management and the city is growing rapidly, so they are succeeding. At that point, following the Haverhill precedent, the local publisher gives a shout and all the other newspapers in that area belonging to the association in California, or whatever state it is, come running in to help this man. They make loans to him, they furnish him with their best advertising and circulation people, give him all sorts of advice, so how could this new group stand against such a combination?

I am a firm believer in the free enterprise system.... What do you do with a group of publishers such as this crowd in New England who simply have taken it on themselves to determine who can and who can NOT go into the newspaper business?

But now has not monopolist Loeb become a chain owner? Presumably his intention is to make the new Haverhill paper his kind of newspaper. He is opposed to the monopolists arrayed against him because they are against competition in Haverhill. He says he is for it. Would he be for competition in Manchester?

The situation in Lima, Ohio, was only somewhat similar. Raymond C. Hoiles, a chain operator, bought the established Lima *News*, a conservative paper with a long record of community service in the kind of promotions that are resonant as a drumhead in promoting the paper — backing civic projects which are beyond cavil.

The Lima *Citizen* was founded mainly by former *News* staff men on money easily borrowed in a situation made emotional by a strike against the *News*. Hoiles had been in Lima long enough to be categorized as non-civic and reactionary. It was said of him that he was trying "to drag the town back into the nineteenth century."

This may be an apt description. Hoiles was against parking projects, public schools, labor, and all manner of things that most people, either out of conviction and courage — or lack of it — feel are not open to question.

One can disagree violently with Hoiles and with Loeb regarding their ideas, but their real crime in the eyes of the newspaper club is nonconformity. Not to belong to the American Newspaper Publishers Association is as heinous an offense as to be opposed to unlimited public education. These things are as right as righteousness and not to be disputed.

The "one party" of the newspaper business is not the Republican party; it is the party of Regression or holding fast. It is the party of social reaction at the cost of war, the party of journalistic license, of monopoly, of profit above all, the party that makes of the First Amendment a shield for all backward practices from child labor to thought control.

I do not agree with either Hoiles or Loeb but I admire them as newspaper publishers who have the courage to refuse to conform to mediocrity — the courage to open their mouths, which is a good deal these days when journalism's high priests do not seem to know that the First Amendment also sanctifies free speech.

10

JASON
AND THE
DRAGON'S
TEETH

THE ASSOCIATED PRESS IS THE greatest news-gathering organization in the world.

This statement has been repeated so often and so easily that one is strongly tempted to dispute so confident an assertion. If "great" means large, it is true. Whether it is judged by the yardstick of membership, resources, or ramification, it has no contenders for the title of biggest. If the standard is accuracy, speed, writing, or resourcefulness there can be, and has been, room for argument. Fictions have been devised and loudly promulgated regarding the unimpeachable reliability of the Associated Press but the score is about even with that of the United Press, now merged with the International News Service. Both have made egregious errors and have tried to live them down, mainly by keeping charges alive against the other service. Both accused International, while it had a separate existence in the Hearst empire, of sensationalism.

All three have kept charges alive against an opponent because there has been a modicum of truth behind all the accusations. United Press was responsible for the "false armistice" in World War I and the Associated Press was similarly at fault in World War II. Each found an individual scapegoat and tried to clear its corporate skirts, but there was so little difference between the two that judgment must weigh premature revelation of what-wasn't-so-but-might-be-soon against breach of confidence and betrayal of a pool agreement among one's colleagues. As to the sensationalism ascribed to International News, one can with no difficulty cite purple passages from the wires of the other two services that would match anything that ever came over Hearst's wires.

The United Press-International is vastly more efficient in the operation of its news and photo circuits because it must be. Because there are fewer members and fewer news pictures sources there must be less waste of time in transmitting pictures over conference telephone wires to maintain volume. A check of machines running side by side shows that the UPI actually telephones more pictures each day than does the Associated Press. Because United Press-International has fewer wires for verbal transmission its news stories must be more terse and compact. International News Service had during its lifetime some of the best reporters in America and abroad, though perhaps fewer than other services. The United Press has always dominated South American coverage. The news writing of the United Press has always been superior to that of the Associated Press, and this continues so with United Press-International. UPI tends to give a story the hard sell, the overplay, and what may be counted sensationalism in some minds, but by comparison Associated Press stories are likely to be understated, dull, and badly organized. They lack flair and zest.

The two press associations eye each other in the obsolete pastime of the "scoop," but in fact neither has left the other very far behind and the race is usually a dead heat. Either will run the risk of hypothecating accuracy to get there first even if with the least. Rivalry of this kind is old-fashioned and amusing.

The Associated Press is the most extensive news service in the world. There are no foreign services that can be considered in the running. However, its great source of strength is also its most conspicuous weakness. It is a co-operative organization. Its permanence is assured as long as there are newspapers in America. It doesn't have to think about money. Its members are assessed for any needed sums. No member knows what any other member pays. That secret is held closer than the most highly classified information in the Pentagon. Many a managing editor does not know what his newspaper is assessed. He can find out if he really wants to, but the matter is held to be none of his business. Unlike the practice of other services or syndicates, no bill ever reaches his desk. The assessment is by draft against the newspaper's bank account. The managing editor cannot do anything about the amount of the assessment, however great or small, and he would be foolish to worry about it because he has plenty of other bills to be responsible for about which he can do something.

The publisher or owner can find out, if he wants to do so, but to him the question is academic. He believes, as firmly as in the four gospels, that he must belong to the Associated Press to survive. A publisher and managing editor with courage and imagination could get out a good newspaper with only United Press-International, under the present definition of newspapers, but most do not. Any wanted sums pour into the Associated Press operating fund and its security is absolute.

The Associated Press has by far the largest corps of correspondents in the world. Its bureau in Washington counts a staff of over a hundred. Not all of its correspondents are full-time reporters. Many of those abroad are native newspapermen with other, permanent connections and have only a contributing relationship to the Associated Press. The same is true in this country. Nevertheless AP has more full-time staff correspondents in the foreign field than any other service, including the Chicago *Daily News* or the New York *Times*. For South American coverage editors have always been inclined to look to the United Press for leadership.

The weakness of the Associated Press is the weakness of democracy. Each one of the 1700 member newspapers has an equal right to ask for what it wants. In fact the smaller newspapers are likely to be more vocal because their own resources fall far short of what the bigger papers are able to provide for themselves. The result is that the service must be a synthesis that will keep the greatest number of members reasonably happy. Inevitably the news report will be a sort of common denominator. Special services are not to be expected. Should one member want the text of a Supreme Court decision, it will be forthcoming only if a majority of the members on the circuit, which is usually coextensive with state or regional boundaries, also want it, and that is not likely to happen very often. The United Press-International, on the other hand, as a commercial service will be at considerable pains to service extra requests of any kind. The wants of a customer buying a news package over the counter are bound to be considered.

The AP does not have democracy's corresponding strengths, where sturdy individual leadership arises.

Since the Associated Press is a two-way co-operative,

each member is bound to make available to all the others the news which it gathers. The contractual term is that a member paper must supply to the common pool all news of "spontaneous origin."

This vague phrase can mean anything or nothing. In effect it reserves for the papers' exclusive use the local stories of specialists, usually written under a by-line. The spot news stories of a superior reporter like the late Meyer Berger, whether he is operating in New York or in a suburb, as in the sensational Unruh killings, are not available to Associated Press member papers. If he had been a reporter in Muskogee or Hartford, the member papers there would be required to file his copy. This is because New York local news is covered by the City News Association, owned by the Associated Press, and therefore supported by all the members. In other words, members the country over pay for and provide coverage in the field, whereas metropolitan members are excused from the contributing responsibilities to which other papers are held.

This is probably the most efficient method of procedure but there is no way of establishing the facts because of the curtain drawn before all assessment matters.

On the average circuit more than half the news volume is supplied directly by member papers. Frequently this news is an accumulation of carbon copies of locally written stories, much of it filed directly on the wire from point of origin without benefit of bureau supervision. Theoretically, the city editor of the filing paper should give special editing to the copy he feeds to the wire but in practice, he nearly always bypasses this obligation. The result is that often all the newspapers on the circuit will have a verbatim account of what the originating paper publishes, a bland uniformity which amounts almost to regimentation. For the folklore that the Associated Press is infallible and its copy untouchable persists among telegraph editors, many of whom send Associated Press copy to the printer innocent of any editorial pencil marks.

Since news writing, like water, does not rise above the level of its source, it can readily be seen that the quality of the Associated Press report is no better than the dead-level of news writing in the average American newspaper and that is far below what it ought to be.

The Associated Press does little editing, either of pictures or news copy. It makes no decision about what is obscene or what is printable. It will send a message warning editors, in effect, that "Here is something at which you might want to give a second look." In most shops AP copy doesn't even get a first look beyond the opening paragraph and that look is only for headline purposes so that the rubric will bear some resemblance to at least the early part of the content. Members thus are actually accepting without question, on the state level at least, the copy as written and the judgment as exercised by member papers on the same circuit.

One serious mistake made by the Associated Press was to enter the feature business — comics, columns, departmentalized reading matter such as articles on hobbies; and "stuffing" for special editions of newspapers, which seasonally shake down advertisers at school opening time, or in the season of brides and home furnishings, or in the vacation season (automobile and travel sections); — all of which are revenue-producers pure and simple. For a price the Associated Press supplies a bundle of copy which can be poured into the forms without being read. This has nothing to do with news, but it helps keep the Associated Press great.

It cannot produce an extremely popular comic, first,

because of the completely neutral level at which continuity humor has to be aimed in order to appeal to all members; second, it cannot give exclusive territory, the chief promotional value of a comic feature. The smallest Associated Press member in the shadow of a big paper would have just as much right to such a feature as the metropolitan paper and that would destroy its value to the big paper, which is willing to pay large sums for territorial rights covering an entire state or more. (Boston papers buy rights for large sections of New England.)

As a news service the Associated Press is in a permanent business, while most editors now realize that as a circulation builder the comic strip is on the way out. Once it was thought that 50 per cent readership was the dividing line between a first-rate comic strip and a poor one, with some rating as high as 70 and 80 per cent in the heyday of this type of feature. Recent studies show that out of 40 strips published in one large city, only 13 rated as high as 50 per cent readership and eight of those were on the ragged edge.

As to columnists, it is just as futile to expect a co-operative organization to sponsor a colorful opinion writer as it is to expect the Associated Press to provide as salty a comic strip as *Li'l Abner* or *Pogo*.

One reason why more and more newspapers are being created in each other's image is that the Associated Press is rivalled only by death as the great leveler. Conformity is the built-in hazard for any rigidly co-operative enterprise. By this agency 700 daily newspapers run virtually identical accounts of the most important news events. This monotone is not entirely the fault of AP. Copy editing today is largely a matter of theory and it is rarely, even on newspapers which pride themselves upon editorial fastidiousness, that the desk changes more than a word or a phrase of telegraph copy, if it is from the Associated Press. Here is cause for misgiving. The sale of the International News Service does not signify that there will always be competitive services. No business, except the Associated Press, is invulnerable.

Growing directly out of its tribulations as a co-operative, the Associated Press organized a program of self-study which could have been one of the most enlightened permanent critiques of journalism. Every circuit meeting of the Associated Press, whether state-wide or regional, used to be a Donnybrook in which Associated Press brass and bureau managers got all the brickbats.

A stroke of genius on the part of canny General Manager Kent Cooper, twenty-five years ago, produced a remedy. Like Jason sowing the dragons' teeth he might have reckoned that if he could get the editors fighting among themselves it would take the heat off the press association management. The organization was to be called the Associated Press Managing Editors Association. Next the Continuing Study was organized, with its own chairman and endless committees, to examine the entire AP news output. These committees included those on: the domestic report, the foreign report, Washington news, sports, quality of writing, election coverage, AP News features, newsphotos, state studies, membership participation, and many other divisions, including even a freedom of information committee.

This seemed to work successfully and the Associated Press Managing Editors' conventions became a hive of industry and oratory. It was really stimulating to these committee members to bring home from the office daily carbon copies of the Associated Press report and pore it nights — analyzing, criticizing, organizing. It did them good; many of them had not handled wire copy for years.

There were round-robin reports to exchange with other committee chairmen; then there were the midyear meetings of all the chairman at 55 Rockefeller Plaza, the cairn of the Associated Press, for a thorough check with AP general executives.

Zeal was unprecedented. Somehow, though, the critical element mellowed. There was on every committee an appropriate member of the Associated Press managerial staff to comment on findings and criticisms. After the first few years it began to become apparent that a pattern was forming: hard work on a committee for a couple of years and writing of enough letters and reports made an editor a chairman; a conspicuously active chairman on a lesser committee soon got a more important chairmanship and a place on the convention program; then there were the chairs of officialdom, ending with the chairmanship of the Continuing Study beyond which there was nothing but the short, crowded ladder which led to the presidency of the AP Managing Editors Association.

These promotions were inevitable, provided one dealt gently with the Associated Press report, its general executives, and all the olympian works of the greatest newsgathering agency in the world. There was the Hazen case, for example.

Charles Hazen had been managing editor of the Shreveport *Times* for eighteen years when, during the McCarthy hearings, he fancied he detected evidence of bias in the writings of Associated Press reporters. He prepared a report of sixty-six pages containing fifty-eight charges with supporting evidence to show that AP writers were somewhat to the left of center.

Hazen was given a few moments to discuss his report at the opening of the Managing Editors' convention in Atlanta in 1950. Meanwhile the Board of Directors had unanimously condemned the report and thrown it out.

Because there was some feeling among editors that Hazen had been steamrollered, the subject was raised again on the final day of the convention. The heavy artillery of the editorial stalwarts had been rolled up and fired at point-blank range. Hazen was crushed and his only vocal ally, Robert Early of the Indianapolis *Star,* was silenced too. The Early resolution calling for a full-scale investigation died when Louis C. Harris of the Augusta, (Georgia,) *Chronicle,* withdrew his second.

Norman Isaacs, Managing editor of the Louisville *Times,* who was anything but a Hazen partisan yet at great pains to see that fairness prevailed, gave the convention something to think about when he commented: "If Charlie Hazen had tried to show bad news judgment by the Associated Press he probably could have made a pretty good case." The resolution of the Board of Directors condemning the Hazen report was unanimously made the resolution of the entire convention. At its next meeting the Board of Trustees of the Associated Press Corporation took the same action, attesting to the unimpeachable rectitude of the Associated Press.

The point is that Hazen by voluminous documentation had tried to show that Associated Press writers were biased and had been unfair to McCarthy. Of this almost nobody was convinced. His own paper had only a single AP wire and the reports received there were greatly condensed before they reached Shreveport. The point that the Associated Press might have shown bad news judgment in editing down the copy was never of any interest to the convention.

The oratorical drubbing that a lone questioning editor got from his hundreds of infuriated fellows was enough to suggest to anyone who witnessed it that in this instance the quality of mercy was quickly overstrained.

Misled as Hazen may have been by the truncated evidence available to him, in subsequent conventions critics of the Associated Press were much more circumspect and cautious. This was regrettable, because such efforts as the managing editors had been putting forth through the years represented, while by no means the only one, what is still the most highly organized continuing study of newspaper practice. Its main usefulness is that a good many editors each year look hard at Associated Press copy. This puts them in a more useful position than the publishers who are the franchise-holders and who, once each year, gather in the Starlight Room of the Waldorf-Astoria to listen to Lloyd Stratton, General Executive, read the report of the General Manager. This begins at eleven o'clock in the morning, and when Stratton concludes the annual meeting is over. Few, if any, of the publishers ever see much of the AP News report, until or unless a fraction of it appears in their own papers.

What difference now in Associated Press reporting after more than a decade of the Continuing Study? One might expect that the writing would have improved, that there would be fewer fresh starts ("new leads") — the AP allows itself four or five on a story of ordinary importance — a better Washington report, more human interest stories, shorter sentences, shorter words, shorter items, and improvements in all of those things of which editors complained before the Study. But the writing is still conventional enough to be recognized even without the identifying Æ logotype; even if the first version is clear, factual, and direct, the Associated Press keeps sending new leads which may be cloudy and ambiguous; there are still items to prove that even the short word, the short sentence, and the short item can be dull. Foreign news is interpreted by deskmen in New York and Washington; campaign coverage is still judged by how near the reporter came to guessing who would be elected; and the sports report proves that Americans are bilingual, being proficient at reading the ring, rink, gridiron, and diamond argot as well as United States English.

In any race for survival it must be remembered that Æ is not a business but a co-operative enterprise with almost unlimited resources. If the day comes when the Associated Press has the field without competition it will create a fearful hazard. Federal regulation of the press as a monopoly might follow.

The Æ logotype signifies the biggest and most securely established press association in the world, and because of that there is real reason for concern lest some day it be left without the dynamic influence of rivalry and initiative. And because there are already signs of its growing narcissistic complex, American editors might well stand in fear of the day when, grinding away at the teletype prayer wheel, they shall be allowed to worship but one true and only prophet.

11

THE

NEWS

FUNCTION

THE WORSHIPFUL RELIANCE OF newspapers upon the Associated Press has causes other than the quantity of its service. It lifts from local shoulders the burden of deciding what is news, its importance, and even, to an extent, its play. This tends to blunt the judgment of editors, not only as to news values but even as to basic news function. Has the business of informing the reader, as the whole duty of the press, become blurred? Has interpretation become a recognized role of the daily press? Is the entertainment factor now fixed as a second function? Is the American — "local as the town pump" — actually as parochial as he seems or is helping him to gain world perspective a pressing obligation? Shall we have critical writing on the arts or will the reportorial account suffice?

The Associated Press has offered most of the answers. News, definitively, is what the Associated Press transmits. Interpretive writing has during the past decade — and under the pressure of the Associated Press Managing Editors Association — been established by the assignment of such by-line writers as James Marlow, Saul Pett, William Ryan, John Hightower, and others in the capacity of "news analysts" to venture farther into the realm of opinion than do many local *editorial* writers. The Associated Press is no doubt keenly aware of the "one world" concept but its spotty performance in the foreign field is justified by the dictum that "there is no readership for foreign news." The entrenchment of entertainment as a newspaper function was assisted by the Associated Press's blessing. The department called "Newsfeatures" issues comic strips, seasonal religious continuities, magazine pieces, puzzles, and all sorts of divertissements in common culture and casual uplift.

In some respects the Associated Press assumes crucial decisions. Whether to use the full text of presidential press conferences and other important speeches or documents is not for the local editor to decide.

William L. Beale, chief of bureau for the Associated Press in Washington, has written:

> There have been occasions when we have filed a complete text of a presidential news conference — for instance, his second term announcement. But more often we file excerpts selected on the basis of news merits. For example; presidential remarks on his own health, or the Middle East crisis, might be lifted out of transcript and filed textually. At other times, if the news content of the conference is thin and repetitious, we file nothing textually.*

This thinking casts its image in editorial offices. Of the seventy-three editors polled in thirty-seven states, only forty-five said they used presidential texts "with some

* *Bulletin* of the American Society of Newspaper Editors, June, 1957.

degree of regularity" or used them "when they were deemed sufficiently important." (If any President of the United States opens his mouth and has nothing of importance to say that in itself is a fact worth the reflection of the reading public! If his actual words are vacuous, the news is that there is vacuity in the White House.) Twenty-one said of gubernatorial messages that they never used texts at all, while thirty-six used them from "sometimes" to "often." I remember the day when a mayor's message was something to print in full.

James Kerney, Jr., then of the Trenton *Times* answered: "How many editors read the full texts of presidents' and governors' ordinary speeches? Or even extraordinary?"

Wright Bryan of the Cleveland *Plain Dealer:* "In general our trend is away from use of full texts. . . . There was a time when the *Plain Dealer,* attempting to be a newspaper of record (whatever that is), printed almost every major text from a governor or a president. Now we try to decide on the basis of interest and usefulness to readers."

Undoubtedly the Cleveland *Plain Dealer* is in a position to pay the cost of getting a full text even if the wire services do not see fit to supply it. However, others would have to abide by the Associated Press decision. On one occasion the Hartford *Times* was refused an important text by the Associated Press. Insistence brought the disclosure that the AP's radio bureau in Hartford already had the text and that a messenger could fetch it. Here was an instance where the broadcaster had access to more news than the newspaper member of the press association.

Among newspapers in state capitals there is, understandably, a more favorable attitude toward publication of full texts. Harry Ashmore, then of the Arkansas *Gazette* wrote: "As a state capital morning paper, we consider the *Gazette* an organ of record. Hence our fairly frequent use of texts." Similarly Frank Ahlgren of Memphis: "The *Commercial Appeal* is a paper of record in this area, and, therefore, we feel an obligation to do more text printing than perhaps mass readership warrants."

On the other hand J. A. Meckstroth of the Columbus *Ohio State Journal* wrote: "If you would fill your newspaper with texts which few, very few, would read, you would be robbing the bulk of your readers of what they want and deserve and you would soon find yourself out of business."

Not so Arthur Laro of the Houston *Post:* "We believe in printing texts for the significant minority of readers who look for them. The publishing of texts adds depth to news coverage. We believe readers are not satisfied with sketchy news coverage. They get the gist of the news through radio and television and look to the newspapers for complete coverage." Alfred Friendly, Washington *Post* and *Times-Herald,* agrees: "We'd like to run texts more often; although their readership may be comparatively small, still a significant group of our audience wants and needs them." Also Harry Montgomery, *Arizona Republic* and Phoenix *Gazette:* "We try to make room for as many texts as possible. I am sure the readership is small, but I feel that this is a service that newspapers should render whenever possible."

These quotations are from editors who make up their own minds. But the Associated Press influence — along with cynicism in general — is not to be discounted. During the 1956 presidential campaign, when every newspaper assigned considerable space to election surveys and predictions, the Connecticut bureau of the Associated Press reported that not one paper in the state had asked for or printed the texts of the Republican and Democratic platforms although they were available.

We are concerned not only with full texts in state documents. Traditionally newspapers once printed verbatim Question and Answer reports of important trials and congressional hearings but this, too, has largely gone by the board.

Raymond Crowley of the St. Louis *Post-Dispatch* wrote: "I know of nothing so dull as the Q. and A. report of a trial." But George Beebe of the Miami *Herald* had this to say: "On major hearings, such as the Kefauver crime and juvenile delinquency committee sessions in Miami, we used extensive Q. and A. The interest in these hearings was high, and we are sure the readership was correspondingly high."

On the surface minority readership seems a valid excuse. But in a democratic society minorities have a right to know what the nation's leader has to say. Nor do such excuses square with the editorial rationalization that broadcasting increases the desire to see the news in printed form. The publisher says so, especially to advertisers, but he is worried about whether it is really true.

Newspapers that plead lack of space for this basic service — and not a few editors do so — are scarcely consistent. When the President of the United States appeared on television to make what he called one of his most important speeches, it was difficult the next day to come by a newspaper that carried the full text. Yet one morning paper found eight full columns of space to print in green ink a map of Ireland with clan names geographically spotted in. It was, of course, St. Patrick's Day.

Most of the ills and failures of modern journalism can be attributed to the fading consciousness of the newspaper function. This is, of course, to supply news. In no other capacity can the newspaper presume to be an educational medium. The power of the press is not to regulate, to reform, to win elections (its persuasive prowess has been greatly vitiated), its power today is simply the very great power of information. To the degree that it washes over into unrelated areas of mass appeal at the expense of news dissemination does it dissipate its influence and betray its reason for being.

The press enjoys its freedom under constitutional guarantee. Its second class mailing privilege is tantamount to a subsidy — a subsidy based on the concept that it is an educational medium. To lose sight, then, of its responsibilities as a fourth estate is a grave matter.

Not all editors and publishers are unconcerned. Commenting on a circulation loss of three million by eleven of the nation's largest Sunday papers between, 1947 and 1954, John Cowles of the Des Moines *Register* and *Tribune* told a Sigma Delta Chi meeting in Columbus, Ohio:

> With a single exception, those newspapers that have had the heaviest circulation losses are *not* newspapers that regard full and fair news presentation as their primary function and reason for existence. Ten of the eleven have depended primarily upon entertainment features or sex and crime sensationalism, or are papers that frequently editorialize in and slant their news columns to present their publishers' prejudices and opinions.

The editor of the same paper, Kenneth MacDonald, in a lecture at the University of Michigan, said that newspapers were not printing enough hard news:

> I use the adjective "hard" to mean all categories of news except entertainment, amusement and trivia. . . . This criticism usually prompts two defensive reactions. The first is that most newspapers have necessarily to appeal to masses of people, and you can't hold masses with hard news. The other is that editors do not have a sufficient amount of space available to them because of the high cost of newsprint.

MacDonald was not very much impressed by either argument because of the implication that a newspaper cannot print a high proportion of hard news without its circulation totals and profit margins declining. "Hard news is the most salable commodity a newspaper has," he said.

Those editors who justify content on mass appeal forget that the "masses" are not today on the same level as they were fifty years ago. The American masses today have at least some opinion, even though prejudicial, about foreign affairs; they once were blissfully isolationist and geographically ignorant. Scores of thousands, if not millions, had never heard a symphony orchestra; today the key-signatures and melodies of the symphonies of Brahms, Mozart, and Tschaikowsky are common knowledge among the school-age young. In science, sports, politics, literature, and perhaps in religion there is a mass sophistication, or at least an exposure, which it would be a gross error to underestimate. Even obscurantist modern furnishings of extreme design, and advanced architecture, are accepted over a popular base; obscurantist abstractions in painting arouse fewer jeers and less puzzlement. The press has done exactly what it warned itself against: Do not underestimate the reader's intelligence, nor overestimate his information.

The press has often shortchanged itself in dealing with events that should be of absorbing interest to any editor. The high-pitched exhortations in behalf of a free press, access to information, and the constitutional rights of journalism indicates some concern over what the courts and the bar are thinking and deciding. Editorials have been written about civil rights, deploring the law's inadequacies. If the Supreme Court found itself unable to deal with communists under present laws, that too was a subject for breast-beating and cries for reform. How did this work in the news columns?

The American Bar Association had a committee working for two years on the problem of tightening up the law under which authorities could proceed against communists. The Supreme Court had been unable to support judgments against alleged communists under the Smith Act. It was supposed that the Bar Association committee would bring in a program to stop up the gaps in the law. The Association's House of Delegates, meeting in Chicago in February, 1959, was ready to receive the committee report.

Anyone who was at all interested, and any newspaper editor should have been, would look to the Associated Press and the United Press-International for an account of this important meeting. Day after day the reports came in — confused and truncated. Quotations from the text of the report made it difficult to understand. Who was on the committee, and which Bar Association president had made the committee appointments? There were tensions on the floor of the convention and sharp words. What was the issue? Headlines indicated that the Association was making an attack on the Supreme Court. Was this so? There was speculation among some initiated readers that not a few southern lawyers were voting en bloc against the background of the civil rights issue. If this was so, the news copy gave no indication of it. Chief Justice Warren resigned from the Association. Why? There was no answer to that and the Chief Justice was cryptic in a situation filled with ambiguities. At this stage my curiosity was such that I was at pains to obtain a complete file of the Associated Press report on this meeting, thinking that perhaps telegraph editors on the papers within reach had eliminated vital parts of the reports for lack of space. This proved to be of little help.

The AP reported in one leading paragraph that the Bar Association "took action at a stormy session of its midwinter meeting in which some members openly denounced the Supreme Court decisions as wrong and said lawyers should be the very persons to take the lead in making criticisms."

This was clear enough, but was it accurate? It was Anthony Lewis, writing in the New York *Times* of Sunday, March 1, who first got the Bar Association action into focus and to state the problems confronted by the Supreme Court. He wrote:

> It would be easy to read too much into the vote. The Association has been a most conservative organization and it has had committee reports strongly critical of Supreme Court decisions in the Communist area before now.
>
> In some ways the whole record of the Chicago meeting could be read as relatively favorable toward the court. The resolutions specifically condemned broadside attacks on the court. The Committee wording was softened on the floor. And the liberalizing trend . . . was signified by the choice as president-elect of Whitney North Seymour of New York, a bar leader who is identified

with civil liberties and who would not have had a chance for an American Bar Association office a few years ago.

The *Times* carried in full the text of the report as adopted by the convention. But on the whole, the business in Chicago, for lack of accurate and comprehensive reports, caused so much confusion and misunderstanding that Ross L. Malone, a president apparent of the Bar Association, was constrained to go over the whole matter point by point in an address which he delivered before the Upper Ohio Valley regional meeting of the Association on March 11 under the title: "The Communist Resolutions — What the House of Delegates Really Did."

> What is surprising [said Malone] is the fact that reaction in so many cases has been based upon apprehension or misconstruction of the action actually taken by the Association. This has been reflected in statements by men in public life in Washington, *by newspaper editorials* [author's italics], and in the voluminous mail I have been receiving . . .
>
> Press reports, editorials and public statements which labeled the action of the House of Delegates as an attack by the Bar upon the Supreme Court were, in my opinion, and I believe in the opinion of the great majority of the members of the House of Delegates, wholly unjustified and contrary to fact.

A persistent editor has the means of getting all this information. It may be an annoyance, but the sources are at his disposal. Not so the general reader who, depending upon where he is resident, runs a risk of getting a completely distorted view. An issue such as this is of some moment to every citizen. It is "hard" news in any sense of the word.

It is easy for a newspaperman to be deluded about the quantity of news in his paper. He is unable to place himself in the position of the man who reads one paper or at most two. The editor reads his own paper *and* his competitors'. He will read daily, with some care, one or more major metropolitan papers no matter where in the United States he is located. Editors have at their disposal, if they want to consult them, the complete outpourings of the press associations; many have access to two. There is the Washington report; for even those newspapers that do not have a bureau are usually represented in some fashion by a correspondent who covers for several small papers. It is not unusual for a managing editor to receive at his desk a carbon copy of every story written for the paper by city and state staff reporters, to say nothing of the products of the women's and sports departments. If he is conscientious he gets proofs of all copy set. Much but not all of this is used. Of the other flood of news copy, only a small fraction ever sees daylight. There is a mass of syndicated material.

With all this volume he is rather thoroughly informed. He should be. But he also is likely to overestimate the amount of news that is actually published. He doesn't miss a thing; he probably doesn't know what the reader is missing.

After years on the inside of all this journalistic turmoil, one still has to put oneself in the reader's position.

All the reader knows is what he reads in the papers — and it isn't enough.

12

"AS LOCAL AS THE TOWN PUMP"

WHEN A GROUP OF AMERICAN, BRITish, and French editors gathered around a green baize conference table in Paris in the spring of 1957, the discussion leader, who happened to be from the United States, ventured that the American press was the most parochial in the world. This struck fire immediately from some of his countrymen, especially from William R. Mathews, editor and publisher of the *Arizona Star* at Tucson, winner of a Pulitzer honorable mention for distinguished editorial writing, and a world traveler.

Later, in the pages of the *American Editor,* he prescribed a means of promoting readership for foreign news. Travel, he advised, and write what you see and hear. "Publish your articles right down column one page one, and keep within 750 words."

He witnessed and described the flowering of nazism in 1937. In July, 1939, his column with a Paris date line was headed, "It is War and War within Weeks." Subsequently he wrote: "My experience enabled me to forecast every war, except the one in Finland and the Spanish

Civil War. It was not altogether chance that prompted me to get to Korea with Mr. Dulles a week before hostilities broke out there, and in Tokyo to see how a war was made that eventful Sunday evening of June 25, 1950."

Mathews is an exception; further, not all foreign news is news of war.

The position that editors take on the subject of foreign news seems amply justified if they are merely to ask themselves what the public will read. They know that there is a very shallow topsoil of interest in what happens in lands across all the seas. They reason, then, that little space is to be wasted in that quarter except for a royal romance, a papal coronation, or a European chapter in the love life of a Hollywood star. They know that in the thinking of the "mass" reader anybody who lives outside the borders of the United States is a foreigner. There is a finality about such a classification from which there is no appeal.

This is a curious circumstance because no people in the world are so widely traveled as Americans. The tourist path is well worn to a rut so deep it is almost impossible to get out of it. Not all wish to get out of it; it is a convenience to resume in Venice or Nice a conversation interrupted on the country club veranda.)

Millions of Americans in the armed services have been traveling to the ends of the earth since the 1940's. Among them is a rare minority who made use of free time to get away from the military installations and barracks long enough to learn something of the people among whom they found themselves. The great number, however, knew little of the places they had been except the names. Servicemen in Frankfurt-am-Main insisted upon buying at the PX tinned beer from home and were satisfied with nothing but American sausages in the city which gave them its name. The American traveler demands bourbon, and if the bartender is so benighted that he cannot make a decent very dry martini, he will be patiently, patronizingly instructed.

The pathetic figure of the tourist has been well described[*] by Walter Hackett, veteran foreign correspondent, who told of the American couple who in five weeks had "done" France, Portugal, Spain, and Italy, and "we still have to go to Austria, Germany, Belgium, Holland, Luxembourg and England." When asked what they had seen the husband answered: "Hell, we've seen everything. Why, we spent three whole days in Rome. Do you know Rome?"

> He goes on to describe another tourist looking out at a field full of crop pickers sweating it out under the blasting summer sun.
>
> "Look at them," she said. "Each a happy king and queen with no worries. How very picturesque!"
>
> Each of those "kings" and "queens" was getting the magnificent wage of sixty cents a day for working at least ten hours; and on this the men supported families living in poverty impossible to describe.

There is nothing even faintly amusing in the fact that while the United States is in a position of world leadership, with all the responsibility that implies, we act as if we were collectively ignorant of the fact that foreign countries are inhabited by human beings.

So it is not entirely the fault of the editor that foreign news gets little attention. It is, though, at least his partial responsibility to provide a modicum of the kind of news

---
[*] In *The American Editor*, October, 1958.

that a well-informed, intelligent citizen ought to have available.

But that doesn't sell papers and if the ought-to-know began to crowd the want-to-know it wouldn't be very long before he would be entangled with the circulation manager.

There is, again, the competition of the broadcasters. While both radio and television can manage a measure of local news, that is not where their main audience lies and technically it is almost impossible for them to go into certain local details such as the obituaries; the routine of births, marriages, and divorces; the civic routine of boards and councils and committees. The press knows this and has taken shelter where the competition cannot follow, like the cat in the apple tree cornered by the barking dog below.

The American newspaper's cherished refuge is the citadel of local news. Curbstone philosophers have said that "the newspaper should be as local as the town pump." That sounds good; it is good and profitable, but it has the effect of making the American newspaper near-sighted. Not every one, of course. The sturdy slogan of the Quincy (Massachusetts) *Patriot-Ledger* is: "Cover the world but don't forget the North Shore!"

There are other enlightened newspapers. G. B. Williams, editor of the Geneva (New York) *Times*, claims that he has increased circulation by special attention to foreign news. The San Francisco *Chronicle* has accented human interest and feature reporting from abroad. The Milwaukee *Journal* frequently devotes a solid page and more to the foreign scene and, incidentally, makes most effective use of color in printing maps.

The San Diego *Union* has a keen awareness of one interest in foreign news. It has a Latin American page every day and a Spanish language review of the week on Sunday, for which there is, of course, a readership based on geographical location. The Minneapolis *Star and Tribune* sponsors large-scale seminars on the high school level to encourage interest in affairs abroad.

These efforts are not representative of the press at large. For the most part only the feeblest attempts are made to interest readers in this kind of news. The cables carry little except reports of crisis and Weltpolitik. Human interest is in scant supply. The press association correspondents travel a worn path to the chancelleries and back to the bureau. Those who can read it rewrite the foreign press.

At the time of the Laos crisis, an Associated Press correspondent traveling in this country admitted that in the Tokyo bureau, where he was stationed, were six men, only two of whom were Americans; and neither of the Americans could speak or read Japanese. The other three rendered into English the product of the native wire services. When the alarm sounded there was no correspondent in Laos.

One of the major chores of foreign correspondents is to entertain traveling clients — publishers and editors — whom they will take to an American bar and thence, frequently to a steak house or a restaurant where one can get a corned beef and cabbage dinner fully equal to anything at home. Here their ears will be safe from anything more troublesome than United States English.

These reporters think of human interest as the patterned item they learned back home, relating usually to animals or children. But since the newspaper back home isn't much interested in foreign animals or foreign children, that category is closed off. The vein of genuine human interest has not been worked at all: What is to be seen on European television? What is the price of gasoline and shoes and orange juice? What does a young married couple pay in apartment rental? Do French people go to French movies or American (and are the French-made films for export only)? There are crime stories that have found high readership in the news weeklies, adventure stories that never reach the cables, mysteries and thrilling rescues, and stories of foreign policy in-the-making.

The pure journalism of such books as John Gunther's on Africa and Russia have been bought by hundreds of thousands of readers at five dollars each. Irving R. Levine's *Main Street, U.S.S.R.* immediately sold more than twenty thousand copies simply because his job as NBC correspondent taught him what readers are really interested in, and he answered questions, colorfully and clearly. Newspaper editors might well profit by the example of such successes.

Not many detective thrillers surpass the story of the bishop's left thumb. It would have had high readership anywhere, but the American press associations didn't get to it. The date line was too remote. This is how it went.

A prominent Lutheran theologian was elected a bishop in Sweden. He was a man of blameless reputation, but politics can affect even ecclesiastical conduct. After the election, somebody thought there ought to be an investigation of certain slanderous letters which had been circulated to damage two other candidates for the office. Someone accused the bishop himself. Charges were drawn up and he had to face trial.

That trial revealed day after day one of the most gripping of detective investigations. It was as sensational and scientific as that which finally trapped and convicted Bruno Hauptmann; in other respects it suggested the final scenes of the *Caine Mutiny Court-Martial* and the disintegration of Lieutenant Commander Queeg.

As in the Hiss trial, there was the pursuit of a guilty typewriter, except that there were two instead of one and also a mimeograph machine which had been rented under suspicious circumstances. It developed that the bishop had made visits to a distant city in disguise and made purchases under an assumed name. The slanderous letters had not been mailed in a letter box, but were handed to a mail-car clerk as a train was leaving the station. The bishop swore the sender was not he and produced an alibi.

While the trial was in progress a couple of university students were experimenting in a laboratory with a new method of recapturing finger prints under circumstances previously considered impossible. The letters were exhibited and revealed — the print of the bishop's left thumb. He was convicted; he lost the appeal to a higher court; and he lost his job.

The Associated Press carried a short item the day the bishop was convicted. It would have been news no matter where it happened. Only the Religious News Service supplied to American clients this amazing story in full. It was merely a kind of crime story. There are many other varieties which would testify with optimism and enlightenment to the strong ties that unite or affect the human family.

It is the absence of knowledge that fertilizes the soil for propaganda — in our time one of the darkest and most poisonous flowers of evil. Newspapers can do much to root out these growths, but they are not working very hard at it. Unless journalism bends its back to combat international ignorance, we must face the inevitability of World War III — call it the Last War. There never was a time when people of the United States had such a reckless attitude toward war — reckless in the sense of indifference and an abandoned insensibility to its consequences. Reckless also because of a docile willingness to be led. They see the prospects of what in the past has seemed to be the benefits of war: apparent prosperity, a heroic role at something less than the full price of heroism. People feel — because military men who are either stupid or without conscience (conceivably both) have told them—that the A and H bombs are security against war. The Atomic Energy Commission declares, in a field where it is not competent, that fall-out has no genetic effects; while geneticists, who are the experts, have been ridiculed and contradicted and, in many newspapers, have had their findings ignored or suppressed. Robert Louis Stevenson referred ironically to the people who went about on the slopes of smoking Vesuvius carrying umbrellas.

War cannot be averted until there is a deeper understanding among peoples, or while the word foreigner implies a wooden image without intelligence, rights, or feelings. It is somewhat sinister that the problem of over-population is now a prominent issue in geopolitics. Population explosion indeed! Perhaps it is merely the detonation cap for the ultimate explosion.

All this remains a newspaper opportunity. Erwin Canham has written in his book *New Frontiers for Freedom:*

> Our world is divided into three parts. At one extreme are ourselves — a very small minority. At the other end are the Communists, an even smaller minority if you count only party members and a

microscopic minority if you count only those holding power. In between these two extremes are to be found the overwhelming majority of the human race. Some of these people, like the Western Europeans, not only lean toward us, but have a long and rich experience of freedom to which we owe an incalculable debt. Some of them lean toward the Communists. Most of them are not yet sure.

We must prepare our own minds first; clear out of our thinking the things we'd like to believe and make room for ascertainable news facts.

A party of editors went to Russia and most of them came back with exactly the same ideas they had before and reported precisely what people wanted to hear. But not Rebecca Gross, editor of the Lockhaven (Pennsylvania) *Express*. She had courage enough to report exactly what she saw in Moscow: That the people were well clothed and looked well fed. For this, the hue and cry was raised that she had allowed herself to be duped.

Miss Gross wrote after her Russian trip:

> It seems to me that American newspaper and magazine editors, and American readers of the news, are making a great mistake when they ask any observer to do anything but tell them exactly what he saw. If they demand that he should bolster their own preconceived ideas, on pain of being accused of treason or stupidity, or both, are they not taking a step in the direction of the policies exemplified for so many years by Communist newspapers, which publish nothing that does not conform to the party "line"?
>
> I hope there is no developing tendency in the American press or the American public to require

reports on the Russians to conform to the "line" that they are necessarily ill-fed, ill-clothed, ill-housed and dissatisfied. Such a trend would remind me of the insistence of the Russians on news reports portraying Americans as downtrodden victims of Wall Street, suffering slaves eager for the liberating day when Communism may triumph over the "contradictions" of capitalism.

As Mathews, the Arizona editor, has said: "It's an American sin to think in absolutes." Classify everybody either as a good guy or as a bad guy. That is what we do internationally — playing a game of cops and robbers with newspaper assistance.

Germans were the blackest of the bad guys during two world wars. They have now — the western half only, of course — suddenly become good guys. The Japanese were not long ago infamously bad guys; they are good guys now, but we are watching. Chinese are no longer yellow but black and white — black on the mainland and white on Formosa; Pakistanis are white — but Indians are gray — the only instance momentarily of departure from the absolute. Between the years of 1941 and 1945 we held hands with Russia and every cartoonist in America put a good boy's pipe in the mouth of Uncle Joe and a benign expression on his face. Still thinking in absolutes, we cannot today distinguish between Russian imperialism and Marxian communism. Tito is of course a good guy or a bad guy as the policy weather vane turns.

There is, of course, international iniquity and international virtue, but one cannot think in absolutes and learn about people.

For nearly half a century now we've been around the world, and almost every nation has at one time or another been in the hate category, but Americans generally have not increased their knowledge of foreigners as human beings.

We are now in the grip of a new isolationism. The United States may be more isolated now than it was in 1920, when the election made clear that the people wanted nothing to do with the League of Nations. There is a difference, however. The isolationism of 1920 was of our own making. The people so decided. The new isolationism is not of our choosing. It grows out of the fact that our allies are going ways separate from ours.

America seems to have lost a large degree of its influence abroad.

Is there any connection between this and our failure to cover foreign news adequately?

Five years ago the Associated Press began what was called the Vanguard service, a promising beginning in this field. The late Paul Mikkleson explained that on a normal day there was about an hour in the morning when transmission pressure was not great. The time was to be used to send foreign news, especially human interest items.

These were some of the stories:

Out of seventy thousand physicians in West Germany, about fifty-eight thousand are largely dependent upon income from socialized medicine.

A man in Gross Unstadt, Germany, makes a living tanning elephants' hides.

In an Arabian village the men chew narcotic *Qat* leaves all day and the women do the work.

Filipinos are growing red radishes instead of white ones with seeds from the United States.

Mexican tortillas are now sold in sanitary plastic bags.

If the Apostle Paul came to Damascus today, he would

walk down the same street by which he entered it after his conversion and he would see essentially the same sights.

Some of these stories could only be described as pert or trivial. It is not likely that they greatly stimulated the appetite for foreign news. They were not widely used in any case. It is the editors who are at fault and the Associated Press cannot be blamed for not continuing a service of which little use was made.

The news stream is there for those who want it. Were it used to greater degree, this stream would swell into a swift, powerful current of interest. In addition to what the general wire services provide, there are newspaper-sponsored services such as those of the New York *Times*, the Milwaukee *Journal* and Chicago *Daily News*. The last-named at one time had assembled what was the most brilliant foreign news service ever built in this country. Thirty-five years ago it was represented by John Gunther, Edgard Ansel Mowrer, Paul Scott Mowrer, Negley Farson, Vincent Sheean, Leland Stowe, and many others including William Stoneman, who is still on its foreign staff. None of these writers ever tried to compete with the political and crisis news of the Associated Press, United Press, and International News. They seldom operated in the capitals but mined out the richer human interest veins.

There is an encouraging gleam, although journalism can take only slight credit for it. While statesmen knit their brows and beat their brains ineffectually in the great game of cowboys and Indians there is evidence that if the cold war ever reaches an armistice it may be on the beachhead of culture.

Note the enormous acclaim accorded the Russian ballet, violinist Oistrakh, and pianist Gilels; and recall the case of Van Cliburn.

Even if Khrushchev saw an opportunity in pinning a medal on an American boy who, in spite of hearings in his own country, went unrecognized until Moscow discovered him, Van Cliburn is more than the mere beneficiary of a propaganda gimmick. The young man, in my opinion, is a great musician. More than that, I see in him the hint of the beginnings of a rapprochement between this country and Russia on the wings of culture. Boris Pasternak's case may be somewhat different, although his disavowal in Russia was said to stem more from the Soviet writers themselves than from officialdom. Let us say that Pasternak was caught in the cross fire of the cold war or, to change the figure, was a sort of literary bridge between the lines.

It is only a slender hope that culture or sports or tourism will create that needed beachhead of understanding. Perhaps American-Soviet differences are too great, but it is not too much to say that culture has made more progress than the intransigence of the statesmen on both sides and the newsmen who watch.

13

REVIEWING

VERSUS

CRITICAL WRITING

IN THE

DAILY PRESS

> He who writes poetry plays
> at bowls and whoever bowls, be
> he king or peasant, must put
> up with the pinboy's criticism.
>
> MOSES MENDEL to FREDERICK THE GREAT

IN THE SPRING OF 1916, I WENT TO work on the Davenport (Iowa) *Democrat*. It was my first newspaper job. The pay was eight dollars a week. On this, of course, I couldn't live and began to borrow money from staff men on the *Democrat*, and also from personnel on the German language morning daily, *Der Demokrat*. I roomed with the city editor of the latter, whose name was Voss, and another German whose name escapes me, a floor walker at the department store of Harned von Mauer. I was greatly interested in German mainly because of my musical studies, such as they were. I used to attend the German repertory theater in Davenport for such plays as Suderman's *Schmetterlingschlacht* and occasionally went to a German-language church. Newspapermen simply walked into theaters free, without credentials, in those days.

One day the Minneapolis Symphony Orchestra came to town and with it a problem. There wasn't a critic of any kind on the *Democrat* or *Der Demokrat*.

Someone had told the city editor that I played the piano and he said, "You will review the symphony concert tonight."

The first time my young ears heard symphonic sound, I was the critic! This was, of course, before radio; there were less than a dozen established symphony orchestras in the country and not all of them toured. The most ambitious phonograph recording was a reproduction of Vieuxtemps' *Polonaise in D* on a half-inch-thick disc which an Edison machine played with a diamond needle.

Voss wanted a review for *Der Demokrat* and I orally recited some obscure musical terms that he put into city-room German and for which his publisher later praised him.

That was the day of James Huneker, E. H. Krehbiel, and W. J. Henderson in New York; H. T. Parker in Boston; and Glenn Dillard Gunn in Chicago. Outside of these luminaries, music reviewing the country over wasn't much different from what Davenport got that night. It couldn't be that bad today, with the tidal wave of recordings and broadcasts.

The first person on the Hartford *Times* who could be called a critic was Dr. Nathan Mayer. Mayer was self-confident and dogmatic. It was not a difficult task for him to write his critique in advance of the event. He knew what the facts and the judgment ought to be. Once he miscalculated. It was a snowy night, but as far as he was concerned, there was no reason why folks should not venture out — everyone except Dr. Mayer. He finished his stint in the afternoon, sent it to the printer, went home to enjoy a few tall drinks by the fireside — and cozily stayed there. The concert was called off, but the Hartford *Times* faithfully reported the next day what it sounded like, or might have sounded like, had it been played.

His successor was Julius Hartt, an old-school pedagogue, whose studio was named for him by pupils who later took it over. Eventually it became Hartt College. Hartt was a sound musician but not a newspaperman. He dipped his pen in vitriol and few performers escaped. In those days the old Hartford Philharmonic Orchestra, largely supported by Mrs. Charles Dudley Warner, widow of the Hartford *Courant's* one-time editor, was playing a season of concerts. The Boston Symphony Orchestra was a fairly regular visitor.

It was the local orchestra, however, that felt Julius Hartt's sting. It was an open secret that he fancied himself as the only competent conductor in sight and yearned for the baton. The Philharmonic finally gave up the ghost, and many feel that Hartt helped in its demise. Ironically, he was succeeded as critic by John Spencer Camp, composer and organist, who had been for a time conductor of the Philharmonic.

But a day of sweetness and light had dawned. Camp's successor was an insurance salesman and a good one. He was repeatedly honored in the Million-Dollar club, which was the distinction of any salesman who rolled up that amount of life coverage in a given year. The reward was a convention trip, which usually meant Miami.

He was given the sideline job of music critic. He had been an organist once upon a time, but more recently a general news reporter. As a news-gatherer he was, in the words of the managing editor, "a long arm reaching out." It was indeed a long insurance salesman's arm and it tapped on the shoulder any musician in town who was about to sing or play a recital, or who had pupils to present.

This maneuver occurred just before the recital date. If the victim bought a policy or renewed an old one, the reward was a favorable review. No sale, no review. Visiting performers like Rachmaninoff, or organizations like the Boston Symphony Orchestra, were always good for a thorough panning; it was a great opportunity to balance off the local bouquets. Besides, the strangers in town were scarcely to be considered good insurance risks or in any degree susceptible to pressure. One of the best-known and most praised pianists in Hartford once complained, "I am the most heavily insured musician in town!"

None of this was unusual. Racketeering and incompetence varied in degree from coast to coast thirty years ago, and if racketeering has disappeared, incompetence continues to reign in almost any city outside of the three or four largest metropolitan areas.

Managing editors simply do not hire critics; they do not have to do so. There is always somebody around the shop who has taken lessons while young and who can distinguish the *Moonlight Sonata* from the *Nutcracker Suite*. There are few managing editors competent — and most of them will admit it — to hire a critic of any of the arts for lack of a benchmark to judge qualifications. They know a good reporter, which is important, for the best critic must first be a reporter. He can report the program, the audience reaction to the music; he can tell the plot of a book or the message of a play; he can tell what a painting looks like even if it is not representational.

But there are readers who want a guide, philosopher, and friend to help them form their own opinions, or who want to be fortified in their already crystallized impressions. Here critical judgment does come into play and here competence is tested.

The reviewer is not to be swayed by public opinion but he ought to find out what it is. "Deference to public opinion is one great source of bad writing," wrote George Henry Lewes: "There are many justifications of silence; there can be none of insincerity. . . . Why should I echo what seems to me extravagant praises of Raphael's 'Transfiguration,' when, in truth, I do not greatly admire that famous work? There is no necessity for me to speak on the subject at all; but, if I do speak, surely it is to utter my impressions, and not to repeat what others have uttered."

To review music offers a problem far greater than reviewing any of the other arts because of the medium's extreme volatility and evanescence. There is no physical thing to be perceived — merely a succession of ordered sounds. Nothing can be proven or re-examined once the concept has had its passage through the ether. The reviewer is as much at a loss to prove his opinion as another is to persuade him of error. He finds music a most convenient vapor behind which to conceal his ignorance. A medium of this kind begets a critical jargon which means little or nothing but serves to screen the absence of cogent ideas. The vocabulary and phraseology are utterly opaque: "puissant," "incandescent," "lambent purity," "vouchsafe," "a communicative clarity that is almost mystical," "lyrical luminosity" — all this is extremely uncomfortable bric-a-brac to live with and it is used only by writers to whom music has given no real thoughts or experience. Of the late Alfred Einstein it was said that "his horizon is broader than that of his fellow critics, hence the absence of big words."

Virgil Thomson, who as the New York *Herald Tribune's* critic was never guilty of concealing a single oscillation of his shrewd mental apparatus, once wrote, for instance: "The piece was a delight ten years ago, and it has worn well; its fancy and general exuberance are still tops." Twice as many words would not convey a better idea of an opera performance than this: "Whatever musical faults the performance bore, it was at all times a lively show. If the present cast, which seems to understand the character of Italian farce, will practice up on its music, 'The Barber of Seville' may become one of the Met's more striking numbers. At present it needs tightening up all over. Even in the comic effects, for lack of timing, the actors have a little the air of just horsing around." You knew what he meant when he wrote of a singer that "she is a top technician and a woman of culture; also she is genuinely musical. The only advantage she lacks is personality; her presence is cool and a little pale."

Such writing is rare. For the most part reviewing is defensive. The critic is determined to sit in judgment, yet he often lacks confidence in his equipment. He strives to demonstrate his competence by parading symptoms of erudition. This is fatal because the reader is not interested in the critic's learning. The critic suspects that if he is competent to destroy, that proves his superiority — so he destroys.

Max Graf reveals: "Berlioz, who was a critic and an excellent writer as well as a composer, once attacked his enemies most violently. He, himself, admitted that the article was 'badly ordered and badly written and overstepped the bounds of polemics.' But Michaud, the editor of the *Quotidien* ('Daily'), to whom he offered his insults, would not print them, saying, 'It is all true enough, but you are just breaking windows!'"

There is also the critic who cannot resist the temptation of a phrase. There is no such thing as a free laugh. It is free only to the reckless writer, and is bound to cost somebody something. Such a critic may be highly thought of for his cleverness, because he is readable. He has style; he has salt; he may have readers. He is his own show. He is himself the only actor, the only virtuoso; the column is his stage. His writing is often more entertaining than the concert or the play under consideration, but it is not criticism. And cleverness is not confined to newspapers.

Frederick B. Robinson, director of the Springfield, Massachusetts, Museum of Fine Arts, has said: "I am confident that any worker, such as myself, in any one of the various fields indicated [art, music, theater, and the dance] would be more than willing to say that the critical service of local newspapers is not adequate. This has always been a perennial bellyache on the part of orchestra conductors, museum directors and theatrical managers."

A baker's dozen of managing editors were asked how music is handled on their papers. These are their replies:

1. "Occasionally we have a guest reviewer, some musician in the community serving by request. Most often some staff member with admittedly more or less sketchy knowledge of music does the job. Our telegraph editor is our theater reviewer."

2. "We do not have the time or space to have anyone especially assigned to music and, besides, there isn't enough of it here to warrant it."

3. "Neither our books nor our music get really critical treatment. We mostly do a reporting job with a slight tinge of criticism."

4. "A pianist, church organist and choir leader who has studied both in this country and abroad, does our reviewing assisted by a teacher in the music department of the University."

5. One managing editor wrote that once during his career, he was told to cover musical events

when he "didn't know the first thing about it and still doesn't." He says he managed "by simply studying the Victor phonograph catalogue, various musical dictionaries and other reference books."

6. "In selecting our present critic, we were convinced that we had the right man when we found that he had been a student of voice at the New England Conservatory of Music for six years, and he was sincerely interested in all phases of music. He can express himself intelligently on the typewriter."

7. The reviewer, when a student, specialized in the history of music.

8. The critic "studied theory and composition and specialized in piano and organ," gets fifteen dollars a week.

9. Reviewer is a singing teacher.

10. Occasional critical articles are contributed by a music faculty "stringer."

11, "On occasion we have published reviews written by a priest. He is qualified by inclination and musical education. He works gratis."

12. An editorial writer does the criticism.

13. "On the whole it is much more comfortable and satisfactory in my opinion to use a staffer on these arts where you find a competent one, because, at least he can write. In times past, with good fortune, sometimes, we fished experts out of our local colleges to handle special fields. These professorial minds do bring a great deal of learning, but on the whole they certainly lack the ability to write a news story. They like to wander all over the place."

When it comes to movie reviewing, all the journalistic media leave something to be desired in that they frequently fail to tell the reader what he wants to know:

do I want to see this picture? Many tend to measure films by what they regard as artistic standards. Except in rare instances the producer's only motive is to entertain; he has no higher purpose. The judgment, then, should be on that basis and not on artistic canons. The reviewer fears he might be thought uneducated if he measures the picture only for its entertainment value. Certainly most movie-goers have nothing else in mind when entering the theater. Even in those instances where the producers film a classic or aim for artistic effect, they surmise that the classic might make money and entertain.

Typical of the cynical review is one that appeared twelve years ago but might have been written yesterday:

> Buckling his swashes with stilted abandon, Louis Hayward leads a group of long-haired villains through a merry chase in not-so-merry England in "The Black Arrow."
>
> ... After half the cast has been dispatched and thrown to the vultures, Richard comes through. He neatly runs a spear through the uncle's body, restores his future father-in-law's estate and marries the girl.
>
> It could be done much better but children should love it.
>
> In order to get things straight he has to kill one man and cause the death of two others, but it's a very happy ending anyway.

This may be considered clever writing but it is supercilious as well. Hence, it is not for the movie-goer at all but for some indeterminate reader of the paper. The critic just doesn't like movies and is inviting the theater managers to make representations to the publisher of the paper, who might be justified in taking action — not because an advertiser has protested — but because the writer was not giving reader service.

Certainly a reviewer is confused about his function when he writes: "I note also that although Arthur Ripley was originally listed as director, the credits on the screen name Mr. Tallas as film editor. I suspect Mr. Ripley wanted to cover his tracks behind him, and I can't say I blame him. And the film is about as atrociously edited as any I've encountered in several years. I wouldn't say it had been 'edited' — hacked would be a more appropriate word."

The jobs of movie reviewer and drama critic should not be combined in one person. While the boundaries of the two fields occasionally overlap, there is the necessity of maintaining a double standard, and no person should be asked to walk that tightrope.

Of all critical writers, the theater critic wields the greatest power. The movie reporter has virtually none, since people make up their minds what picture they want to see on the basis of the stars, the story, and the advertising. The music commentator has but little more. His greatest usefulness is educational. The book reviewer's influence has lessened since the book-club technique transferred much of the critical decision to the board of editors. But the drama critic makes and breaks shows. This is because of the intense centralization by which the theater is both victim and beneficiary. Broadway — and off-Broadway — *is* the American theater and theater-goers do read reviews and are guided by them. While there are a few significant instances in which the critics' judgments have gone unheeded, the fate of a new play is usually in their hands. Managers know it. Drama criticism elsewhere in the United States can be discounted (except in try-out cities) because by the time a show goes on the road, its success has already been demonstrated and it has been vaccinated against any critical virus it may encounter. Still a show is not beyond improvement on the road.

In the *Bulletin* of the American Society of Newspaper Editors, Howard Lindsay wrote of drama critics: "It would be, I feel, of greater service to the newspapers and to the theater, and more becoming to their craft, if the drama critics pontificated less and made it clear that their reports and their opinions were colored by their personal predilections."

His collaborator, Russel Crouse, added:

> So far as New York is concerned, I think the average of criticism is extremely high.... I have, however, noticed a growing tendency in recent years on the part of at least some reviewers to write about the play they wish the authors had written or the play they would have written had they been writing a play on the same theme. This, I feel, is slightly unfair. I believe critics should judge a work for what it is. I feel that an author has the right to treat a subject his own way and should not be penalized for not treating it in the exact way a particular reviewer wishes he had.

In book reviewing the daily newspaper does its best critical job. This is because news writers are themselves literate, if not literary. They, like the author, are concerned with putting words together in cogent succession. All writers, and that includes the reporter, have the problem of involving the reader and retaining his attention.

Book reviewing in the daily press does leave much to be desired; there is a wide range of competence and conscience. In many news rooms it is done by staff men.

The literary editor may have full- or part-time responsibility but in any event his control is of limited effectiveness. Often books are assigned and the reporter never finds time to write the review — especially if he is not paid, as many are not, except in receiving the book. (Books have a way of disappearing from the literary editor's desk during his absence and in that case, they are usually *spurlos versenkt*. Even lock and key does not always suffice to prevent such disappearances; the mail boy can be intercepted.)

College students serving summers as copy boys and girls like to review books as a means of getting to the typewriter keyboard, and in that case there may be the factor of immature judgment. In fact, almost anybody around the shop can ask for a book to review and get it. The literary editor always has more books on his hands than he can get reviewers for. The reporters will have had their pick and reporters are choosy. The critical results of such a process are inevitably spotty.

Such reviewers as the late Carl Victor Little of the Houston *Press*, John Hutchens of the *Herald Tribune*, and Leslie Hanscom, late of the New York *World-Telegram & Sun*, have been praised for their ability to put their opinions into readable prose, perhaps because they meet journalism's standards as well as the bookman's.

Book publishers are less concerned with favorable reviews than people suppose. Frequently, an unfavorable review sells more books. Pyke Johnson, Jr., long-time publicity director for Doubleday, has written: "Any reviewer who writes for a publisher, or for his own advertising man and not for his reader, is wasting time and space" — a dictum that might well be applied to all newspaper reviewing.

Johnson once gathered interesting data on book reviewing. There are, he found, some twelve hundred bona fide book reviewers in the country. That includes magazine writers, broadcasters, and lecturers, so we see that this form of journalism is not confined to the daily press, either. He reports that booksellers feel that newspapers are doing the best job and that lecturers, with the exception of ministers, are least effective. The bookstores were not enthusiastic about radio reviewing, although television has come to be a different story.

Booksellers feel that the national publications, the *New Yorker, Time*, the *Atlantic Monthly, Harper's Magazine*, the *Saturday Review*, and the Sunday New York *Times* have the greatest influence with the buying public. Local reviewers carry more weight in the Middle West than elsewhere.

Publishers on an average send out about 120 copies of a new book for review. Only about 40 reviewers in the United States can expect to get a copy of everything published.

Pyke Johnson observed that

> the average book reviewer, with only a few exceptions, finds reviewing a secondary occupation in his life, wherever it may rank in his interest. He may be a Sunday editor or assigned to the cable desk. He may be in charge of reviewing music, movies and the theater; he may be a college professor whose sole connection with the paper is the book page. He may be a society editor, or a professional writer who has turned to reviewing to supplement the income derived from his royalties, or he may be a relative of the paper's owner.
>
> In short, the only thing that any book reviewer has in common with his colleagues — and with pub-

lishers and booksellers — is an interest in books, and a desire to see that the largest possible number of copies of the best books get into the hands of readers. . . .

Book reviewers are not among those having the highest incomes. Of the book editors queried, only one-third paid their reviewers, and of these, only about half pay all their contributors. The fee is around $10 for a regular review, slightly more for a special article. But the most the average reviewer may expect to receive for his work is a copy of the book, and sometimes not even that. . . .

About two-thirds of the book sellers queried felt that books were not being given adequate coverage in local review media. Exceptions . . . included specific praise for the . . . Washington *Post*, Chicago *Sun-Times*, Louisville *Courier-Journal*, St. Louis *Post-Dispatch*, Richmond *Times-Dispatch*, Milwaukee *Journal*. The strongest criticism came from the Pacific Northwest, where the booksellers felt that the reviewers were overly pre-occupied with books of purely local appeal and so failed to give satisfactory attention to books of wider interest. . . .

Book publishers are aware of the fact that, for the money spent, the total cost of sending out a review copy of a three-dollar novel is not over sixty cents, review copies bring them the greatest return in terms of space and readership. "Books, however, are more than a means of grabbing space," comments one publicity director, "they are news and channels of education and enlightenment. Reviewing edges into the public service field." Nonetheless, it seems true that until the day when publishers can afford to scatter advertisements with the generosity of that other cultural medium, the movies, the burden of bringing books before the public rests largely on the shoulders of the papers.

Newspaper publishers, outside of the metropolitan areas, have little interest in book reviewing. There is no revenue in it. (Yet books are *Number One* among all linage classifications in the New York *Times*.) Even local bookstores rarely spend any money in advertising. As a feature of the newspaper, then, it is there largely because an editor wants a book page.

If a publisher is at all concerned about book reviewing it is because book reviews as well as music and art criticism (which bring in even less revenue) are likely to establish the paper as a solid, family paper and thus attract advertising from other makers of consumer goods. Many are not unaware that the book clubs bring into the Sunday supplements a substantial measure of book advertising.

Complaints about unfavorable reviews are not likely to cause the publisher much concern, certainly not to the degree that a reviewer's slam at a film can cause. Hollywood is a good advertiser. The amusement rate is usually a premium one. This is the reason why movie reviews are as bad as they are; the advertisers are to be mollified and they know it — even in some metropolitan offices they expect to be listened to.

Thus we see that much of literary criticism is left to the magazines. (Curiously, the *Saturday Review* migrated to independence from the daily newspaper field, since it was born as adjunct of the New York *Evening Post*.) For the rest, outside of three newspapers with complete book sections, the readers are looking to the periodicals and the broadcasters for the most generous amount of information and opinion.

Ralph Thompson, editor of the Book-of-the-Month Club, does not let the newspaper off so easily. In an article in the *Bulletin* of the American Society of Newspaper Editors he hit so hard that several editors ran a temperature in the following issue. Indignation has an exceedingly low boiling point in editorial offices when the press critics start shooting.

Thompson started off with a big bang:

> There are probably more lame, careless, lazy or pussyfooting book reviews printed in American newspapers in the course of an average month than there are hairs on the average author's head. This curious circumstance tends to confuse the lives of authors, to abrade the tender hide of publishers, and so to alarm certain retail booksellers that they withdraw to back rooms to dream up new ways of saying that business is bad. But it seems to have no comparable effect, material or spiritual, on the editors of the newspapers involved. How many times a year do such editors take a long, cool look at their literary departments?
>
> One ought to be able to expect, in a literate and prosperous country of 165,000,000, at least a couple of dozen adequate review departments (apart from the nationally syndicated columns) — one, say, in every other one of the 48 states, or one to each of the 24 principal cities.
>
> What we have instead is a scandal. It is acknowledged by the entire book trade but out of delicacy rarely mentioned in print. One has to guess at figures, of course, but a fair guess would be that we have about one adequate review department to every 20 million inhabitants — a grand total of maybe eight in the length and breadth of the country. Of these, moreover, only three of four manage to maintain reasonably high

professional standards. The rest range in quality from good, not so bad and passable down to wretched, dreadful and horrible. There are signed reviews by the carload in major American newspapers that no self-respecting instructor in English would accept from an athletic sophomore.

New York does much better than other large cities, and as the publishing heart of the nation it ought to. In four of the five other principal American cities it is a rare review that is neither sedulously tailored to the pattern of a publisher's blurb nor just plain rambling, woolly and offhand.

One curse of newspaper review departments everywhere is the office boy with nothing to do for the next couple of hours. Another is the local clubwoman whose children are now grown but who still adores Thomas Hardy. Among the others is the girl graduate who did a thesis on William Faulkner last June, the novelist who is stuck on the third chapter of his first novel, and the expansive city-room type who recently bought a new house and still has a couple of bookshelves to fill.

Good reviewers, to be sure, are hard to come by. So are good linotype operators and good sports writers. As already suggested, they may have to be pursued — in universities, schools, libraries, churches, editorial offices, homes, hospitals and jails — and once caught up with they may have to be nursed along, petted, edited and paid. As a notion, we cannot possibly be as hard up intellectually as the general quality of newspaper book reviewing today would imply.

Four book-page editors came back bruised and perhaps justifiably outraged. There is a natural pride in any newspaper worker and those who are giving their craft a real try are quick to fire back.*

One raised the point that book publishers do not advertise "in the provinces." The revenue factor should not be a consideration in the news department, but he put his finger on a key to the problem. Newspaper publishers are by and large unconcerned about the standards of reviewing; as long as some attention to culture is there. They are tone-deaf to the appeal of reader service. If an improvement does not sound the chimes of the cash register, they can't hear. That is the sole reason why newspapers were so slow to print radio news, and then television news. In both, public interest has been, and is, deep and abiding. Program schedules and personalities in the broadcasting field are news and service in anybody's definition, but publishers were skeptical until the broadcasters began to spend at least a little money.

The Toledo *Blade* has an art editor, Louise Bruner, who sees still another problem. In the pages of *Editor & Publisher*, she lectured the copy desk for failure to recognize and appreciate the nuances of critical writing. She complained:

> Our quarrel is not with publishers and top editors, who generally endorse culture along with clean government and motherhood. It is the desk men, who think of news only in terms of crime, sports and politics, who commit mayhem with our copy and treat us like well-meaning, but addled, nuisances.
>
> While they brag of not knowing a thing about

* All four are doing good jobs and ought to be named: George H. Esselburne, of the Buffalo *Evening News;* Margaret Parsons, of the Worcester *Telegram* and *Evening Gazette;* Paul Flowers, of the Memphis *Commercial Appeal;* and *Evangeline Davis,* of the Greensboro (North Carolina) *Daily News.*

art (my field) or music or the dance, readers of this kind of news are no longer a few eggheads. Museums now draw a bigger attendance than baseball. The crowd at a recent art auction was so large and so plush that the director of the Metropolitan Museum had to sit on the floor.

The Detroit Institute of Arts has established 13 suburban centers. In the first four hours of the Picasso show at the Chicago Art Institute, 6,000 persons paid fifty cents each for a look. Preview visitors to Cleveland's local May Show spent over $19,000 in the two hours before the public opening. Twelve universities, including Harvard, offer intensive courses in cultural subjects for men of executive potential, who attend at their companies' expense and receive full salary while they are learning.

Slick magazines, published by grocery chains for the average housewife, include a piece on art in every issue.

When a museum acquired a full-length painting of a reclining nude, rear view, the managing editor ordered the print sent through for one column. "Which half?" asked the art critic, "Head to derrière or derrière to toes?"

The society page carried the tea party angle of an exhibition of portraits, at which the painters were the honored guests. Among those listed as present was Renoir!

Newspapers, be it said to their credit, make no pretensions in the arts. What they are doing is *not* criticism; it is *reviewing,* and that is what they call it. Most editors, no matter how unschooled they are in the arts, seem to know that criticism calls for more background, more knowledge, more talent than they usually manage to hire. They know that they have no copyreaders competent to edit criticism; they know that oftentimes an honest and unsparing criticism *qua* criticism would probably cause them no end of trouble. They have, besides, a worshipful attitude toward the reportorial craft. Let reviewing therefore be reporting and only that.

This rationalization takes no account of the fact that their readers have not been standing still culturally during the past fifty years. It would be hard to find today a reporter who had never heard a symphony orchestra; less than half a century ago, millions had never set foot in an art museum and had few prospects of doing so; there were no book clubs with members in the millions; only aristocrats had ever seen anything on the stage besides vaudeville; television drama had not yet been imagined. There is today growing enlightenment which deserves something better than homogenized "reviewing" by incompetents who are either afraid of the shadow of their own opinions or too fond of them.

There is another roadblock to adult criticism in the daily journals. The drive for economic and social fringe benefits has cost more than mere money. A pension program is almost a necessity for the modern newspaper, which cannot hope to attract young talent without it because this is one of the first queries that the potential recruit is likely to make. The cost — and it is high in any event — of a pension plan is scaled to the average age of the employees. This results in a hiring premium on the very young and puts a heavy discount on the availability of the mature, experienced workers — especially women candidates. The museums are full of women who are potentially expert art critics. They are not hired by newspapers nor are they likely to ask to be hired. Besides the disadvantage of their womanhood, they might be disqualified because they are over thirty.

It is rarely that a person under forty, man or woman,

has the capacity to be a critic. A university graduate, far above the average in intelligence, began his career as a drama reviewer by declaring that *Death of a Salesman* was far superior to anything Shakespeare ever wrote. He may be right but it is certain that he will have to wait a couple of hundred years for justification. Yet news writing, even criticism, demands reasonable judgments here and now.

Apprenticeship in critical writing on the arts cannot be served in less than a decade. Meanwhile, age creeps on and the things that ordinarily only age can add — maturity, judgment, balance, perception — are washed out under the exigencies of the pension plan.

As long as the current fear of maturity continues, the newspaper is trapped in paradox. Bernard Berenson would not have been considered by today's managing editor as an art critic. He was, actuarily, incompetent during the last and most fecund sixty years of his life!

14

THE

NATURE

OF

CRITICISM

NOTHING ANNOYED FRANKLIN P. Adams in the days of his "Conning Tower" in the New York *World* and later in the *Herald Tribune* so much as the praise given a poem or a well-written article with the words: "It's too good for the newspaper!" Nothing, F.P.A. thought, was too good for the newspaper, and he was right and will be as long as there are newspapers.

There is mistaken reasoning in the idea that criticism must step down to the merely reportorial level because criticism in the best sense of the word does not belong in the daily press. We have seen how ill equipped most reporters are to address themselves to an art exhibition, a festival concert, the ballet, or even the drama. Our reviewer-critic is "somebody around the shop." His reportorial competence is supposed to suffice. And thus managing editors, city editors, and all the journalism textbooks insist upon "reviewing" as quite sufficient. Because of the worshipful attitude of the public toward the verity of type, the reviewer's by-line takes on a mesmeric authority which too frequently does not exist.

Let us make a distinction between "reviewing" and criticism. Criticism has the disadvantage of living under a bad name. In common speech it has the flavor only of fault-finding, its somewhat less than incidental function. To criticize a person is to imply that we not only are about to find out what is wrong with him, but that we have already found out; that we are therefore negatively committed to him and his actions.

To try to translate such a definition to the field of critical writing about the arts is a manifest absurdity. Writing about values in the theater, in music, in painting, in poetry or in books presupposes a love of the theater, of music, of painting, of poetry, of books, or whatever a person is regarded as competent to discuss.

A critic in the fullest sense of the word is the real amateur: the man who is in love with a medium. The dilettante I would define as one who is casually, superficially, or intermittently committed. There may be some reluctance about accepting "amateur" as the definition of a critic since this word, also, has negative, feeble connotations. It is not used here to imply inexpertness.

The dedicated critic is in favor of the art he contemplates. He wishes the artist well: long life, fruitfulness, and the great good fortune of being comprehended by as many people as possible.

Because of this devotion he is likely to be demanding. He sets his standards high. He will not feel indulgent toward merely a good try, a good intention, a second-best result. It is the loving father who takes his offspring to the woodshed as need be. (Although such a figure of speech in the art of child rearing is frightfully out of date it will have to stand.) Perhaps the critic, for that reason, may have more than a normal consciousness of sin — other people's sin. But that should not obscure the fact that he is primarily concerned with salvation of the good, the beautiful, the original.

Considering, then, the aims of criticism, there are a number of misconceptions as to whom critical comment is directed. Many artists and actors seem to be of the opinion that criticism exists for their benefit — literally their benefit, because they are happy to find commercial uses for any favorable comment that is published. Not only the artists but their managers cull these comments assiduously for use in press-books and advertisements. This is perhaps the lowest use to which criticism can be put.

Only slightly less selfish is the performer who believes that the critic has an obligation to remedy his (the performer's) faults. If a singer doesn't know how to manage his voice correctly, he should go to a voice teacher; similarly, if a pianist's technique is untidy, he needs more tutoring and harder practice. It is not the critic's duty to tell him how to fix what is wrong. Critics often make very poor teachers, anyway.

Quite simply, criticism in the newspaper should exist primarily — one might say exclusively — as a reader service. There are several classifications of readers whether we are considering a concert, a hit play, a fire, or a prize fight: (1) those who were present at the event, (2) those who were not present but interested, and (3) those who were not interested but might become so if the intelligible writer has the gift to bring them into the circle.

Those who were present may have a pretty good idea of what happened. Their opinions may have been formed already, although a man likes to have a little assistance in shaping his own opinion. He might have enjoyed the concert or the play; he may have been awed by the drama of the fire or the prize fight. Most people, however, want to be confirmed in the opinions they already have. Perhaps some few want to be disabused of notions which they fear are not quite valid. The person who was transported by the music, who laughed heartily at a comedy, may not have rationalized his emotions; and the counsel of a trained observer helps him to evaluate the art or the entertainment with which he was confronted. If the critic has no other competence, he undoubtedly has been to more concerts and more plays than most. Exposure means experience — and experience is a qualification for the reporter-analyst.

The persons at a fire may have wondered why streams of water were not poured on the south side of the building but he will not know until he is told that there was either a shortage of water or a shortage of pressure. The fire may have looked to him like a holocaust, but he will not be able to fix in his own mind the extent of damage until he sees the official figure of a half million dollars or whatever the estimate of the authorities may be. What was the technique of the knockout blow? It is not always apparent even to the ringside observer, but if the fight reporter cannot tell you he would be better employed doing something else.

As to the second classification of reader (those who were not there), one of these simply wants to be informed about something in which he has an interest but which he was unable to see or hear. He may be keenly interested in a musical performance but, unable to attend because of unexpected visitors, lack of money, fatigue, or other reasons, he wants to know what happened and so turns to the critic's report. The ordinary report cannot tell him.

We say of any news account that it must answer every reasonable question that the reader might ask. This fits the case perfectly. To that extent, then, the critic must be a reporter. Incidentally, some of the best American critics first served their apprenticeship on reportorial staffs. E. H. Krehbiel, long-time critic of the New York *Tribune* was a police court reporter. The managing editor of the San Francisco *Chronicle* said that Alfred Frankenstein, its distinguished music and art editor could do an excellent job reporting a baseball game. The Baltimore *Sun*'s H. L. Mencken is perhaps the best example of all.

Such outstanding reviewers will, then, answer every reasonable question that might be asked by the reader who was not present at the event.

The third, disinterested, group may, in some minds be reason enough for ignoring the others. But the disinterested and the apathetic can be stirred to interest, and the journal that does so becomes for that reader an organ of surprise and discovery. Not a small gratitude to evoke in these days, when it is apparently so difficult to capture anyone's attention at all.

How many people really *care* about the people and actions of most news events until the newspaper or its competitors has made them care?

We also have to fix in our minds the purpose of the performance itself: Are we confronted with art or with entertainment? Obviously, one does not bring the same criteria to a performance designed to be pure and simple entertainment that one brings to a classical art. But the two may overlap to a degree depending on the hearer. Duke Ellington was once asked to distinguish between his music as entertainment and the music one hears at a symphony concert. His answer was another question: "Isn't a symphony concert entertainment?" A perfectly valid query, because a symphony concert can be mere entertainment to one listener while another is transported by the nobility of the composer's creation. Isn't Paul Dukas's *The Sorcerer's Apprentice* entertaining? Assuredly. It is also the work of an artist whose composition is an intellectually ingenious structure. The same may be said of Strauss's *Til Eulenspiegel*. It tells a story. Beethoven entertains us with his *Pastoral Symphony*, and it is also a lofty orchestral composition, even if it hasn't the architectonic proportions of the *Eroica*.

What now of the competition of television? Walter Hawver, who does a column for the Albany *Knickerbocker News* recently took stock after his first year on the job. The statistics were impressive (or terrifying, depending upon one's point of view). Hawver reckoned that he had spent some 1200 hours viewing TV and that his 275 columns added up to 232,000 words, or the equivalent of three fair-sized novels. He watched about 500 dramatic shows (roughly one-tenth of the total output), 100 or more variety programs, most of the "spectaculars," and took at least one look at every known species of day or night program. When time permitted, he moved away from his set long enough to talk face to face with some of the people involved.

His approach to the formidable task of covering all forms of television entertainment was realistic. How can one man, he asked, qualify to deal with a ballet, *Richard III*, the opera *Antigone*, a documentary on Africa, a new play, not to mention sports and national events? He fixed upon a simple guide: "The job of the TV critic is not simply to ask: Is this good theater, or good music, or good documentary, or good comedy? His basic question is whether it is good television entertainment."

That goes to the heart of the matter.

It does limit the newspaper's potential.

It is often said: "After all, criticism is only one man's opinion." Obviously. But what are the qualifications for this opinion? How does a critic establish himself? Paul Henry Lang, then editor of *Musical Quarterly*, suggested:

> We should begin with the simple equipment of a practical musician. . . . A musician is not necessarily a person who can play a Paganini concerto at the drop of a hat or compose a symphony faster than Miaskovsky; but he should be able to read a score, and what is more important, hear it. . . . He ought to be a man who at one time or another, went through the holy sensation of moving four parts along the staves, such movement resulting in a piece of music that makes sense."

There have been eminent critics who were also creators — Hector Berlioz, Robert Schumann, Richard Wagner, George Bernard Shaw. But as in the cliché, a person doesn't have to be able to lay an egg in order to judge an omelet. Virgil Thomson established himself as a composer before he began his critical writing. His contribution to criticism may be as important as his music.

But by some mysterious magic, a man becomes a critic the moment he is appointed to the job of writing for a daily newspaper. He is an expert in the public mind, even to those who do not like experts. An expert has been defined as a man who has made every possible mistake in whatever is the field of his endeavor. Most critics worth their salt eventually commit all the errors to which critical flesh is heir.

People really have a high opinion of critics. They believe the critic is judicial, unprejudiced, unemotional. One must not be misled by what he says in his sarcastic moments. It may be something he has had for breakfast or something he has had for culture.

Sarcasm is evidence of either. The real truth is that while the critic tries to be judicial he does not always succeed. The critic *is* swayed by his emotions; and he *does* have his prejudices. All this is because he is a sensitive human being; and if he were not a sensitive human being, he couldn't be a very good critic.

The British author Halliday Sutherland once wrote:

> He who thinks himself unprejudiced is suffering from self-deception. We are all prejudiced by our nationality, heredity, education and beliefs. We are all prone to look with a partial eye on those who share our opinions and to regard with suspicion those whose views differ from our own. Recognition of these facts should make us examine evidence as fairly as the frailty of the human mind permits.

We really do not believe ourselves to be unprejudiced. It is an idiom of our language to begin with the phrase "I may be prejudiced BUT ——" It would be more honest to say: "I AM prejudiced AND ——"

Editors ordinarily give their critics and department heads a free hand, especially in the sensitive area of opinion. But if the critic strays too far off base, what can the editor do? Throw out his review? Edit his piece?

Norman Cousins, editor of the *Saturday Review,* faced this problem when his able movie reviewer, Hollis Alpert, found *War and Peace,* the six-million-dollar, star-studded, three-and-one-half-hour, color-and-wide-screen version of Tolstoy's novel food for lengthy carping.

The *Saturday Review* ran Alpert's piece intact. But next to it Cousins entered a piece under the caption

"Editorial Dissent." Agreeing with many of the critic's complaints, Cousins suggested that Alpert may have failed to place the flaws "in proper balance, with respect to the scope of the undertaking and the actual achievements of the film...." After reporting his delight over the film's many memorable scenes and its dramatic use of the full potential of color, Cousins said he felt "it would be unfortunate if his [Alpert's] criticism had the effect of keeping anyone from seeing a picture light years in quality beyond the average Hollywood product ... a sincere effort to deal with the mammoth and the minute with the sense of equal beauty."

He closed on a friendly note: "Nothing in the foregoing should be interpreted as any loss of confidence by the editors in their motion picture critic. All the meaning — and all the fun — would go out of artistic criticism if critics always had to agree with their editors — and vice versa."

There is one problem for the critic which is not apparent to the general reader. It is this: When he has expressed himself on the Fifth Symphony or the Ninth, when he has dilated upon the marvels of *Tristan* for more times than he can count, what is there left to be said? There it is, a noble art work, recognized by everyone and established. Its proportions and details are as familiar as the house we live in. How is the critic to approach it afresh?

Of course, if the performance is so obviously poor that it departs from the intrinsic outlines of the classic, it is fairly easy to so report. The tradition is clear. It takes, perhaps, a little courage to find fault with shortcomings, but, on the other hand, the creator and the interpretations are fairly well established. If a certain movement of a symphony is marked *allegro*, it is to be played rapidly; how can one quarrel with that? There are degrees of fastness, of course, and here we enter the realm of opinion.

There is ultimately no criterion. Since all works of art inescapably have a historical position, some of these details of presentation and interpretation must be adapted to the perspective of the age in which we live. To say that all art is historical is to enter dangerous territory, but the thought is worth following. Here is where it takes you:

There is no such thing as a guaranteed immortal work of art. We enjoy musical classics of a century or two ago, but our enjoyment derives from an attitude not unlike that of the antique collector. A Puritan candle mold or warming pan, or a cobbler's bench, are matters of great interest to us now. But the candle mold and other appurtenances of an earlier civilization have no meaning except as we rationalize them in terms of the age in which they were used.

The symphonies of Mozart were not composed for the modern concert hall. They were composed for the eighteenth-century salon and that means that they were never intended to have a mass appeal. Their aristocratic tone is unmistakable. If they have general appeal today, that is because we are able to make the historical projection. Just as the average movie-goer enjoys period pictures dealing with the age of ruff and powder and patches, so, too, can he enjoy historical music of this kind. Most of the operas of Händel are completely dead and buried; so for the most part are the operas of Gluck and Monteverdi.

But you say the sculptures of Greece endure and are admired even in our day. True enough. Isn't a large part of our enjoyment derived from our veneration of the Greek ideal? Can the same person admire, equally the art of Praxiteles and that of Jacob Epstein? Naturally, but we can enjoy them both by reason of this same historical adjustment. It is no reflection upon the Hellenic ideal that we no longer put up public buildings in the style of Greek temples (except in Washington, D.C.).

When we move into the theater the problem is slightly different. The chances are that the factor of sheer entertainment is likely to loom a little larger. Some people, no doubt, go to the theater to be edified and educated. But mostly the motivation is an evening's diversion. Theater tickets cost more than admissions to concerts or museums or the average-length book. For hit shows the price can be prohibitive when the speculators have done their inflationary work. Isn't it, then, the business of the critic to give some idea as to whether the show is worth the $7.50 top or whether a man gets his money's worth by giving $25 to the scalper? The critic must guide us to worth, in art and in money.

It might be said with some justice that the critic is scarcely in a position to judge the latter since he pays nothing for his seat. It is also true that the person who gets in free is likely to be more critical than he who has a four- or five-dollar stake in the performance. He who spends money for the show or the concert is going to try a little harder to enjoy it. This is completely irrational; but so is human nature.

Opinion *is* news, but to be news it must establish its competence and earn its authority. It is one of the newspaper's few legitimate opportunities to make news.

It is upon competence that people lean for guidance, for confirmation of their own opinions or for the replacement of their opinions by new thoughts. Just as the editorial page, in order to guide, persuade, instruct, explain, must demonstrate intellectual leadership — the ability to think out clearly the elements of public affairs, history, political science, and sociology — so too does art criticism call for authority.

If newspapers are to address themselves to the arts and recognize none but the reportorial function then the reviewer must limit himself to counting the house, listing the program or cast of characters, reporting encores or obviously fluffed lines — and all this is not enough.

Criticism is not too good for newspapers.

15

WORN-OUT
TOOLS

THE AMERICAN PEOPLE ARE BI-lingual; they speak a form of English and they understand headline-ese. Some even manage to follow sports writing but that like the dialect of the headlines, is merely a reading language. God forbid that these strange tongues be given voice!

The techniques of the newsroom are perhaps even more obsolescent than the machinery of the composing, stereotyping, and press rooms. The headline, the structure of the news story, the conventions of human interest, the reportorial approach, were only superficially useful in their day, which has long since gone by, but newsmen cleave to them.

Every journalist knows that the display headline was so designed that he who runs may read and perhaps pause at the newsstand to buy, but this is insufficient appeal to the man who today picks up the newspaper from his doorstep. Perhaps display headlines continue in use because there is still a newsstand sale in the metropolis. The big city way, of course, has always been the model for provincial minds and in spite of the fact that the big journals are in real trouble, home-delivery journalism somehow cannot see the light.

The doctrine holding that the first paragraph of every news story must contain the five basic facts of time, place, person, result, and reason confronts the reader initially with a rhapsody of confusion. It so fantastically ensnarls the narrative elements that he who cares at all must read the story twice to comprehend. The most engrossing story loses all its drama. There is very little news that is not dramatic unless the writer is insensitive to dramatic elements or unable to put them in order.

Photography is so cliché-ridden that what few news pictures convey a generous message are fortuitous. This is not the fault of photographers so much as of the habit patterns of those who make assignments and those who seek publicity. At the doorstep of photography also must be laid a large part of the responsibility for public resentment against invasion of privacy.

In addition to this devotion to worn-out techniques add the misuse of mechanical aids such as the telephone and the automobile.

To interview a man over the telephone is to fail to employ that most reliable instrument, the eye. It is to forfeit whatever testimony there is in a man's handshake, the aromas of his cigar or after-shave lotion. None of these alone may be greatly important but taken together with his normal surroundings, they will provide a concert of sensory impressions quite beyond the power of the telephone to convey. This is a two-way street. If the reporter has any prepossession or persuasion, if he dresses well and is mannerly, then his own presence is likely to favor a rapport with his source that may get him a better story. The much-too-useful telephone touches off a defense mechanism in the interviewee — a constriction that can be felt, an evasiveness, an instinct to outwit. You are not a man asking questions, but a Voice with the power to put answers directly into type.

The automobile can cost the reporter his mobility. If the mayor drops dead on Main Street, the reporter driving by has first the problem of parking his car. A good reporter should wear out more shoe leather and make the seat of his pants last longer.

One excellent reason for headline reform is that a very large percentage of newspaper error can be traced to headlines. The constricting nature of the narrow newspaper column, as well as certain arbitrary rules of symmetry, constitute a straitjacket which makes it almost a miracle to achieve a heading faithful to the text below it. Every idea must be paraphrased in the shortest possible word that even approximates fact. Since there is no such thing as an absolute synonym the headline writer is faced with a conspiracy to defeat accuracy. This problem has produced an argot that bears only a bastard relationship to the English language. Its absurdity is manifest if it is read aloud.

The headline is the most vulnerable chink in the newspaper armor. It makes correct quotation almost an impossibility; it accounts for most distortions and misconstructions; it offends intelligence and rips the envelope of context; it is a constant libel risk. By actual check, it trips up more frequently than that sturdy refuge of all incompetence, the so-called "typographical error."

The headline is the spoilsport of the gay human interest yarn and the marplot of the carefully written dramatic story. It is the incubus of a responsible, conscientious copy desk where the trained editor sits in judgment, skepticism on his right hand, common sense on his left. Whether there is one man or ten around the rim, the copy editor is the reporter's best critic, the writer's conscience. The copy desk is the sacrificial altar of the sacred cow, the abiding place of curiosity, discretion, cynicism, sympathy. The men at his desk give the paper its flavor: newshounds all, with noses in the air for the scent of human interest or libel. But they cannot win against the treachery of the traditional headline and they are not to be blamed for its obscurities and its imbecilities.

There are gaucheries for which they are responsible, however. Occasionally a reporter is inspired to write a narratively constructed news story. For instance, a congregation is kept waiting Sunday morning for the arrival of the minister. He has served them forty-five years without missing a service, for illness or any other reason. The minister's wife is there with their son, daughter-in-law, and three grandchildren. She goes to the church door and gazes up the street. The phone rings in the church office and an elder goes to answer it. He is absent several minutes before he returns to the whispering, uneasy congregation. It is eleven o'clock when he returns ...

The story goes on in this fashion for several hundred words and the reader by this time would have been sitting with the anxious congregation, except that whatever skill the writer manifested has been completely nullified by the headline: CRASH KILLS PASTOR ON WAY TO CHURCH.

Dr. Benjamin Spock wrote in the *Ladies' Home Journal:*

> Certainly the newspapers consider punishment [of children] especially physical punishment, an endlessly hot and fascinating topic. Whenever an

educator or psychologist or physician in a long careful speech about the management of children makes an incidental reference to the naturalness of occasional punishment, this side remark is what always gets into the headline as "Expert Advocates Corporal Punishment."

It was the headlines, and they could not have been other than deliberate, in the Sheppard case in Cleveland — that made hay for those who talk of trial by newspaper:

QUIT STALLING AND BRING HIM IN

SAM DECLINED JULY 4 LIE TEST

SAYS DR. SAM TALKED DIVORCE

TESTIFIES SAM CHANGED STORIES

CHARGES SAM FAKED INJURIES

SAYS MARILYN CALLED SAM A 'JEKYLL-HYDE'

The headline's literalism too often sacrifices the power of the non-specific, the suggestion that gives wing to imagination. If, for instance, this book were to carry a headline instead of a title, it might be:

NEWS-WEEKLIES DISPLACE NEWSPAPERS

— but that is not the gravamen of these pages. Or he might write:

PRESS FAILS IN TECHNOLOGY

— which is but a detail of the argument and, as every headline must be, an oversimplification. Conceivably the headline might say

WRITER RAPS CHAINS

— except that the author is not criticizing chains alone or (he hopes) not only "rapping" his life work.

So he doesn't try to write a headline. His book is entitled *The Fading Newspaper* because that is what he sees in all these manifestations. He also feels that the title may be sufficiently arresting to those who are creating newspapers and those who are reading them to help them stop to think. A good attack on the problems raised here might be begun by headline reform.

There are people who read no further than the headlines; they may be a majority. But there are others who still look to the press for information, education, and considered opinion. Editors often wonder why educators, scientists, and academicians generally seem to have a contemptuous opinion of the press. Some have an important message to disseminate but are often frustrated by the cavalier way in which the daily press seeks to impart it.

This vandalistic treatment does not begin with the headlines; often the headline merely completes the damage. The distortion takes place in the whole technique of oversimplification. It is merely the nub, the kernel, that is wanted. The husk, the ear, the maturing product are of no use to the reporter who spots a fuse that he can ignite. The headline writer strikes the match.

Not many years ago Dr. Rensis Likert, Director of the Institute for Social Research at the University of Michigan, released for publication the result of a survey, covering a period of years, investigating the reasons for high and low productivity in industrial plants. The study began in 1947 with an initial grant from the Office of Naval Research. The result was a book called *Productivity, Supervision and Morale in an Office Situation.*

The magazine *Business Week* carried an account of this

research in some twenty-five hundred to three thousand words. This account was as comprehensive as that amount of space permitted. It was accurate, fair, and in general got to the heart of the findings. *Business Week's* account was slightly out of focus — and only slightly — because of the headline. The caption was "Best Workers Gripe the Most."

Now the findings of the survey (greatly oversimplified) were that workers most devoted to their vocation and to the company were apt to be more critical of management than the low-production workers who did a routine job. The latter didn't seem to care very much what sort of company they worked for. They had no organization pride. So the headline was slightly off center because of the use of the word gripe. Griping, criticism and apathy are not the same. It is impossible to gripe constructively; but one can criticize constructively.

Business Week sent out a news release which, though shorter, was nearly as accurate as the original article. But the caption for the news release was still more out of focus:

Biggest Gripers
Are Best Workers.

The thought has now been completely reversed. The story traveled far and wide over this country and was reprinted abroad. The United Press rewrote the release and came up with this lead: "The man or woman who complains the most about his job, his company and his boss usually makes the best worker, a four-year study showed today."

Later: "A Prudential spokesman said the report might produce startling results. 'On the basis of the study,' the spokesman said, 'it may be that instead of firing a guy who threatened to punch his boss on the nose, we should have promoted him.'"

The Prudential spokesman was fictitious. Neither Prudential nor the United Press was able to produce anybody who ever said anything approaching that quotation.

There were other rewrites of the press release: "It's the wise boss who promotes the guy that gripes all the time instead of firing him, for the chances are he's a superior worker."

At this point the editorial writers came to bat. A brief editorial in the Philadelphia Inquirer ended with this paragraph: "If the University of Michigan's researchers are right the key to success is to gripe. We find it hard to swallow. When social research or any kind of research produces such peculiar results it looks as if some money needed for worthwhile phases of education is being sadly wasted."

The Portland *Oregonian* editorialized: "If a tune you heard on the radio the other night keeps running through your head, don't whistle it at work. The boss may jump to the conclusion you like your job and fire you. Better to snarl at the old so-and-so. He may have read a report by the social research institute of the University of Michigan and decide you are a griper and, therefore, entitled to more pay."

The editorial concluded: "The fact that research men spent four years on such a dull subject is evidence that they like their work. We think they should be fired."

The Binghamton *Sun* picked up the fiction: "If employers generally accept and decide to put in practice the results of a four-year survey just completed by the University of Michigan's Institute of Social Research, we may expect the employe who threatens to punch the boss in the nose to be promoted instead of being fired."

The point is that no reporter and no editorial writer checked back with the Institute of Social Research as to the accuracy of these statements or checked the authenticity of spokesmen.

To wrap up a news report and editorial comment on a four-year research job without stirring from the reportorial desk or the editorial ivory tower, or so much as reaching for a telephone, is of a piece with the journalism in which a great many thinking people are losing faith.

This is the essence of sensationalism. It does not take crime and lust to be sensational. The deliberate distortion of serious, meaningful labors can be equally startling. This incident illustrates that the editorial writer, too, can be sensational and flippant when vital news stirs no cogent thoughts. Ruminating before his typewriter, he might at least check the facts.

The structure of the conventional news story is a phenomenon in that it is the only form of writing which does not presuppose wholeness. It prescribes a beginning but no ending. It lacks form. One of the secrets of craftsmanship is that the creator is able, before he begins, to see his job in its entirety.

The news story is concerned only with details, chiefly in the first paragraph, on the curious assumption that no reader — and perhaps not the newspaper — will get to the end of the story. The story has no sum; its appeal is partial. It is the height of frustration for any writer to have to work on the assumption that his reader has not the time to hear him out.

Just about all that is wrong with news writing today can be traced to the so-called pyramid lead, with its primitive, breathless, hit-'em-in-the-eye approach — who, what, why, when, and where, the five W's, all in a single sentence.

What else has the paper to say? (asks the reader). That's the gist? Well then, a friendly goodbye to you!

But wait ——

Very well, but now you're repeating yourself. Go on, though, if you must ——

— this also happened —

Now you have me confused as to what happened when, says the reader, baffled.

This "pyramid lead" is responsible for the sins of incoherence, inaccuracy, loss of the unities of time and place, poverty of expression, and finally for the death of the story itself through sheer exhaustion and general debility, a guttering candle finally blown out. The term pyramid lead is not a particularly good one because the word pyramid connotes a solidity which the device does not have. The news pyramid stands on its apex.

The term "jackpot lead" might be a better one. For instance: the reporter hurries back from the scene of a fire or an accident, the carnival, or the caucus and on his way mentally churns up his facts in the business of finding a beginning. Usually he has it by the time he reaches his typewriter, but sometimes, especially if the deadline isn't breathing on his neck, he will sit and ponder, chew a pencil or chain-smoke. He may make a try or two, ripping out the copy paper and giving it a crumbling toss in the general direction of the wastebasket.

Suddenly he has it! The lead — it's done!

The rest is easy. The typewriter pours out a cascade of clattering, clinking facts until the last feeble fraction of a datum has been accounted for.

What is this marvelous device? He has pulled some sort

of trigger; he has tripped an escapement, hit the jackpot, and the payoff is at his feet in a glut of disorder trailing off into nothing.

This is the jackpot lead. To write it the reporter seizes upon the most dramatic detail in a sequence of events which make the whole story. It is likely not to be the first incident in the chain — more probably it is the climax. By putting this first, he immediately dislocates the time element. Sooner or later he begins to tell things chronologically. That makes it necessary to repeat certain facts told before — or to omit them. The reader is confused. He begins to ask what happened first; and what next?

The combination of the stentorian headline and the five-W lead destroys the writer's most valuable ally — suspense. Clifton Fadiman once made a nice distinction between *attracting* attention and *engaging* attention. The awkward structure of the conventional news story attracts attention and simultaneously destroys whatever interest the reader might have had in the subject. When he is told, in barn-door type,

SCREAMING WOMAN
KILLED BY THUG

the screaming headline kills the event.

News writing has been the subject of much study in recent years but the results have not answered the questions as to why news writing should be different from any other kind of writing. The principles of communication apply with equal force to all mediums. Writing is merely a means of getting thought or information from one mind to another, and the shortest distance between the two is the straight line of precision, clarity of expression, and involvement of attention to the end. Whether in a novel, a sonnet, or a news story the principles are the same.

It is only the conventions of journalism that confuse the problem. The very pattern of news-story organization makes it almost impossible to report fairly what a speaker says. Malperformance in this job is the shame of the craft. A speaker spends most of the time allotted to him preparing the minds of his listeners for the impact of his message. Usually the most dramatic point is near the end. The reporter is trained to spot the dramatic point; he is required to put it first in his report. Thus before he begins he has torn the news from its context. Out of context it has a different force and inevitably is misconstrued. The hex of misquotation was upon the speaker before he began. The difficulty has been recognized and roundly deplored in the craft but probably will not soon be corrected.

The broadcasters have much to teach newspapers regarding the technique of interviewing. Regardless of the sequence of questions, the person interviewed can make the emphasis he desires; he is "live," he has the expressive power of his voice to underline his meaning. He can backtrack and repeat what to him is important. To a large degree the organization of the message is in his own hands. A misquotation can be corrected on the spot.

In preparation for the interview, by knowing the interviewee's background, and pursuing promising lines of discussion, some of television's newsmen have brought new life to the interview form. (See next chapter.)

Fear of assuming responsibility has led to another device that muddies the newspaper's stream of good writing — the habit of attribution. There may be only a single speaker involved but any news report of the event will be peppered with "he said," "declared the speaker," "the speaker asserted," and so on endlessly. This merely impedes the tempo of the story.

In crime reporting the news writer feels safe only if he attributes every sentence to the police. This affords him no protection whatever, for the police memorandum is not privileged and officers of any rank will not hesitate to contradict the news account if it suits them to do so.

Reporters defeat themselves with excessive attribution. Seasoned news sources, on beats regularly visited, are used to being quoted. Most of them like it. There are many others who are publicity-shy, who hold no official position that requires them to speak for publication, who get buck fever when they see their name in print, and are likely to keep their mouths shut the next time a reporter shows up.

One reporter who managed to write an extended series of articles on education without a single attribution sent a memorandum to his managing editor:

> In writing the series on education, I have not made a single personal attribution. I wrote this way because it seemed to me I could present a more effective, more accurate picture by forgetting about attribution. The problem was to determine the general pattern of educational thinking and operation. The significant materials were a sentence here, a phrase there — part of this classroom, part of that. To clutter the story with an attribution for every statement would have made the thing an utter mess — impossible for the reader to assimilate and most vulnerable to distortion.
>
> I feel this is something for the newspaper business to think about: If reporters are so untrustworthy that they must present direct evidence for everything they say, it's time newspapers got some better reporters. (Personally, I think it is.) It seems to me that nobody ought to be sent out on a job unless the editor has absolute confidence in

that man's ability and integrity. The day is past when newspapers can send a crew of half-trained men to collect scraps of information and set them down, willy-nilly, each scrap neatly pinned upon a source."

To insure accuracy, there is one obvious method — but it is one that newspaper people stoutly refuse to consider. Raymond F. Blosser, manager of the New York Central Press Bureau, once suggested to a newspaper audience that

one approach which might be tried more often is to let the source of your more important stories see them before they hit type, or at least read them to him on the telephone, except on the occasions when the story is so "hot" that you really must rush it into print.

Is this censorship? No. It couldn't possibly be censorship as long as you retain the right — as you certainly should — to be the judge of what changes you will buy, and what changes you won't buy. You might think it would lead to endless haggling, but I don't think it would. Obviously there will be people who won't be happy whatever you do. But this need not prevent you from letting your better sources know that you're really interested in being accurate by checking important stories back with them while there's still time to avoid actual mistakes.

I feel that newspapers are too sensitive in almost invariably refusing to let a person or a company know what's being written before the story gets into print. You of the editorial department expect people to cooperate with you, and on many occasions, to drop everything else to do it. At the same time, you force these same sources to accept your accuracy on faith, though they may feel that your record isn't nearly good enough to justify that arbitrary requirement.

I have heard newspapermen complain through the years about the inaccessibility of businessmen. They vary, just like all people. But if the modern businessman is out of reach, the chances are that the greatest single factor is that he's been burned at least once by an inaccurate reporter, and has no intention of letting it happen again.

The newspaper man's objection to this routine is a matter of pride. By not trying it now and then, he forfeits the chance to prevent the source's pulling the rug out from under him with the cry of "misquotation," a refuge that is often used insincerely.

Photography is too old a craft to be abused in the unimaginative fashion of which most newspapers are guilty. This is usually not the fault of the photographers but of their bosses, who make the assignments and who in turn are subordinate to the pressures of publicity seekers, politicians, women's clubs, merchants, brides, check donors, foundation-stone layers, and ribbon cutters.

As with most proverbs attributed to them, the Chinese probably never said that a picture is worth a thousand words. A great many news photos require up to a thousand words to explain what they presume to depict. There is usually no difference between one picture of an auto wreck and another; they differ as little as plane wreck pictures and neither conveys sufficient information regarding the accident.

Photographs may lie unconsciously. The false testimony of the camera lens regarding what proved to be one of the safest and most beautiful parkways in the country cost a governorship. Cameras have lied repeatedly regarding race and labor friction. The camera can willfully exaggerate slum conditions in the fairest city in the land. It can poison with heavy-handed, lifeless chiaroscuro the subtlest prose.

The news camera, too, is responsible for more public dismay and resentment than any other newspaper tool or technique — in its invasion of privacy. The picture which creates in the beholder the feeling of intrusion upon grief or private anguish, the feeling of "here I should not be," ought never to be taken.

The news camera has brilliant uses. The news cannot be fully reported without it. But words can do things which a picture cannot. A picture is valuable when it concerns that which can only be pictured. The Dutch master painted a portrait of an old woman cutting her nails — certainly a homely scene and a commonplace act — but no words could do what the artist did with light and shadow. On the other hand, a sensitive reporter I know of often begged that his feature stories *not* be shown to the picture editor because he felt that he had made his own pictures with words. And usually he was right.

Television makes the same mistake — of attempting to do what another medium can do better. A symphony does not become more enjoyable when the camera moves about from choir to choir showing first the woodwinds, then the strings, then the horns. That is because one does not see Mozart's G Minor symphony. It is for the ears, the imagination, the intellect — through the channel of sound alone.

But television is learning by its mistakes much faster than the newspaper.

There is an area in which the television camera is useless and that is the field of minor local events. For such dramatic episodes as the coronation of a queen, a congressional hearing that has captured the public attention, or a national political convention, television is the magic carpet which beings every viewer directly to the scene of historic events. When a princess marries, television cameras make everyone a member of the wedding. But the local bride, the local obituary, the council meeting — these are for the daily paper. The local face, the local group, the familiar terrain, must be seen with fresh words and with fresh eyes.

The great bulk of local advertising will remain in the newspaper. The classified section — for the man who wants to sell his automobile, rent his house, or hire a housekeeper — represents a great market-place for the exchange of human needs. It is one of the most eagerly read sections of the paper (ironically enough, by a *minority* group — those who want to buy) and there is no medium to compete with it.

Where other mediums have tried, they've fallen on their faces. When television first caused a reaction among newspaper publishers and circulation managers, it was one of we-must-get-into-the-home-before-they-turn-it-on. They looked for means to establish earlier deadlines, speed up the press run, cut corners.

The way to meet competition is not to cheapen the product. The way to meet it is, plainly, to make it better.

Instead of waiting around for an anemic technology to bring salvation, the newspaper had better sharpen its old tools and throw out those that no longer work.

16

SCIENCE

AND

JOURNALISM'S

INQUIRIES

Perhaps you have heard that: a crocodile weeps when it has eaten a man; a hedgehog sticks grapes under its quills and carries them home to its children; a crab waits until an oyster opens its shell and then puts a stone in the opening so that it may eat the oyster; a buried crab becomes a scorpion; and barnacles change into geese.

It is easy to see how such explanations were passed down from one generation to the next, but not so easy to see how they got started. They are due, in part, to inaccurate observations or the lack of observation. In the beginning someone did not take the time and pains to discover the real facts, and perhaps, being eager to appear wise, advanced a theory to explain what he had seen. His friends believed him and passed the story along as true.

LAKE, HARLEY, and WELTON in *Exploring the World of Science*

THE MANAGING EDITOR ASKED THE City Editor if he thought newspapers generally took a scientific approach to newsgathering.

City Editor: "Journalism isn't a science."

Managing Editor: "Why not?"

C.E.: "Because we're dealing with human beings all the time. Science is concerned with graphs, formulae, and chemicals, the nature of material things."

M.E.: "We're dealing with human beings only a part of the time. Much of our news concerns inanimate things: nature, fire, flood, and earthquakes, to say nothing of creatures other than human beings. Aren't you going to run any more dog pictures or stories?"

C.E.: "Still, we're not a science."

M.E.: "You'll remember that I didn't say journalism was a science. The purpose of my question was to inquire if we could not use the scientific approach."

C.E.: "Explain."

M.E.: "I cannot understand why there should be anything antithetical about science and journalism when both begin and end with the business of asking questions and rejecting what is false or unprovable. If there is any dissimilarity at all it is because journalism stops asking questions too soon. The flame of inquisitiveness burns intensely for a while, but it burns out too quickly and is very loath to correct mistakes, which science is bound to do."

The City Editor, by way of reply or corroboration, produced a staff memorandum written by Charles H. Spilman, executive city editor of the Providence *Journal* and *Bulletin*, after a disastrous hurricane and flood. The caption was: FLOODS HAPPEN TO PEOPLE.

> I think we have a tendency in a terrible disaster to forget that it is happening to people. We see the smashed buildings, the raging water, the glaring flames of fires, but we forget that people lived and

worked in those buildings, that the bigger story is what happened to the people rather than what happened to the buildings.

The physical destruction is so stupendous, so overawing, that we are bemused by it. We have to make a positive effort of will power to remember the people.

We should remember that we ought to present a picture of what has happened. We need to make our stories visual, so the reader can actually see through our eyes the terror and the immensity of the storm.

For instance, "The Social District was flooded by four feet of water and all residents have been evacuated" is good solid fact, and quite enough if all we want is to present a record for posterity.

We said the water was four feet deep. It would have been better to have written that it was up to the tops of parking meters.

We said the water was full of debris. The reader would have been informed better if we had said the flood carried parts of picket fences, beams and planks snatched from a lumber yard, sections of advertising signs, empty oil drums — what we had seen specifically. "Debris" doesn't evoke a picture.

Here is another example of how superior the specific is to the general:

We weren't content to say, "About 150 people were sheltered in the South Main Street Armory." We wrote in addition: "It was the first time in 40 years that Emiliene Turcotte, 70, has spent a night away from home. . . ."

We let one couple relate their experiences in detail. The reader then could imagine that something similar had happened to others. He could "see" what had happened.

> We should soak up the details, pick out an individual, or a couple, or a family and hear what they say, and how they say it. Rather than write "weary civil defense workers," we have to see "civil defense workers, some sagging in exhaustion against doorways, others gulping coffee in the hope it will keep their red-rimmed eyes open a little longer . . ."
>
> The stuff is there. We just have to stop long enough ourselves to see and hear and remember. The writing then will be easy.

That's about what John Hersey did in the Hiroshima story and in his Winsted flood story for the *New Yorker*. His is a splendid reportorial technique — witnessing a vast event through the eyes of one or a few victims.

Whether we can conclude that Journalism is a science or not, there is no reason why scientific methods cannot be applied to that part of journalism which is the business of asking questions. Other disciplines find that they must employ scientific procedures. To appreciate their importance we must realize that there is no such thing as the ultimate question.

A large part of any reporter's activity is concerned with the interview, whether the journalist is asking questions of a visiting celebrity or trying to get out the facts by talking to routine sources at city hall. It is not unusual for a fairly young reporter to be sent out to interview a personage whose utterances may be newsworthy. It doesn't help much even when, as is often the case, the city editor tells him what to ask. A sort of pretested routine — usually a questionnaire of clichés — cannot be expected to produce much besides stereotyped answers. This procedure also carries the hazard of questioning toward a preconceived position. The result is bound to be a scattering of loaded and leading questions, both of which are easily scented by persons accustomed to facing reporters. They shudder at giving sensible answers to a person who is not equipped to ask intelligent questions in a field that is foreign to him.

The press is alone in its dismal, slight preparation. No trial lawyer would consider himself equipped if he did not have academic training in the art of cross-examination. He has the advantage of textbooks on the subject and his theoretical equipment is soon developed in practice.

Similarly, the social case worker. No competent person in this service would dream of facing the individual's problem unless he or she had a trained knowledge of how to ask questions.

The market researcher and the poll-taker have refined their procedures to the point where they know that the framing of the question is so important that if it is improperly done, wildly fantastic statistical results will appear.

Census-takers know that the interviewee is likely to fail to report infants when asked how many people live in the house; that he gives the wrong answer as to the number of sleeping rooms, forgetting that a sewing, storage, or playroom is being used for sleeping purposes.

The Art of Asking Questions, a book on public opinion and market research by Stanley L. Payne,* boldly seizes the title *art* as opposed to *science*. The problem of science, says Payne is to ask the right question at the right time. It is a matter of developing a hypothesis into fact or refuting its validity. Payne is less concerned with question sequence than with question wording. The reporter, however, must be concerned with question sequence if he is to flush a covey of newsworthy answers.

*Princeton University Press, 1951.

Payne says that failure to understand the question does not bar glib answers. For instance, when asked "Which do you prefer, dichotomous or open questions?" the respondents soberly express a choice from which he concludes that "the more meaningless a question is the more likely it is to produce consistent percentages when repeated."

Sam Gill has said that when asked questions about the phony "metallic metal act," seventy per cent of those questioned gave definite answers as to whether the states or the national administrations should have jurisdiction. Payne also goes on to say that "Isn't that question loaded?" is in itself a loaded question whereas either "Is that loaded?" or "Is that loaded or not?" is considerably less pointed toward a preconceived answer.

The reporter has much to learn from these considerations. Suppose, for instance, the interviewee is willing to yield up what the reporter wants. Well, what *does* the reporter want? Is he leading to an objective; talking to a position? If so, isn't he asking for a propaganda answer?

The reporter should quickly find out whether the interviewee trusts him. He certainly will not be trusted if he pretends to have a knowledge that he does not possess. An admission of ignorance is far better than pretense. Better still if a reporter has the actual knowledge that inspires confidence.

There are, of course, differences between market researchers, pollsters, social workers, lawyers, and the journalist. The former are asking their questions of the public — many people disparate in education and social and economic status. The newsman, as a rule, faces people who make news, and who are for the moment, at least, his "superiors."

The social worker faces usually a lower stratum of

humanity — those who want or need something. The defense lawyer cross-examines to win acquittal for his client, the prosecutor to win conviction for the state. The poll-taker is neutral.

There are some similarities, however, in what all questioners are apt to encounter. The prestige factor is one. The interviewee may hope for gain in some instances or feel reluctance as a giver of facts in others, but with nearly all who are subjected to questioning there is the temptation to transfer a flattering self-image whether of guiltlessness or economic status. The similarities of the questioners' problems, like the differences, are mostly matters of degree.

An important faculty is the reporter's ability to listen. Just what did the man say? Most interviewers talk too much.

"Interviewing as applied to journalism is unique in that the audience is the general public. The reporter must discover what is of interest to many people. He must know how to listen rather than talk." *

An abiding concern of the interviewee is the hazard of misquotation. This is a genuine worry born out of more unhappy experiences than American journalism should have permitted. The danger of misquotation is far less if the interviewee is given his chance to expound his cherished opinions. He doesn't like to have them mutilated by leading questions, by what the reporter deems to be interpretation or even background.

Preparation for the interview is important. A striking example is cited by Ben Reese, co-chairman of the American Press Institute, and formerly managing editor of the St. Louis *Post-Dispatch*. He writes:

* *How to Interview*, by Walter van Dyke Bingham and Bruce Victor Moore, Harper & Brothers, 1941.

A handout reached the *Post-Dispatch* city desk saying that Lady Asquith would speak before a St. Louis organization three weeks later. I called Paul Y. Anderson to the city desk, asked him what he knew about Lady Asquith; he knew she was the wife of the British prime minister.

I instructed Anderson to read everything about or by Lady Asquith that he could lay his hands on, in our morgue and in the public library, and prepare questions to ask in an interview upon her arrival.

Lady Asquith rode a mile from Union Station to Hotel Statler. Two women from the *Globe-Democrat* and *Star*, and Anderson, met her in her hotel room. The first question asked by one of the women was typical: "How do you like St. Louis?" The Lady had just arrived and seen one mile of St. Louis. The women asked all the questions, mostly foolish; Anderson none.

Three reporters departed together, walking out of the hotel together. Anderson circled the block, re-entered the hotel, phoned Lady Asquith and asked if he could see her again and ask her questions he had refrained from asking in the presence of the competition. She welcomed him.

Anderson wrote a 2½ to 3 column interview for the same day used with a 2 column cut. A corking fine job, based on his knowledge of the lady, her activities, her interests, her writings.

Next day I received a note from her inviting me to a causerie she was having for Mr. Anderson, "the greatest reporter she ever met."

One of the best reporters I know — and he chooses to be anonymous on the ground that his newspaper might not approve of his method — has said:

A reporter may — and must — synthesize. I do an interview. Theoretically, I ask the questions, make a note of the answers and write them down, with solid notes to protect me should I be attacked later for misquotation.

Actually, I do no such thing. I recreate what, in my judgment, the subject said; something of his feeling; and I draw in a sketch of his personality — my own sketch.

On every one of those grounds I am weak if I am accused. I cannot, for the most part, produce notes to substantiate the exact quotation, for the very good reason that it is, literally, not an exact quotation. Only the quality of my perception makes me accurate in my representation of the subject's feelings, much less his personality.

And yet, if I am any good as a reporter, there will be no complaint. My story will be quite accurate. For I must go beyond the actuality of the moment. I must see beneath what the subject tells me under the stress of an interview; I must read beyond his probably halting, uncertain speech. I must somehow know that person, and I must recreate him in print.

In defending his anonymity he declared: "There are certain persons in this business who have passionate devotion to objectivity, incontrovertible things like statistics and 'exact' quotations. What would they think about reporters who fancy themselves as seers! !"

Erwin D. Canham has said much the same thing in describing his early training under Paul S. Deland, then city editor of the *Christian Science Monitor*:

A reporter had sometimes the obligation to protect a public man from misstatement or rash impulse. We must weed out his meaning and reflect it truly. More than once as a young reporter I have turned in an interview to Mr. Deland, only to have him bounce it right back to me with the comment: "I expect the man said what you have quoted, but that isn't what he meant." Then he would explain the viewpoint and commitment of the public figure, which I would recognize as valid. I would go back to the interviewee to get a better quotation, or put his real meaning into indirect discourse.

It may seem that there are two different and contradictory approaches: stenographic accuracy versus the distillate of a person's meaning.

They are not incompatible. Scientific training in so important and elusive a skill as interviewing should not hamper the the reporter's pursuit of the essential truth.

The alternative to the scientific approach is the mechanical: the application of formula, of habit thinking, of button-pushing conclusions, the easy acceptance of the plausible. Formula says that certain combinations produce human interest: boy and dog, sex and money, mystery and murder. People, the formula says, say what we expect them to say.

If science isn't working for the newspaper outside the newsroom, its order and logic aren't working for it inside either. Methods of advancement in the news department are scarcely scientific. One of the great drawbacks of the business is that the expert writer and reporter usually ends up at an executive desk where he does everything but write and report. He makes more money, and that is the way of advancement.

There are three separate functions in the news department. They call for three usually separate talents: observing and writing; editing; management of people.

The reporter who learns how to get his story, how to

write clearly and intelligibly, how to look civilized and treat people with reasonable courtesy, will get along. When he has become the seasoned, valuable reporter, he looks ahead to something else. Very properly so. Any self-respecting newspaper in the country is willing to reward him. But how?

If he is by then superannuated, with failing eyesight, and wears rubbers to work, he will become a copyreader. In this job he will die after, perhaps, having had a staff dinner given in his honor, with libations, on his forty-fifth anniversary.

Or, if he is still vigorous, he may become a rewrite man or assistant city editor. From that point, he has reasonable hope of becoming city editor and even managing editor.

There is always the editorial page.

So journalism has managed to demand the all-purpose newspaperman: he can write, he can ask questions, he can edit, he can be a counselor. From his chair at the city desk, he can become an administrator, or a thinker, and eventually grand keeper of the ivory tower.

Reporting has little if anything to do with copy editing.

The approach of science is: Query, observe, experiment, reject, confirm. Not merely in a figurative sense is reporting the business of questioning and observing. Editing is in high degree the art of rejecting the non-essential, the inapplicable, the invalid. In a positive sense it is exploration. It is also the skill of getting below the trajectory of events — news that warns — in advance of its happening. That has been the genius of the canniest magazines in recent years.

The editorial science then is to plot the curve of human society, its mores, and economics.

The third function, that of management, one might say, with perhaps some oversimplification, is the geometrical business of finding the shortest distance between two points. This can be applied to personnel, to procedures, and to costs, which seem to have become more desperately unmanageable in the newspaper business than in any other.

Since these journalistic functions are so disparate in their nature and call for entirely different temperamental equipment, it would seem the part of good sense to set the course accordingly. The man who elects journalism because he believes himself to be a writer has lost his way if he finds himself in the managing editor's chair. He still, somehow, must be promoted.

The trouble comes from the reasoning that desk jobs are somehow promotions. That is not necessarily true. Neither is it sound reasoning to develop a man to where one decides he is so valuable in a position that one cannot afford to advance him. Here is where money gets into the picture. There should be no "junior" ceiling on the salary of a writer.

It has been said, whimsically, that reporters ought to get more money than managing editors. If this merits a serious answer, it is simply that an editor is paid to manage the costly and sensitive apparatus of good reporters.

17

THE BEATS

THERE ARE FASHIONS IN NEWSPAPER "beats." The latest cry in press coverage throws an incandescent spotlight of attention on science reporting. Fighting for glory, in the reflection of another dazzling light, is the field of education.

The Sputnik caught newspapers, like other disciplines and persons, totally unprepared. Except for a handful of the metropolitan newspapers, none had a capable science reporter. The Associated Press had a veteran writer in the person of the late Howard W. Blakeslee who was succeeded by his exceedingly competent son, Alton Blakeslee. The New York *Times* had its William L. Laurence. The rest of us scrambled.

It is curious circumstance that science and journalism (the writing part) are almost antithetical in their appeal. I can remember men with every imaginable auxiliary interest — sports, stamp collecting, bridge, music, agriculture, bull fighting. I have hired men trained in law, theology, and medicine, men with a fantastic catalogue of hobby interests, but I have never in over forty years been approached by a job candidate who said he was a chemist, physicist, or a scientist of any description — or who understood their language. Like every other managing editor I immediately set about trying to find a reporter who could write ably and understandingly of the nuclear age. It was a universal lack; it is being remedied everywhere. Science is the fashionable beat on most newspapers today. Yet it was fifteen years ago, the day after the first atomic bomb, that newspapers told the world that a fantastic new atomic age was upon us.

Since education was immediately made the scapegoat for Sputnik, that too came in for newspaper attention. This was a belated discovery — about thirty years too late. No educational movement in modern times has been so devastating or newsworthy as permissive or "progressive" education. How radical it was can never be discovered through the files of newspapers because this tidal wave was never really reported. Editors had been content to see that school board meetings were properly covered — where they were open to the public; that a reporter dropped around now and then to the superintendent's office. Other educational news related to bond issues and the signing of contracts by personnel.

When education was made to take the blame for American failures in the space age, simultaneously newspapers began to be aware of the classroom as a source of news. They were not at first welcomed everywhere, on a curious theory of educators that it was none of the public's or the parents' business what children were being taught in the classroom. There may have been a narrow edge of revenge in this, since in many homes the rearing of children in manners and responsibility had been abandoned to the schoolroom.

When the reporters arrived, however, they must have

perceived that the story, neglected over thirty years, had passed them by. Progressive education had crested and was already subsiding, at least in many parts of the country.

At any rate, newspapers are now alert to the challenge of both science and education news and are today spreading themselves to till these fields.

Politics can be said never to have been neglected. The American press was born in the hotbed of colonial political agitation; it thrived in the violent cross-currents of political philosophy in the formative days of the Republic. Most of the great editors of the nineteenth century breathed, even snorted, politics. Today politics accounts for more column space and headlines than any other human activity.

Perhaps there is too much of it. Certainly much of the "news" about it is hollow. It is fair to wonder if popular interest is not limited to the closing weeks of a presidential campaign, just as the interest of many readers does not turn to boxing until a week or two before a title is at stake. Isn't much of the real news made in the time between campaigns? Popular interest in political matters has dissipated somewhat with the washing out of demarcations between the two major parties. The tariff and states' rights no longer divide them. Centralization of power in Washington made its greatest advance under a Democratic administration, followed by a Republican president who urges governors to assume more responsibility for the states and flirts with free trade. In social reform both parties constantly strive to steal each other's thunder (if not lightning). Campaigns are now fought on a popularity basis and the public interest is as in a beauty contest.

On the local level, the city manager system of government has become widespread. City manager administration is not good for newspapers. It is "businesslike" and being businesslike it is government, by executive order, by directive — authoritarian, in essence. Those newspapers who let the city manager have his way — and most newspaper businessmen believe that the managership is by its very nature good — find that it is needless to send a reporter on the rounds through city hall. No commissioner is permitted to speak for publication; all the affairs of his office must be cleared by the city manager before being released to the press.

Newspapers fall in with popular thought. Managership rids a city of politics, and politics, the reasoning goes, is by its very nature bad. This idea cannot be sustained; it is a cynical and superficial view. Politics is the essence of democracy; it is the drama of government. To eliminate political action is to discourage the natural interest of the people in their government. No wonder that newspapers conduct persistently their get-out-the-vote campaigns in a spirit of civic virtue and altruism. Why should it be necessary to *get out* the vote? The absence of voters at the polls can only mean indifference. The feeling of the city-managed citizenry is that they have hired a housekeeper for city hall and what goes on there requires no further attention.

From the newspaper standpoint, if there is an overemphasis on politics it is because political news is easier of access than any other kind. The paper cannot escape it. Politicians are vocal. If they are not called or sent for, they will obligingly call in person or phone the city desk with their latest public pronouncements. The political reporter begins to believe he is the only one who can safely do all his reporting from his desk. It isn't so.

Crime reporting is an area in which newspapers have been forced to take more criticism than any other. That "newspapers are full of crime and scandal" is a popular truism whether warranted or not. The defense is that the news must be printed for the public's protection. To many its very publication is sensation, without regard to the manner of telling.

Actually sensationalism is a matter of the detail selected. Facts of murder and sex can be told unadorned, but they seldom are.

There is also a geographical element. Ostensibly crime reporting is a protection for the public. If a penitentiary prisoner has escaped it is, of course, important that householders in that region be warned that the dangerous character is abroad. There is, however, no reason why a lurid sex murder in California should be reported in full in New Hampshire, unless, of course, the principals are national figures. But to make VIP's across the country of people whose only claim to attention is that they tangled with blood and sex is in its very essence sensationalism. It spreads sordidness for its own sake.

The heart of the matter is that news should be measured not by its potential radius of interest but by its potential depth of interest. To make news of crime is to widen the radius unnecessarily to matters that have neither social nor legal significance but are easily ignited. It is just the opposite of the challenge of foreign news, the significance of which far exceeds normal interest. Here the challenge is to secure depth as well as radius. This can be done in the telling. The satisfaction of prurient interest in crime requires no skill. It makes sensationalism inevitable.

Perhaps in no other field is today's newspaper so efficient as in sports coverage. The dedication of the writers is complete; to write sports is to be a Big Man because the readers accept his authority and competence without question. Sports is an abiding interest. Even in the highly competitive cities that remain, the newspapers may skimp on all sorts of news-of-record in favor of sensation yet none will take any chance of losing sports-page readership. Afternoon papers today have little left except analytical and "dope" stories because few sports events break on afternoon time. But this type of analysis has solid acceptance. The writing comes under the heading of criticism in the best sense of the word. The writer must be authoritative and equipped to gain readership for his expert opinion. Mere "reviewing," as is allowed in the arts, is not enough.

Newspapers generally are aware of the advantage of cultivating youthful readers. They are the subscribers of tomorrow and it is important that they acquire the newspaper-reading habit early in life. Advertisers like them, too. It is difficult to avoid being patronizing in this appeal and few succeed. Young people hate the word "teen-age"; they resent fiercely being corralled in a "youth department," just as women readers do not like to be thought of as limiting their interest to the women's department. One newspaper believes it solved the problem by referring to the young people's page as "Under Twenty."

The obituary page and the sports pages have a much greater readership among women than the pages designated for them. Television made sports fans of uncounted thousands of women, especially for the wrestling and boxing shows. They probably read editorial pages more than men do; certainly they read the letters to the editor. A woman's magazine editor said that women's interest rank about in this order: decoration, food, clothes, marriage problems — with child care last. Newspaper columns on child care are avidly read by young parents and are outranked in popularity, among the middle-aged, only by obituaries.

Thus the difference between magazines and the everything-for-everybody newspaper.

Taking an all-over view, there seem to be beats and beatniks in news coverage: the solid ground and the temporary fashion. To much attention is given to protective coverage, beats where the yield of important news is not high but which city editors are nervous about leaving unprotected — police court, federal building, chamber of commerce, hotels. These require coverage but they also require manpower. They should get their due but no more than that; the energy and attention left over might be better employed in digging out the news that isn't handed out . . . and in writing it up in better style.

18

PUBLIC

RELATIONS

THE DRIFT OF NEWS AWAY FROM the daily journals is matched by the movement of talent into vocations that have the face of journalism, if not the heart, and by the migration of seasoned talent into jobs that pay salaries with which newspapers cannot or will not compete. The lure, whether money or glamor, is provided by public relations and the industrial press. In recent years a sophisticated awareness has developed that the manufacturing and marketing of goods and services depend for success upon public attitudes; that public attitudes are pliant and can be shaped. This discovery is paired with a realization that success of capital in a highly developed and competitive industrial era is closely related to employee attitudes. These factors have produced the public relations phenomenon and the industrial press.

Curiously, both are first cousins of newspaperdom. The newspaper's stock in trade is the purveyance of information — general information for the general public, the Public Relations doctors purvey particular information regarding a single business or person for general consumption; the industrial press, particularly the house organ, provides company information for company employees, the sales force, and clients. All of them call for skills in gathering and presenting information, which is the essence of daily journalism.

Cold as editors have been toward journalism schools, they have also maintained a hostile or standoffish attitude toward public relations men, as exemplified in the condescending descriptions, is "press agents" and "house organs." The editor, however, knows that he cannot afford to go to war with either.

Though he harbors an under-the-skin superciliousness about "press agents," the editor is well aware that he has in them an ally. He uses them almost daily and there is good reason why he should. He doesn't have a staff big enough and to cover adequately all the ground of industry, science, and particularly government. Covering Washington alone without recourse to the "handout" would be unthinkable. The business of government is so ramified and specialized that reliance upon departmental spokesmen is essential; industry likewise; and, more so even than the others, science, in which daily journalism is admittedly only emerging into competence.

The editor protects his *amour propre* by the precautionary dictum that every handout must be checked for accuracy and for "the other side of the story" — an excellent precept, but the press the country over is filled with handouts printed verbatim, a practice that extends to not a few editorial pages.

The danger may be less than some responsible editors' suspect. This is because the best public relations men have discovered that the best public relations is to take the public into their confidence. That is to say: telling the whole story truthfully and without reserve makes friends and builds confidence. True, they are committed to a single employer and his cause; they are advocates, but for the most part they have become responsible ones.

Significantly, the public relations operator to hold down his job at all must be a good newspaperman. He is well paid, but he must earn his money. If he doesn't, he may have to go back to his newspaper job. The topflight newspaperman remaining in journalism runs a great risk of not getting what he is worth (although there are some who get a salary of $50,000 plus or minus). The end result is that in the newspaper ranks are too many men not competent enough to go after public relations money, while the misfits in public relations don't stay there long and are likely very soon to be found back in the city room.

Newspapers can correct this grave professional handicap. It is nothing that money will not redress. The newspaper salary should be so high that a newspaper cannot afford to retain incompetents. That leaves quite a long distance to go.

It is a fault in the editor's rationale when he looks down upon public relations as something foreign to journalism(an attitude reflected in the action of the journalistic fraternity, Sigma Delta Chi, in closing its ranks to further admissions from the public relations field.) Gathering information and dispensing it is journalism. Public relations can be discounted for its limitations but not outlawed, for there are similar limitations in the reporting by the daily press.

Pretentions to objectivity are somewhat qualified not only by the inhibitions and predilections of the chain newspapers but by the prejudices of individual editors and owners. The time has long since gone by when a newspaper in a region even moderately populated by

Roman Catholics could report comprehensively either news or sentiment about birth control, divorce, public transportation for parochial schools, or even the issue of separation of church and state. Nor is it likely that a newspaper will editorially favor higher corporation taxes in what ever community it may publish. Much has been declared and written regarding the impotence of local advertisers to influence reporting or editorializing, and this can be vouchsafed in deadpan honesty. It is perfectly apparent that neither trouble nor dictation can come from that direction as long as city editors and editorial writers know what areas of news and opinions are best avoided. The supposition that the press agent is concerned with only the one corner of the human establishment to which he is attached and that the newspaper is concerned with all of society will hardly bear consistent, close examination. Newspapers avoid particular areas as a kind of no-man's-land where the discreet instinctively do not tread. Public relations men carefully stake out their area of coverage and make no pretensions about the rest of the journalistic map.

Most practitioners in the industrial press set up a demarcation between company and product promotion and news of the employee community. Publications in the latter class are house organs pure and simple, a term which public relations people object to on the ground that an industry or utility is not a "house" and, in their too-finicky definition, a company publication is not an "organ." This is an indication of sensitivity and self-consciousness in a calling which has been described by one of its number as "somewhat too young to be wholly in focus."

By any name, the house organ does cover an area that once provided grist for a newspaper mill which no longer grinds so "exceeding fine." These smaller publications contain hodiernal news about people: who caught a big fish, who has a new baby, who is building a house or going on vacation. Newspapers used to live on, even compete for, this kind of news.

In the days when there were two daily papers in Beloit, Wisconsin, I was required to spend most of my reportorial time at the railroad stations, accosting everyone in the waiting rooms to inquire for publication where they were going, why, and for how long. (They were usually going to Baraboo, Janesville, or Milwaukee.)

This is no longer news in dailies of any size. Some weeklies are still fattening on it, and nearly all company publications. For many people their industrial life is their whole existence, except for recreation and home events. These items serve an employee relations function, giving recognition to people doing menial or major jobs. They get a sense of well-being, a feeling of acceptance, and overcome the complex of the "small cog in a big machine."

In the biggest corporations, with publications of mammoth circulation, the content is somewhat different but to indicate what they are printing one has only to cite a few titles: Ontario Hydro *News,* Swift *News,* Bell *News,* Phil *News,* Telephone *News,* Transit *News.*

There are about ten thousand of them in the United States and Canada, six for every single daily newspaper. Their total circulation is a hundred and fifty million, nearly three times as great as the total daily circulation of the newspapers in the United States.

These publications report company research and scientific news. Charles J. Morse, publications manager for Peoples Gas Light and Coke Company of Chicago and editor of *Gas News,* wrote in *Quill* magazine of the industrial press as "one of the youngest and fastest growing branches of the Fourth Estate." He wrote that most of the magazines and *newspapers* were pinpointed to certain audiences and had widely diversified purposes. "There are internals directed primarily to employees and stockholders; externals mailed to sales prospects, agents, dealers, wholesalers, customers and others; and combinations intended for one or more of the first two groups. There is also a sprinkling of trade, association and syndicated publications in the lot."

They range in circulation from five hundred to more than a million. Most of them, if not all, are on slick paper and some in four colors of a virtuosity that makes newspaper color look slightly sick. The printing is in letterpress, offset, rotogravure, and planograph.

How newspaper editors must bite their nails at such adoption of the term Fourth Estate.

The migration of news into company publications is hardly of competitive significance. In its larger aspects, products and technology, the daily press never pretended to coverage; the lesser function of employee relations, the personal news field, has been long since largely abandoned on the ground of triviality by daily journalism.

The real competition is for talent. Regardless of the rationalizations of Sigma Delta Chi or the irritation of editors looking for recruits, the young career seekers leaving college make no distinction between journalism of one kind or another. Public relations, the industrial press, news broadcasting by radio or television — all is journalism in the minds of the aspirants. I have never encountered one who felt that he was being debauched or prostituted by choosing any of these channels over the daily newspaper. To the job seeker, all other things are equal — except the money. The remedy is to be found nowhere except in the newspaper countinghouse. There is nothing unreasonable about this since newspaper owners and publishers, and now editors, freely and unblushingly refer to the newspaper as, not secondarily but first and foremost, a business. Its primary objective is to stay in business. Its next is to serve a community, if that is possible and consistent with a profit on the investment. As a business, then, the modern newspaper is in competition with other journalistic business for brains, imagination, and competency.

There are editors who are beginning to see the light as the sun of the public relations man rises ever more brightly on the horizon. Andrew Bernhard of the Pittsburgh *Post-Gazette* admits that the public relations man, who now often rates a vice presidency and who regards himself as a personage to be interviewed, is impressive. With his aloof attitude

> it never occurs to us to attribute to him the base motives we imputed to his seedy predecessor. . . . The President who used to think it was nobody's damn business what went on in his company knows better today. He knows that legislatures, congresses, tax officials, a thousand local, state and national boards, bureaus and commissions have the right to poke noses into his books. He knows that an unfavorable public attitude toward his company can bring government locusts down on him to run him into disaster.

It sometimes seems that the larger the business the more enlightened is its understanding of the integrity of the news as a channel to public opinion. It is the giant industry with branches all over the country that has learned to respect the entirety, the wholeness, of news. An explosion in one of its plants is a signal for a telephone call to the local city editor to send reporters and photographers to get, unhindered, all the facts. A company facing indictment under the anti-trust laws immediately posts notices on the bulletin boards of all its plants to tell employees in non-legal language just what an anti-trust suit is. The newspaper has developed no effective substitute for such procedures.

Because experienced and skillful newspapermen acquire and retain the choice spots in public relations it is not to be wondered at that the journalistic functions the ex-newsman performs are likely to be meticulous, sound, and craftsmanlike. His reporting must be accurate or he may be sharply taken to task by the medium he wants most to reach, the daily newspaper. If he has overlooked suspect and it will likely land in the city editor's wastebasket. To influence public opinion he must be convincing.

Against these attributes we can easily find newspaper performances that are sadly wanting in accuracy, through indifference or carelessness; details that are easily available but do not fit within the space deemed sufficient for the story; a common neglect to follow up a continuing story; and, in editorial-page performance, a job considered done when opinion has been expressed, no matter how equivocal and how lacking in concern for the effectiveness of the paper's persuasive and hortatory functions. The public relations man who cannot shape opinion loses his job; the editorial writer starts another editorial.

It is to be regretted that editors have permitted their attitude toward public relations to have become so clouded, for there is no business which has greater need details, his whole story, whether prepared or verbal, is of improved public relations than the American newspaper. The pity is the greater since there is almost no field of endeavor which operates in such intimate contact with the public or is so desperately dependent upon its good opinion. The press has been either completely mute or ineffective against such denigration as that to which it was subjected by Franklin Roosevelt; its only reply was to attack Roosevelt, rather than to examine the justice or injustice of the charges. This produced a fashion in press-baiting that has not ceased. The reaction was identical when Adlai Stevenson casually referred to the "one-party press." The salt would not smart so badly had there been no deserved open wounds to find. Again the counterattack merely spread the charges among many who were perfectly willing to believe it.

The press has its experts: typographical wizards who know exactly where the reader's eye first falls upon the page; pollsters who know the ratio between those who are attracted by leg-art and those who read editorials; circulation scholars who know how to buy new subscribers; and promoters who can find new sources of revenues.

As it should, the press believes in advertising and will spend money to advance the fictions of its infallibility, of the omniscience of its reporters, and of the far-reaching outposts of its influence. The press believes in these things and thus fulfills an important condition of effective advertising. But advertising by itself, as certainly every publisher should know, is not the first step toward public favor and respect. It begins with the product.

The problem probably is not one to be solved by advertising, the frontier at which countinghouse vision stops. The real difficulty is that people do not understand what newspapers are for; their mission; their responsibilities; what newspapers have already done for the public besides giving junior a shiny bike for a certain number of new subscribers.

And if this diagnosis is correct, we must ask: Do publishers and editors know what the mission of a newspaper is? Do they know what it was born to do, can do, and has done, or are their eyes blinded by the single obsession of staying in business? Is the mission of the press so mysterious and pentecostal that we ask respect for its hallowed name even after its tongues of flame have burned low?

Newspapers, in the main, either despise "public relations" or overdo it — by proclaiming their own automatic virtues. They might, instead, learn from some of the better PR men. Instead of abandoning their migrating purpose, personnel, and readers, they should fight to recapture them. And instead of fighting their critics, they should join 'em.

19

JOURNALISM

AND THE

ENGLISH LANGUAGE

IN AN AGE WHEN THE THREAT OF extinction facing mankind is scarcely less appalling than the deliberate corruption of human understanding by means of propaganda, it is dismaying to find scholars enlisting themselves in a cold war against honest, communicative language. Scientists are determined not to be understood and describe their research in a more opaque argot than that of bureaucratic directives; educators demonstrate their erudition by the use of an invented academic patois. They war upon clarity and simplicity because they are ashamed of nakedness — of the disrobing power of simple language to expose their mental processes. They shrink from journalism; they hate newspapers, except, perhaps, the New York *Times*.

In totting up the demerits of newspapers, we must here counterbalance their liabilities with their old-fashioned virtue, in textual matter if not always in headlines, of defending the integrity of the language. The greatest official libel that ever found its way between the covers of a book was the definition in Webster's dictionary of the word *journalese* previously quoted. Let me remind the reader: "English of a style featured by the use of colloquialisms, superficiality of thought and reasoning, clever or sensational presentation of material and evidence of haste in composition, considered characteristic of newspaper writing."

We are approaching the end of an era. Each of the periods of our language has lasted four hundred to six hundred years: Old English, roughly from 500 to 1100; Middle English from 1100 to 1500. Modern English has now had its four hundred years and a little more. Maybe time is up. Evidence could be cited in the development of radio and television, with their oral journalism, and the growing emphasis upon visual aids. The language is rapidly being vocalized.

The press, including all printed matter, is the last bulwark of the English language. As, more and more, communication, education, and journalism become oral and visual, the printed word disintegrates or is corrupted by indifference and vocal abuse. Language structure is undermined and verbal precision is blunted. Were this merely the vernacular rearing its head it might be easier to accept although just as difficult to combat. The matter is more serious. The fact is, many teachers and educators on the college level are not only unconcerned but are guilty of abetting this corrosive process.

The educators are entitled to their "in-group" talk just as are other specialists. It is the lingo of the "club," exclusively understood and possessively used. But the matter does not stop there. Educators bend words to new purposes which they think they have invented, blithely turning their backs upon excellent, sharp-edged and time-tried words whose meaning is clear. The psychologists are the worst offenders. Their textbooks are peppered with such bloated words as *conceptualize, privatization, objectify, maximize,* just as business men never finish anything but finalize it — including the language. The psychologists prefer *schema* to *scheme,* which means the same thing. They see "value constellations."

Scientists, historians, and engineers help in bastardizing the language. For them the primary techniques of grammar and spelling are unworthy of notice. There is instead concern for a syntax that is impressive rather than communicative. The college sound is to be achieved by interlarding Macaulayan periods with such suet as *essentially, primarily, substantially, in the last analysis,* and the long-leaping cadence — square pegs in the round holes of meaning.

The vast forces of business and of government are embarked, too, on a full-scale assault upon literacy: business because it has found that its elementary decisions can be made to seem intricate, communicable in a push-button assembly of clichés; and government because it is staffed by numerous public servants who think it their job to prevent the public from finding out what the government is up to at the moment.

That wonderfully expressive word "gobbledygook" had to be invented to cover a situation which arose at a time when, in the early Roosevelt days, government was being run by large numbers of displaced college professors. The coining of the word proved how splendidly malleable the English language is; just as it encloses the most magnificent literary treasures, it is also the repository of the most vivid, trenchant, and useful slang around which the tongue of man can wrap itself.

Obscurantism in the arts has been with us a long time. We have grown accustomed to it. In fact, a fairly broad public has joined in the hide-and-seek game that some creative artists are playing among the trees of a forest as purposely savage and dark as that which Dante enters in the first canto of *The Divine Comedy*.

It is still not difficult to find bad writing in newspapers; it never will be long as they must be produced in a hurry. But, by and large, newspapers today are using the printed word in its most understandable form and thus are among the last defenders of literacy. Books and magazines must, of course, be given their due, but the literacy of most depends upon the individual writer's integrity and ability. The book and magazine industry has sponsored no united front against corrosive influences and there are, of course, obscurantists among novelists, poets, and magazine people.

I know of no discipline which has during recent decades devoted such earnest and continuing study and research to the writing of communicable English as the newspapers and the journalism schools. They are fighting hard against the inroads of intellectual illiteracy. The problem has been the subject of countless seminars, such as those at the American Press Institute at Columbia, in journalism schools throughout the country, and in national and regional meetings of editors. The journalism schools cannot take time to teach the elements of English. Yet they cannot permit their graduates to look for jobs without them.

If we are going to permit the language to become completely oralized, it is useful to remember that spoken language has in the past triumphed over the written word. The Anglo-Saxon tongue was preserved for several hundred years by people who neither read nor wrote, while their masters were communicating in Latin and later in French. Both of these admixtures greatly enriched English, without greatly diluting its Anglo-Saxon bloodstream.

But there you have it: as men speak so they eventually come to write. And that thought is likely to cause a shudder among people who respect clean, sweet writing.

The English language does not vocalize well. It is a drab monotone, without melody. But what a luster it has on the printed page!

Scholars distinguish between substance and means and there is no question that they should be concerned with substance. But there is great danger in neglecting the means. If the medium is lacking in clarity and precision, the substance will decay. The beauty and essence of good writing presupposes clear thinking and without clear thinking there can be no teaching worthy of the name, whatever the subject.

Newspapermen haven't all the answers and the pressures under which they work often produce results that are far from admirable, but they know what they are up to and do not intend to be deflected in their objective of finding the most direct line to the reader's mind. Over the country copyreaders who know English grammar, daily bending their backs over news copy, continue to wear out more dictionaries than students and teachers. They may miss some of the blemishes but their objective is decent English. Managing editors take time to write and circulate staff memoranda concerned with improved, literate performance. Conventions of editors are preoccupied with writing as writing. Direct, understandable communication *is the substance* of journalism.

The newspaperman has no occasion to write any other way than simply. He has nothing to hide. If he is in possession of the facts, he has only to marshal them in orderly fashion. He is trained to see and report news and once he has done that his mental problem is solved. Muddy writing comes from muddy thinking — nothing else. If the reporter does not mix his opinions with the news there is little chance of his getting mixed up in his thinking.

The trouble comes in other departments of the paper: in interpretive writing among the columnists, the editorial writers, the reviewers and analysts. Their job is to express opinion, and unless they think clearly, the prose will be clouded. It often is. Helping to cloud his thought is the writer's feeling that he must write "up," be strenuously lofty. This is singularly true of the critic, but common also in the columnist and the editorial writer. It is one reason, also, for the obscurity of professional language. Scholars who thus offend are too much concerned with demonstrating their arcane superiority, which they, like the critics, seek to prove even before it is questioned. What they say and what they write must sound important, brainy, cryptic. That is the reason for their allergy to "journalese." News writing is transparent; and they call it oversimplified. It is direct; and they call it childish. It is usually correctly spelled; but spelling is arbitrary and therefore unimportant. The transparency of newspaper English exposes the man who does not know grammar. Its simplicity unclothes the brain where no thinking is in progress.

In the newspaper offices of the country are men — editors, copyreaders, rewrite men — who are defending the English language for its own sake.

Lord Conesford has written: "There are three good reasons why we should fight for our language: the need for clarity of thought; the need to be understood; and the duty to enrich and not injure the noblest language and the richest literary heritage in the world."

20

THE

RELIEF

CORPS

ONE BRIGHT MORNING IN JUNE, 1959, A PARTY of four talent scouts from one of the biggest metropolitan newspapers in the Middle West arrived at the campus of the University of Michigan and headed for the journalism department. An assistant managing editor represented the news room, a second executive was an envoy of the advertising office, and the other two spoke with authority for both these and other branches of the business. They had also been to the Missouri School of Journalism. They interviewed men and women about to graduate and some of these got jobs.

About the same time a scouting party for a metropolitan newspaper in California looked around in the School of Business Administration, and I know of at least one graduate who got a job; he was taking, in addition to courses in his major interest, one or more courses in journalism. He is resolved to own a newspaper some day and I'm sure he will.

The director of an eastern journalism school once told a group of editors that it would scarcely pay them to look over the remaining crop at semester's end because "the good ones have already been snapped up by interviewers on the campus." The smart newspapers are on the job. These happen to be the big newspapers; the journalism graduates are getting their chances at the top level. And there are not enough graduates to go around.

Other publishers and editors who complain that journalism students are going into public relations, broadcasting, and advertising do not seem to realize that many of these students could be interested in newspaper careers, if there was anyone around to convince them.

The editor who is waiting for just the right bright young man to walk into his office will finally get to see only the candidate who could not quite make the grade in public relations, broadcasting, or advertising. Too many salesmen for city room careers are at home rocking in their swivel chairs and editing their papers in the best traditions of 1900, unaware that the appeal which drew them to daily journalism has migrated to other offices.

The prejudice against journalism schools goes back to their very founding. Perhaps it arose because until recently, relatively few of either the most notorious or as the most distinguished newspapermen had gone to college. Their education began in early years on pavement beats, badgering politicians and city hall understrappers, outwitting policemen, and picking up tips with the free lunch in saloons. Their graduate studies were in the editor's chair, where they cultivated a tiger's thirst for the hot blood of circulation, and where the ethics of the scoop began just after piracy left off. They came to know more in some respects about human foibles and motivations than the psychiatrists; their knowledge of law was sufficiently pragmatic to show them where it would bend; geography ended at the newspaper's circulation frontier; and they were too preoccupied with the history of current politics to be concerned with a larger view. Many cultivated gastric and metabolic gifts to the point of virtuosity. They were suspicious of the whole breed of professors. When the academicians addressed themselves to journalism the cold war was on.

Editors generally directed withering blasts at the schools of journalism and their product with the declaration that they were "trade schools," teaching "techniques" — headline writing, photo-cropping, page make-up, and a glossary of phony argot that was never heard by deskmen or printers. The editors would be pleased to teach their own techniques, thank you.

They were sure of themselves because the proof of the trade-school approach was all there, chapter and verse, in the journalism textbooks. Besides they knew that many of the journalism faculty members had spent the most fleeting apprenticeships, if any, in practical newspaper-making. In too many instances it was impossible for the professors to conceal their highly theoretical connection with the business. That settled it; a great many editors decided they would have little or none of the schools' issue. Not willing to go on record in opposition to college education as such, they cried instead for "the liberal arts man." This slogan, though somewhat shopworn, is still heard among the die-hards.

The truth is that today editors know as little about what is being taught in journalism schools as the original, and some present-day, curriculum builders know about news-room procedures. The greatest gain, however, has been for liberal arts colleges, chiefly because journalism educators discovered, long before the editors did, that a heavy accent on the liberal arts was right for the aspiring reporter. They go even further, broadening requirements beyond the area of the social sciences and humanities. They appreciated the importance of at least rudimentary training in the the natural sciences even before the editors, along with everybody else, where thrown into hysteria by Sputnik.

Comes the dawn dragging, for the editors. Now, more are alert and are giving the campus crop an appraising look. Perhaps the credit goes to publishers — and certainly they have need of any credit they can get for what is *right* with the business. Many have seen that the rush is on, and those managing editors who sit at their desks waiting for job applicants are accosted largely by the leftovers.

To a high degree the journalism graduate is making good. He is, if one may try to get a little more milage out of the word, dedicated; equipped almost as far as college can equip him. But just as newspapers are chronically weak in the follow-up of news stories, so also are they neglecting to follow up the academic preparation of their recruits. They have forgotten their assertive *"we'll-teach-the-techniques."* Ask any managing editor about his training program and he'll answer: "Yes, we have a training program." Press the question. "How does it work?"

"Well, we just train 'em."

"Who does?"

"The city editor — when he has the time. But you've got to realize that the modern city editor has a lot of obligations that the old-timer didn't have. But we — well, we train 'em."

"Anything on paper?"

"No — it's not formalized."

There it is. The training and attention that the new man gets is no training at all or very slight. The novice is "coached" by anyone around the plant who thinks the young man can be hazed and taken advantage of.

He is usually flattered if the book editor offers him a first novel to review. The city editor — or even the managing editor — is not above sending young Greeley out for a sandwich, reasoning that the kid's time doesn't cost the company as much as the executive's. That isn't in the long run quite true, but newspaper executives aren't the only ones with rubber consciences.

Any newspaper that hires a college-trained man — many recruits have master's degrees — should in fairness to itself and in the name of simple efficiency set up a curriculum on paper, with a supervisor assigned to carrying out the plan. This should include required — and optional — reading on organization practices and background; the history of the city and its social complexion. It should provide for assignments, helpful criticism, testing, and variety. A newspaperman who never worked in the circulation department cannot appreciate what a deadline is. He may be able to tell time and know that by 11:24 he must have finished his last take of copy to catch an early edition, but he doesn't know why. He will know why only when he has sat with the truck driver and seen him fight traffic, observing all the red lights and traffic laws. He will know what it means for a route man to cover a 140-mile circuit dropping "singles" in each tube along the highway. He will know the added pressure a seventy-two-page paper means when he sees an undersized school boy wrestling with sixty copies. This is only a part of his indoctrination. Some of the best reporters I know began in the circulation department.

Our young reporter will probably never war unthinkingly with the advertising department if he accompanies an advertising solicitor on his rounds for a few weeks and begins to realize that here is a reporter for one of the most important news areas within the paper's scope — the market-place. He will come to realize that Thursday afternoon's and Friday morning's food advertisements have a higher readership than comic continuities. If he considers newspapers a service he will realize that they also serve who sell advertising space.

If he thinks he knows something about news photography he'll know a lot more when he interns in the photo-engraving room and learns the difference between a sixty- and an eighty-screen photo-engraving, or what is meant by mat shrinkage in stereotyping. He will learn the composition of the press blanket and the functioning of the composing-room machinery. If this does nothing else for him than win the respect of composing-room personnel it will be worth his and the paper's time. Sooner or later, he will be sent there for make-up purposes.

These excursions are merely supplementary. His news-room training should be supervised by a man whose business is supervision. From him, the cub will learn newspaper style, the cultural climate of the city, the political traditions, the geography, the history. He will become familiar with all the local source books, the newspaper's library, and the scope of the "morgue." If he spends one, two, or even three weeks in each of the other departments of the paper he should then spend at least ten or twelve in the news department. No productive work should be expected of him during this period. If he writes a usable story, well and good, but that is not yet his function.

This may take half a year but when he is through he is ready to go to work to the profit of his paper. (Even then he is hardly through.) Unless something like a reciprocal training program of this kind is instituted there is no bridge between the candidate's academic start and his ultimate professional usefulness.

Many of the remaining daily newspapers today are being skippered by men who, if they were to seek a position today with no more equipment than they had when they got their first jobs, could not compete with the journalism graduates of the 1960's. Hiring me today, with only the qualifications I had when I walked into the office of the Davenport *Democrat* in May, 1916, would clearly prove that the managing editor was off his rocker.

Newspapers did not pay much in those days but a city editor was often indulgent toward anyone mad enough to go to work for him. He was fully aware that the experience was worth a good deal, and if he happened to be one like the late Hugh Harrison, who didn't go to luncheon clubs, he took time to teach the novice. He also knew that he could fire the impossible one in a hurry. Today, hiring a man is a serious, costly commitment. There is little room for gamble. The hiring editor expects at least an educated man or an educated woman — educated in the principles of intelligible writing and the bare necessities of grammar and spelling. These qualifications the young man who quit after high school once had. Today he does not have them. College has scant time to teach him the rudiments; neither, certainly, has the city room. He or she must know English grammar, spelling, organized writing, direct, communicative discourse. A good many journalism graduates do know these things — but they are more and more self-taught.

Most journalism aspirants knew their own minds in their teens. They've fallen in love with language and its power. They fraternize with words and their meanings.

Not all journalism students are such dedicated beings, but neither are they all completely naive as to the pressing problems which the daily newspaper faces today. When first I met with some of them I felt, in the painful knowledge of what lay ahead, twinges of conscience as to whether they were ready for the realities of today's newspaper. Would they choose a career in journalism if they knew the extent of the compromise, the complacency, the commercialism, the neutralism that infect the daily press? I soon learned that these students were aware of the problems and of the conditions and that they were not to be dissuaded. They had decided upon their careers, not because journalism was profitable, or easy, or free from unpleasant tasks; not because the press was either courageous or heroic; not because it was a prestigeful or lucrative vocation, or because newspapers even deserved as much respect as the reading public gives them.

They believe, I have found, in the kind of journalism that the mind's eye has disclosed to them. They are committed to the difficult, better way; to the newspaper of the heart's desire. There is no evidence that journalism students are training to be the hacks of tomorrow. The hacks are still and always can be hired off the streets. The journalism schools that are not training their graduates to take hold of the reporting jobs, the executive jobs, the policy-making jobs of tomorrow have no right to exist. There is no warrant for the school that is merely training the journeyman reporter.

There is reform ahead — a reform that needs and will have revolutionary force. The effete and the aging are forever looking to the younger generation — where else is there to look? The relief corps happens not to believe in newspaper chains or newspaper monopoly; they have little use for the playpen journalism of comics and puzzles; they believe in news and seem determined to follow journalism whether the pursuit takes them into newspapers, magazines, electronic mediums, or the industrial press.

As there will always be an England, so there will always be newspapers. They never die — fade as they will — and, like soldiers, they brag about it.

APPENDIX I
WHAT'S IN THE NEWSPAPER

IT IS A RARE MANAGING EDITOR WHO thinks he has enough space in his paper. His daily cry is for More! Should he fortuitously, by a jump of two or four pages, get an unexpected windfall of a little more than he can conveniently use, it is likely to occur on a dull day and he is too discreet to complain. The squeeze will be on again tomorrow.

All non-revenue-producing space in the paper is charged to the news department, and even some paid space. He will receive from the business department a daily report on what he can expect — be it 90 columns or 140 — and the following day he will receive another statistical report on how much he actually got. Sometimes they are in fairly close agreement, unless a late, unscheduled advertisement has been accepted over the deadline. His paper will have a policy of fixing the minimum below which the news content should not be allowed to fall. This may be as low as 110 columns on a paper of a hundred thousand circulation; it may be as high as 135 or 140. One newspaper in this class measured as high as 160 columns of news for a 72-page paper.

The managing editor will scream at 110, because his news editor, the city editor, the state editor, and the sports editor are screaming at *him*. The woman's page editor will say nothing because, even if she has a great surplus of space which can only be filled by quick use of scissors and canned fashion releases or recipes, she cannot lend an impoverished department any of her space. The advertisers on her pages expect that the space they buy will be next to "women's" reading matter. In other words, her space allotment is revenue-related. It would be of no avail to tell the otherwise so canny advertiser that women read all the pages, including sports. If I were owner of a woman's specialty shop I would insist that my advertisement run on the obituary page, which has the heaviest reader traffic — as the phrase goes — among women, even over the food-fashions-furnishings features.

This inflexibility extends to other departments as well. Haberdashers ask for sports-page position and automobile dealers like that location also, ignoring the simple, demonstrable fact that many decisions about the clothes men buy, as well as their automobiles, are made by women. But of course everyone cannot have the obituary page; in fact, nobody wants it. And nobody seems to ask for the editorial page — the only one advertisers cannot have.

As the managing editor looks at the space report, and notes before filing it that his space ratio to advertising is thirty-five per cent as against sixty-five, he knows that he has a good professional home and is being well treated. Not a few papers are steadily dipping below these percentages in favor of advertising, but our man is reasonably content if his share doesn't get into the twenties. The editor of a monopoly newspaper in a good-sized eastern city told me recently that his space ratio was twenty per cent against eighty for the advertisers on a heavy business day.

It is a common complaint against prosperous evening newspapers that "there is too much advertising." Actually, by comparison with weekday morning papers, these afternoon dailies might be running more news but, distributed over seventy-two or eighty-four pages it doesn't show. It is also difficult to display the news effectively in so bulky a paper. While there is amusement at times about the bulk of Sunday papers nobody but the newsboy complains nor does anyone complain that there isn't enough news in them, despite the fact that few carry any news of "spontaneous origin" that wasn't in the Saturday afternoon papers.

What the managing editor too seldom does is to question how he is using the space available. In years of going to editorial conventions — working over every problem of the business, whipping frenziedly every dead horse that the news department has ever been astride — I have never heard the question raised as to what proportion of space in a well-run newspaper comics should be allowed to usurp.

That is merely an obvious and elementary question. There are many other parasites living on news space: other forms of entertainment, other space stealers representing a yielding to pressure. Promotional space grabbers. Pseudo-news that gets in under progressively elastic definitions of what constitutes news. If the managing editor ever sits down quietly in his corner to ask his conscience if he is making the best possible use of available space, he is very quiet indeed and has not taken anyone into his confidence. He knows that such a study must reveal that the publisher has particular friends, and causes, and pet features. One publisher I know would not think of beginning his day without first conning the astrology column to find out what last night's stars have in store.

Would there be travel pages if travel agencies and airlines didn't advertise? Would there be recipes in the paper if food advertisers didn't come in with a bang on Thursday afternoon and Friday morning? Would there be a stamp column or a dog column if there were no related revenue?

An evasive answer comes quickly and emphatically: recipes are read avidly and filed away by every housewife; travel copy has widespread appeal (although the advertisements are more deeply read for prices and schedules). And so on through all the ordinary and fantastic interests of man.

There is no dispute whatsoever. The question remains: shall it be in the paper just because it has readers and/or advertisers? Everything that people read is not news and that is the basic commodity newspapers have elected to purvey. It is what they are supposed to be made of and inescapably all this mass of canned copy is encroaching upon news content. Not the nose only, but the camel's hump is already under the tent and the editor's feet are out in the cold.

Perhaps no two people in journalism can ever get together on a definition of what is news. The question lies daily on the bargaining table in every news department in the land. Any yardstick used to measure hard news will be disputed. If a new hotel is built and the advertising department solicits all the contractor's suppliers, a special section appears devoted to this phenomenon and the nonadvertising columns are filled with descriptive and complimentary material relating to the project. A new building is news in anybody's city, but would there have been a special complimentary *section* if the suppliers had refused to buy space?

In 1959, graduate students in the Journalism Department of the University of Michigan undertook a study of the news content of several newspapers in the Middle West and a few farther away. A syllabus was worked out as a basis for classifying the various kinds of news and features occupying non-advertising space. Because there were inevitable differences of opinion, a beginning was made with a Trial Syllabus allowing for individual evaluations.

The dominant conclusion of the study was that about half the space allotted to the news departments of all the newspapers was taken up by reading matter and pictures other than "hard" news. ("Hard"news may be thought of in the Associated Press definition as "news of spontaneous origin.") It is difficult to classify the remainder except as (the natural follow-up) "soft" news — comics, puzzles, and every kind of divertissement — much of which is well read but by no stretch of the imagination can be thought of as informative news.

It was decided at the outset not to attempt a final, refined judgment about what is generally considered hard news, or to indulge in controversy about what reading matter is or is not to be so classified. For that reason the entire content of sports pages was classified as news, in spite of the fact that much of the reading matter of all sports pages actually is opinion, promotion, critical analysis, personality exploitation, and, in many instances, counsel (in the form of how-to-do-it). This may have been somewhat unfair to women's pages, real estate sections, travel sections, and many other departmental interests. There was also this determinant: today very few professional and college sports events occur in time to be reported in the afternoon papers. Their sports pages are therefore limited to speculative, evaluative material, personality columns, and a few news stories. A sharper definition would have eliminated a large part of the sports content from the hard news count.

Other departments with a similar character were analyzed as to content, spontaneous news being separated from counsel. For instance, a column telling how to play a bridge hand is counsel; a column giving the results of a bridge tournament is news. This extends to certain other local columns that contain congratulatory references and pictures of golden wedding anniversary couples. One column consisting entirely of a rewrite of a bank-issued pamphlet on the origin of money and its use through the ages could not, of course, be considered news.

It was difficult to classify pictures because this is an area where pressures build up to publish complimentary photos, the most obvious "set-ups," as well as photos involving the presentation of plaques or checks, committees of club women arranging teas and other nondescript matter which under only the most charitable construction could be called news.

Common sense judgments were used. If a sensible person could rationalize an item, picture, or promotion as NEWS it was so classified. The hard news category consequently contains much dross. Even so, the results should induce editors to re-evaluate the columns awarded them to fulfill the paramount obligation of keeping the public informed.*

* See complete syllabus, Appendix II.

THE FINDINGS †

In his study of the Manila *Bulletin,* Anden (see footnote) rejected such definitions as "News is what the city editor says is news," and "News is an account of an event which a newspaper prints in the belief that by so doing it will profit." Instead he adopted that of William S. Maulsby in his book *Getting the News:* "News is an accurate, unbiased account of the significant facts of a timely happening that is of interest to readers."

In the Manila *Bulletin,* the ratio over six days was 27 per cent advertising against 73 per cent "news." Hard news represented 51 per cent of the paper's over-all content and 22 per cent was non-news reading matter. It is of interest that Anden found nothing to be classified as revenue-related reading matter. Even a pink-page shipping section with its two-page business news insert, while carrying much advertising, printed nothing but hard news in the form of ship movements, cargoes, regulations, and other intelligence.

The Port Huron *Times-Herald* during the period studied ran 44 per cent news, 56 per cent advertising. The allotment of news space was shared 27 per cent for hard news and 17 per cent for reading matter otherwise described. Barnes found that

> the study demonstrates the difficulty of classifying pictures. Because of pressures to which a newspaper yields, pride of friends or cultivation of special interests, mug shots out of the morgue can scarcely be classified as news. Likewise, to avoid

† The group and the papers studied comprised: Tony Anden, Manila *Bulletin;* William E. O. Barnes, Port Huron (Michigan) *Times Herald;* William E. Bradford, Des Moines *Register;* Don Kaul, Lansing (Michigan) *State Journal;* Wono Lee, Bay City (Michigan) *Times;* Jack C. Neal, Kalamazoo (Michigan) *Gazette;* Karsten Prager, Ann Arbor (Michigan) *News;* Roy Reynolds, Macon (Georgia) *News.*

controversy, the content of business pages, sports pages and much of women's pages was rather arbitrarily classified as hard news, although much of this material might well be termed promotion or revenue-related.

The Des Moines *Register* was found almost to reverse the ratios of the other papers studied. This was "unusual, not to say amazing," Bradford commented in turning up a percentage of 58 for reading matter against 42 for advertising. He went on: The highest figure for advertising appearing in any of the week's issues was 51% while the low was 28.5%. . . . The Des Moines *Tribune*, which is the afternoon sister of the morning *Register*, had a slightly higher percentage for advertising for the same week: 48% for advertising against 52% for all reading matter."

The hard news content of the *Register* ranged from a high of 41.5 per cent to a low of 27 per cent.

The ratios varied greatly from day to day in the Lansing *State Journal*. Kaul says that

> revenue-related news ranged from a low of one column to a high of 21 — when a special supplement was published. . . . On Monday it carried no reviews while on Thursday there were three columns, mostly on television and movies. The paper published four and a half columns of civic promotion on Monday, and none two days later.
>
> The figures for the week show a ratio of a little less than two-to-one in favor of advertising over news; and that only half of the news department space was allotted to spot news.

In the Bay City *Times* it was found that for every column of hard news, slightly more than a column was published of reading matter otherwise described. The news to advertising ratio was 44 per cent to 56 per cent. Lee had no qualms about ruling out pictures of "handshaking, plaque-exhibiting, tea-pourings" and classified as illustrative art a photo ran with a St. Lawrence Seaway feature and a drawing of a calico pony in a "Junior Editor's Quiz."

Six editions of the Kalamazoo *Gazette* divided 62 per cent advertising and 38 per cent news. Of the 604 columns assigned to the news department, Neal classified 48 per cent as hard news and 52 per cent as "soft." He concluded that "announcements of women's club meetings are not news. . . . Members are not dependent on newspapers for this information."

The Ann Arbor *News*, which had been analyzed by all the graduate students first as a pilot study, consistently provided a relatively high news content. Separately analyzed by Prager during the week agreed upon, the ratio of news to advertising stood at 40 per cent to 60 per cent. Of the entire non-advertising content 64 per cent merited the description hard news and 36 per cent was distributed among other categories.

The Macon *News* ranged in size from 12 to 38 pages with news columns ranging from 24.4 columns (Monday) to 38.4 columns (Friday). The proportion of news space did not fluctuate appreciably in relationship to advertising. On Tuesday the advertising content hit a low of 59.2 columns with but 40.8 columns of news. On Thursday advertising hit a peak of 188.8 columns while the news content was well under 50 columns. The hard news content, Reynolds found, was slightly more than half as much as other reading matter, the percentage being 36 per cent to 64 per cent.

Even if every question were to be resolved generously in favor of classifying reading matter as news, the survey showed that the problem would remain. The managing editor must face the reality that he has limited space with which to fulfill the newspaper's function of giving its readers the news of the day. Perhaps it is sufficient. That is for him to decide, but he has no warrant to ask for more space, nor explain why any sort of legitimate news is crowded out, until he has conscientiously re-examined the forty columns of farrago dished up for readers in lieu of news.

He is not, of course, the boss, the circulation manager has a stake in comics, lucky bucks, prize puzzles, and other circulation bait. Similarly the advertising manager is expected to better his last year's figures, because costs are going up. The press room foreman and the mailing room superintendent want an earlier deadline because the production job requires it. If the managing editor wants a replate (the making over of an already-produced page) he is likely to find that there are other bosses just as close, or closer, to the publisher, than he is.

APPENDIX II
SUGGESTION TOWARD A SYLLABUS FOR USE IN STUDY OF NEWSPAPER CONTENT

EDITORIAL PAGE: Because the editorial page is traditionally the OPINION department of the newspaper, it is, in all cases, to be discounted as news content in its entirety. In many instances there are informative articles, advice, and feature stories on the page. There is news even in letters to the editor. But in this study the page is not analyzed for news because it still continues to be the organ of opinion, persuasion, advice, exhortation, explanation, and analysis. Where opinion columns are published among the news columns they are to be classified as OPINION OFF THE EDITORIAL PAGE, of which there is an ever-increasing quantity.

REVENUE-RELATED READING MATTER: This category soaks up news space like a sponge. It is not oversimplification to lump into this classification everything that would not be in the paper if there were not some advertising revenue, actual or hoped for, connected with it. This would rule out as news virtually all special sections.

Anyone who has been assigned the chore of getting out

such a section knows that he often works completely in the dark about how much space he has to fill. The size of the section depends upon the estimated response of potential advertisers to the salesmen's solicitations. If a content of sixty columns is scheduled, the "editor" knows that he need not be surprised if within a day or two of the deadline he is given a new estimate of forty-five columns. He may already have fifty columns in type (and this production will be charged against the news department) but that doesn't matter. The estimate may be further reduced. If on the other hand, it goes up there is a wild scramble for filler. Perhaps there will be no section at all and what business has been flushed will be poured into the regular paper. This overset hazard will have been foreseen by the "editor" who was careful to provide only copy that has no time element and can be fed unostentatiously into regular issues of the paper, if necessary. The type cannot be thrown away. When the reader finds a free-wheeling article among the foreign news on how to clean a kitchen ventiliating system he will know that a special section on household appliances was overset.

Under the heading of revenue-related reading matter will be found columns devoted to stamp collecting, the care and feeding of pets, garden "news," fish and game "news," and travel copy.

ENTERTAINMENT: This classification has made the most serious inroads on the news department's reservation. Somehow, entertainment has in recent decades been construed as a major function of the newspaper. Comics are probably responsible for this conviction. They may have had their day. Walter Lister, managing editor of the Philadelphia *Bulletin,* has described them as the "sick chicks" of the business. The reason for their continued encroachment may be circulation department pressure.

Here again, readership alone should not be the determinant. It does not require a survey to prove that people are hungry for games, puzzles, believe-it-or-nots, astrology and all the mish-mash that comes under Entertainment. The question is not: do people read it? The question is: is it NEWS?

Many papers devote a solid page to cartoon continuities and gag strips, telling themselves that their comic proportion is the page's eight columns against whatever the day's news hole may be. Editors forget the cartoon panels scattered through the classified-ad and other pages, which increase the "funny" cargo to ten or twelve columns instead of eight.

COUNSEL: People look for information and guidance from "experts" today on innumerable subjects: from Billy Graham on religion, the heart throb sisters on love problems, counselors on bridge, dogs, children, etiquette, and medicine. This is highly sought-after material but it adds nothing to the news content of the paper. Where a columnist actually digs up and presents news — which is rare enough — he can be classified as "news," but column advice on antiques, veterans' affairs, social security, insurance matters, and retirement problems are something else.

PICTURES: It is necessary to break down this category into smaller units. Newsphotos — clear depiction of an important event — are hard news. Ribbon cuttings, tea pourings, plaque presentations are not. Pictures used to pay off retiring employees, who might be better rewarded by a more substantial financial provision, don't qualify.

Other sub-classifications are: 1. PRESENTATION ART —

Checks change hands, demi-celebrities are greeted, women's committees meet to "plan," chairmen and their lieutenants line up for a new assault upon the pocketbooks of the citizenry as described. 2. MUG ART — The morgue (library) is full of one-column engravings of civic personalities. These cuts have been used countless times but each time the climber advances another stage on his road to local fame his picture is inflicted upon all the newspaper's readers. 3. PLUG ART — When the theater department runs a cut of Brigitte Bardot, or Marlon Brando, or the local theater manager, it is free advertising. 4. PROMOTION ART — This means art published in the interest of newspaper's circulation or advertising departments, or as publicity for staffers.

MECHANICAL AIDS: The flag or nameplate of the paper which appears on page one and on the first pages of other sections; the masthead of the editorial page folio; the date line which appears at the top of every page.

SHOPPING COLUMN: Nearly all papers have them. Girls make the rounds picking up linage at a premium rate to intersperse with helpful household hints or other bait presumed to add readership. Most managing editors do not know or have forgotten that this space is charged against the news department. In the same category are suburban "small ads." In the bedroom towns some of the advertisers prefer to see their announcements in with the news instead of in the classified department.

READER GUIDES: Any well-run newspaper organizes its content for convenient reader consumption — page one index, promotional guides to inside content, the church calendar, movie and television schedules.

MISCELLANEOUS: Recipes have high readership. Recipes are cut out and saved — sometimes treasured. But they are not NEWS. If a flour company prize of $25,000 is won by a local woman, that is news. But not a new recipe for sauerkraut à la mode or how to make false apple pie out of soda crackers.

CIVIC ENTERPRISE: Every newspaper devotes a relatively large amount of space to causes. It just can't afford to be outside the pale. The innumerable disease campaigns may contain news as teams are named, results reported, progress made. But by far the larger amount of space is given over to pure promotion, charitable in spirit but devoid of news value.

APPENDIX III

CODE OF ETHICS

OR

CANONS OF JOURNALISM

of the American Society

of Newspaper Editors

The primary function of newspapers is to communicate to the human race what its members do, feel and think. Journalism, therefore, demands of its practitioners the widest range of intelligence, or knowledge, and of experience, as well as natural and trained powers of observation and reasoning. To its opportunities as a chronicle are indissolubly linked its obligations as teacher and interpreter.

To the end of finding some means of codifying sound practice and just aspirations of American journalism, these canons are set forth:

I

Responsibility — The right of a newspaper to attract and hold readers is restricted to nothing but considerations of public welfare. The use a newspaper makes of the share of public attention it gains serves to determine its sense of responsibility, which it shares with every member of its staff. A journalist who uses his power for any selfish or otherwise unworthy purpose is faithless to a high trust.

II

Freedom of the Press — Freedom of the press is to be guarded as a vital right of mankind. It is the unquestionable right to discuss whatever is not explicitly forbidden by law, including the wisdom of any restrictive statute.

III

Independence — Freedom from all obligations except that of fidelity to the public interest is vital.

1. Promotion of any private interest contrary to the general welfare, for whatever reason, is not compatible with honest journalism. So-called news communications from private sources should not be published without public notice of their source or else substantiation of their claims to value as news, both in from and substance.

2. Partisanship, in editorial comment which knowingly departs from the truth, does violence to the best spirit of American journalism; in the news columns it is subversive of a fundamental principle of the profession.

IV

Sincerity, Truthfulness, Accuracy — Good faith with the reader is the foundation of all journalism worthy of the name.

1. By every consideration of good faith a newspaper is constrained to be truthful. It is not to be excused for lack of thoroughness or accuracy within its control, or failure to obtain command of these essential qualities.

2. Headlines should be fully warranted by the contents of the articles which they surmount.

V

Impartiality — Sound practice makes clear distinction

between news reports and expressions of opinion. News reports should be free from opinion or bias of any kind.

This rule does not apply to special articles unmistakably devoted to advocacy or characterized by a signature authorizing the writer's own conclusions and interpretation.

VI

Fair play — A newspaper should not publish unofficial charges affecting reputation or moral character without opportunity given to the accused to be heard; right practice demands the giving of such opportunity in all cases of serious accusation outside judicial proceedings.

1. A newspaper should not invade private rights or feeling without sure warrant of public right as distinguished from public curiosity.

2. It is the privilege, as it is the duty, of a newspaper to make prompt and complete correction of its own serious mistakes of fact or opinion, whatever their origin.

VII

Decency — A newspaper cannot escape conviction of insincerity if while professing high moral purpose it supplies incentives to base conduct, such as are to be found in details of crime and vice, publication of which is not demonstrably for the general good. Lacking authority to enforce its canons, the journalism here represented can but express the hope that deliberate pandering to vicious instincts will encounter effective public disapproval or yield to the influence of a preponderant professional condemnation.

INDEX

Abbot, Willis J., for ASNE code, 55
Abraham bargains for the righteous in Sodom, 61
Acme pictures taken over by UP, 97
Adams, Franklin P., 187
Adams, Walter, co-author "Monopoly in America," 115
Advertiser, Montgomery, Ala., 32
Advertising-news ratio, 22
Aetna Life Ins. Co.: affronted by scandal sheet, 85; site of Wadsworth house, 94
"Afghanistanism" (Jenkin Lloyd Jones), 64
Afternoon dailies, 23
Ahlgren, Frank, 145
Alpert, Hollis: a coda for his review, 195; movie critic, 194
American Association for the Advancement of Science, 99
American Bar Association: Smith Act, 15; Warren resigns from, 150
American Editor, The: founded, 100; quotes W. R. Mathews, 153
American Legion, pressure from, 47
American Newspaper Guild president addresses ASNE, 38
American Newspaper Publishers' Association, 38: like opposing education, 129; W. Loeb non-member, 125
American press is parochial, 20
American Press Institute: co-chairman Reese is quoted, 222; seminars for good English, 248
American Society of Newspaper Editors, 14: amendment voted, 56; code of ethics, 281; "conceived . . . in irritation," 44; hears integration report, 33; its integrity committee, 42; invites critical speakers, 37; Krock, Arthur, comments, 53; represents best press, 38; Sulzberger explains, 103; Wallace, Tom, predicts, 54
Anden, Tony, in student survey, 267
Anderson, Paul Y., interviewer, 223
Andrews, Roland F., swashbuckler, 95
Anglo-Saxon tongue, 248
Antigone, reviewing problem, 192
Arizona Republic & Phoenix *Gazette,* use of texts, 145
Arizona Star, Tucson, editor comments on use of travel, 153
Art of Asking Questions, book is quoted, 220

Ashmore, Harry, quoted on text use, 145
Asquith, Lady, interviewed by PYA, 223
Associated Press: accuracy of report, 150; AP New England group, 100; assessments classified, 132; Bar Association coverage, 149; comic strips, 136; content study, 38; Continuing Study, 140; co-operative nature, 133; counsel John W. Davis, 55; editors' reliance on AP, 142; entertainment and features, 135; founding of APME, 137; Hazen case, 138; McCarthy bias debated, 139; members file news, 134; "papers of record," 145; premature war's end, 131; report on bishop's trial, 159; science reporters, 228; text of speech refused, 144; underbids on picture wire, 97; use of texts, 143; world's greatest, 130
Associated Press Managing Editors' Association: committee reports, 38; convention trip cancelled, 99; end of objectivity, 62; founding by Kent Cooper, 137; hears prediction, 15; interpretive writing by APME, 142; "resemble . . . flagellantes," 37
Asylum Street newspaper site, 83
Asylum Hill aristocrats, 90, 94
Atlantic Monthly: article blocked, 99; influence of reviewing, 178
Atomic Energy Commission, genetics, 160
Attribution, excessive use of, 211
Atwood, M. V., 5 points before ASNE, 55
Aviation Week, quoted on crash, 31

Baraboo, train travel to, 239
Barber of Seville, V. Thomson comments on interpretation, 171
Barnes, William E. O., content study, 267
Beale, William L., on filing texts, 143
Beebe, George, on Q. and A., 146
Beethoven, as entertainment, 192
Bell *News,* house organ, 239
Bellamy, Paul: asks committee discharge, 43; on critics of press, 42; for ethics amendment, 56
Beloit, Wisconsin, two dailies in, 239
Bennetts, personal journalism, 70
Bent, Silas, as critic of press, 44
Berenson, Bernard, maturity and age,

Berger, Meyer, not filed for AP, 134
Berlin, President speaks on, 14
Berlioz, Hector: composers as writers, 193; as a critic, 171
Bermuda liner, Morro Castle follow-up, 31
Bernhard, Andrew, on public relations, 241
Bible, reprints on Christmas, 61
Bill of Rights, not for press alone, 18
Bingham, W. van D., *How to Interview*, 222
Birdsall, Daniel C.: capital of $10,000, 83; political scandal, 85; started paper, 82; threatened with prison, 86
Blade, Toledo; art editor comments, 183; Block defends monopoly, 114; editing political news, 120
Blakeslee, Alton, science writer, 228
Blakeslee, Howard W., AP expert, 228
Block, Paul, Jr., 114: in Niemann reports, 119; uniformity in press, 117
Blosser, Raymond, on accuracy check, 212
Blücher at Waterloo, 26
Book-of-the-Month Club, 181
Boston, Old Editor visits, 79
Boston Symphony: a critical technique, 169; visiting orchestra, 168
Boy, 11, kills family, 28
Bowles, Samuel, editor's dilemma, 56
Brahms, a familiar, 148
Brickman, David, defends editor, 102
Brooklyn, a Gannett paper in, 95
Bruner, Louise, art editor, 183
Bryan, Wright, on printing texts, 144
Bradford, William E.: content study, 267; news-advertising ratio, 268
Bulkeley, Morgan G., "crowbar governor," 85
Bulletin of the American Society of Newspaper Editors: book club editor on critics, 181; comment on drama critics, 176; poll on color in newspapers, 110; quotation from, 45
Bulletin, Manila, analyzed for content, 267
Burr, Alfred E.: refuses to turn Whig, 92; silent on political scandal, 85; threatened by mob, 82
Burr, Willie O., remembers father's vigil, 82

Buster Brown, entertainment a press function, 108

Caine Mutiny Court-Martial, 159
Camp, John Spencer, conductor, 168
Canham, Erwin D.: *New Frontiers for Freedom*, 160; on interviewing, 224
Capp, Al, editorializing in comics, 38
Chamber of Commerce, pressure from, 47
Chandler, Norman, on fewer papers, 15
Chicago Art Institute, Picasso show, 184
Childs Restaurant, on diet, 124
Christian Science Monitor, 14: resolution of its president, 55; student and faculty readers, 47
Chronicle, Augusta, 139
Chronicle, San Francisco: foreign news, 156; its music and arts editor, 191
City News Association, 134
Citizen, The, Lima, Ohio, 128
Civil Aeronautics Bureau, 31
Civil Defense, indifference to, 66
Civil Liberties Union, 86
Civil War: Crane's story of, 27; newspaper opposes, 82; state of reporting, 40
Civic enterprise, space devoted to, 277
Clark, Charles Hopkins, 95
Clark, John M., on Hutchins Commission, 8
Cleveland, Sheppard: case reporting, 203; May art show, 184
Code of ethics of ASNE, 39; text of code, 281
Collins, Dr. Joseph, speaks at ASNE, 43
Color printing: editors comment, 110; run-of-paper, 108
Columbia University, 8
Columbus, urban uniformity, 74
Comet, Halley's, journalism at time of, 69
Commercial Appeal: book reviewing, 183; "paper of record," 145
Congress, Lincoln Day tribute, 15
Connesford, Lord, 250
Connecticut delegates in Chicago, 85
"Conning Tower," column of F.P.A., 187
Continuing Study of APME, 137; evaluation of, 140; how the committees work, 138
Content analysis of papers, 261

Cooper, Kent, organizer of APME, 137
"Copperhead sheet," 82
Courant, Hartford: Burr rejects offer, 93; editor goes to *Times,* 91; former-editor's widow, 168; friction on League of Nations issue, 95; "oldest paper ... in United States," 90; silent on scandal, 85
Courier-Journal of Louisville, book reviewing, 179
Counsel, in content analysis, 261
Cousins, Norman: addendum to movie review, 194; no loss of confidence, 195
Cowles, John, Sunday circulation loss, 147
Cowles papers, in Iowa and Minnesota, 119
Crane, Stephen, in war reporting, 27
Crop pickers in Italy, 155
Crouse, Russel, on drama reviewing, 176
"Crowbar governor" in Connecticut, 85
Crowley, Raymond, on reporting court trials, 146

Daily News, Chicago: in foreign field, 133; its news service abroad, 164
Daily News, Greensboro, book reviewing in, 183
Dana, Charles A., day of personal journalism, 70
Daniels, Jonathan, in rebuttal to Hutchins, 44
Dante, *Divine Comedy,* 248
Danville, Illinois, has Gannett paper, 95
Darrow, Clarence, before ASNE, 43
Davenport, Iowa, a novice critic in, 166
Davis, Evangeline, as book reviewer, 183
Davis, John W., counsel for AP, 55
Davis, Richard Harding, in tradition of, 95
Death of a Salesman, 186
Deland, Paul S.: training described, 224; "what the man said," 225
Democrat, Davenport: city editor assigns, 167; equipment when hired, 257; had no critic, 166
Demokrat, Der, German-language daily, 166; a second music review, 167
Detroit Art Institute's 13 suburban centers, 184

Dickinson, John, on Hutchins Commission, 8
Dispatch & Pioneer Press, St. Paul, 106
Dukas, Paul, his music entertains, 192
Dulles, Foster, editor with him in Korea, 154
Duluth paper has local autonomy, 106
Doubleday, publicity director writes, 177

Early, Robert, resolution on Hazen case, 139
Edison phonograph discs, 167
Editorial in *American Editor,* 100
Editorial page: in content analysis, 273; department of opinion, 58
Editor: and the community, 75; editor's isolation ends, 76
Editor & Publisher: art editor lectures copy desk, 183; prints Tripp letter, 101; replies to Tripp published, 102
Editors, U.S., British and French, 153
Einstein, Alfred, no need of big words, 170
Eisenhower: covering President's illness, 25; a reporter's competence, 26; text of speech omitted, 14
Ellington, Duke, on symphonic music, 191
Entertainment in newspapers, 274
Epstein, Jacob, historical adjustment, 197
Eroica, symphonic structure compared, 192
Esselburne, George H., book reviewing, 183
Evening News, Buffalo, book reviewing, 183
Evening Post, New York, its literary adjunct, 180
Exploring the World of Science, 216
Express, Lockhaven, Pa., its editor in Russia, 161
Eyerly, Frank, in Hutchins rebuttal, 44

Facsimile, experiments in Miami, 112
Fadiman, Clifton, "attracting" and "engaging," 209
Farson, Negley, as foreign correspondent, 164
Faulkner, William, girl reviewer's thesis, 182
Fifth Symphony, how many times

reviewed, 195
"Fifty Pieces," the symphonic repertory, 73
First Amendment: guarantee to the press, 18; other rights protected, 49
Flood story, reporting in Providence, 217
Flowers, Paul, on book reviewing, 183
Forrest, Nathan B., the "mostest," 26
Fourth Estate, industrial press, 240
Foreign news, parochialism, 20
Frankenstein, Alfred, reporter and critic, 191
Frederick the Great, critic's warrant, 166
Free and Responsible Press, Hutchins report, 8
Friendly, Alfred, on publishing texts, 145

Gannett, Frank E.: buys the Hartford *Times,* 90; no liquor advertising, 87; on local policy, 95; Senate investigation, 96
Gannett Newspapers: local harmony, 94; in a new locale, 91; the presidential bee, 96; sale of preferred stock, 93; Clifton Sherman comments, 92
Gas News, industrial press, 239
Gassett, Ortega y, on the common people, 69
Gazette, Arkansas, on using texts, 145
Gazette, Haverhill: encounters competition, 126; not an AP paper, 100; regional support for, 127
Gazette, Kalamazoo: in content study, 267; "hard," "soft" news ratio, 269
Gazette, Emporia, White buys paper, 81
Gazette, Mason City, use of color, 110
Geneva, President's firm stand, 14
Gilels, pianist acclaimed, 164
Gill, Sam, on asking questions, 221
Gillilan, Strickland, addresses ASNE, 43
Globe, Boston, a reporter writes, 102
Globe-Democrat, women reporters, 223
Gluck, few of his operas survive, 196
Gospel of St. Luke, reprinted at Christmas, 61

Government, local, and the people, 78
Graf, Max, comments on critics, 171
Graves, Col. Edward M., takes over paper, 84
Gray, Horace M., *Monopoly in America,* 115
Greek ideal: sculptures endure, 196; temples of Washington, 197
Greeley, a personal journalist, 70
Grogan, Frank, takes over *Telegram,* 86
Gross, Rebecca, reporting Moscow, 161
Group, no chain papers, 90
Grouchy, performance at Waterloo, 26
Guantanamo, Crane's reporting, 27
Gunn, Glen Dillard, a Chicago critic, 167
Gunther, John: book journalism, 158; on Chicago *Daily News* staff, 164

Hackett, Walter, describes Italian peasant, 155
Hall, Grover Cleveland, monitors press, 32
Hall, W. Earl, comments on color, 110
Hamilton and the kept press, 40
Hanscom, Leslie, as book reviewer, 177
Handel, his operas are dead, 196
Happy Hooligan, early comic strip, 108
Hardy, Thomas, clubwoman's favorite, 182
Harper's Magazine: article criticizes press, 42; influence of reviews, 178
Harrison, Walter M., amending ASNE by-laws, 54
Harrison, Hugh, city editor Davenport, 257
Hartford, local papers file for AP, 134
Hartford Philharmonic Orchestra, 168
Harned von Mauer, 166
Harris, Louis C., in the Hazen case, 139
Hartt College, its origin, 168
Hartt, Julius, old-school teacher, 168
Harvard University, 8; offers cultural courses, 184
Hauptmann, Bruno, reference to trial, 159
Haverhill, becomes two-paper town, 128

Hawley, Joseph R., editor of *Courant*, 85
Hawver, Walter, pressure on movie critic, 192
Hazen, Charles: critic of AP, 138; evidence of bias in news, 139
Hearst: and International, 130; personal journalism, 70; used chain for power, 87; and sensationalism, 131
Heath, William H.: organizer of NESNE, 99; an outspoken editor, 126
Hemphill Noyes, selling *Times* debentures, 91
Henderson, W. J., an old-time reviewer, 167
Herald, Miami: facsimile developed, 112; on printing texts, 146
Herald-Tribune, New York: its book reviewing, 177; critic Virgil Thomson, 170; of eastern papers, 14; FPA and "Conning Tower," 187
Hersey, John, his Hiroshima story, 219
Hiss, Alger, pursuit of evidence, 159
Hocking, William E., on Hutchins Commission, 8
Hoiles, Raymond C.: chain owner, 128; as a non-conformist, 129
Hold-up of $20,000 supposed, 29
Holmes, Oliver Wendell, 94
Hood, Maj., aids William Allen White, 81
Hooker, Thomas, founder of Hartford, 94
Hoover, chain papers in his day, 104
Hough, Henry Beetle, recalls Old Editor, 79
Houston, a typical U.S. city, 74
How to Interview, 222
Huneker, James G., as music critic, 167
Hunter College, 8
Hutchens, John, book reviewer, 177
Hutchins Commission: reception of the report, 42; study of press, 7
Hutchins, Robert M.: commission chairman, 8; a critical speaker, 38; manuscript shown, 45; second ASNE appearance, 44

Idlewild air crash, 31
Inquirer, Philadelphia, 206
Integrity Committee ASNE, 42-43
Institute for Social Research, 204; editorial reaction, 206; a four-year job, 207
to United Press, 137

International News Service, 130; sale
International Paper Co., 96
Ireland, feature story in green, 146
Isaacs, Norman, defends Hazen, 139
"Is the Chain a Menace to American Journalism?," 104
Italian Airlines crash, 31

Janesville, Wisc., travelers to, 239
Jason and the dragon's teeth, 137
Jefferson and the partisan press, 40
Johnson, Pyke: on book reviewing, 177; a secondary occupation, 178
Jones, Jenkin-Lloyd: "Afghanistanism," 64; "drowned in sea of choice," 37; "Gee-whiz journalism," 40; press self-critical, 36
Journal-Bulletin, Providence, 62; "floods happen to people," 217
Journal, Milwaukee: on book reviews, 179; on foreign news, 156; its own news service, 164
"Journalese" definitions, 46

Kansas," "What's the matter with, 82
Kaul, Don, content analysis, 268; in student survey, 267
Kefauver hearing, Q. and A. used, 146
Kerney, James, Jr., use of texts, 144
Khrushchev and culture rapprochement, 165
Knebel, Fletcher, on Eisenhower's illness, 25
Knickerbocker News, Albany, 192
Knight, John S., "eastern seaboard editors," 14
Knox, Frank, on chain newspapers, 104
Kobler, John, on Marland story, 31
Krehbiel, E. H.: as court reporter, 191; music critic, 167
Krock, Arthur, satirical article, 53

Ladies Home Journal, 202
LaGuardia, Fiorello, read comics, 16
Lake, Harley, & Welton, 216
Lang, Paul Henry, critic's qualifications, 193
Langley plunges into Potomac, 28
Laos crisis coverage, 157
Laro, Arthur, printing of texts, 145
Lasswell, Harold D., Hutchins Commission, 8
Laurence, William L., 228
Lazebnik, E. A., propaganda chief, 117
League of Nations, policy split, 95

Lebanon, old barn migrates, 94
Lee, Wono: analysis of content, 269; in student survey, 267
Levine, Irving R., 158
Lewes, George Henry, critic on sincerity, 170
Lewis, Anthony, Bar Association report, 150
Lewiston, Maine, man comments, 89
Liebling, A. J., speaker at ASNE, 38
Likert, Dr. Rensis, on news distortion, 204
Li'l Abner, a salty cartoon, 136
Lima, Ohio, two-paper town, 128
Lincoln: paper opposed him, 82; tribute by Sandburg, 15
Lindsay, Howard, on drama critics, 176
Little, Carl Victor, book reviewer, 177
Little Rock and objectivity, 34
"Local Autonomy," a Gannett policy, 91; local sentiment, 93; policy pursued, 96
Loeb, William: his non-conformity, 129; non-member of ANPA, 125
Long Island local crash coverage, 31
Look magazine, covering Eisenhower illness, 25
Lutheran bishop, his left thumb, 158

Macdonald, Kenneth: on "hard" news, 147; "the most salable commodity," 148
MacLeish, Archibald, Hutchins Commission, 8
Main Street, Hartford, newspaper scene, 83
"Main Street USSR," reader interest, 158
Malone, Ross L., comment on lawyers' action, 151
Manchester Guardian, Lincoln story, 15
Mansfield, Conn., murders, 28
Marlow, James, news analyst for AP, 143
Marland, Lyde, and Governor, 31
Martha's Vineyard, Old Editor in Boston, 79
Mason-Dixon line, desegregation, 32
Mass production and mass mind, 71
Masthead, NCEW publication, 64
Mathews, William R.: foreign news and war, 154; thinking in absolutes, 162, traveling editor, 153
Maude the Mule, an early comic, 108
Maulsby, William S., defining news, 267
Mayer, Dr. Nathan, early music critic, 167
McCarthy, Senator: the Hazen report, 139; hunt for bias, 138
McCormick, Col., and personal journalism, 70
McKnight, C. A., director, School News Report, 33
Mechanical aids, content analysis, 276
Meckstroth, J. A., publishing texts, 145
Mencken, H. L., as a critic, 191
Mendel, Moses, advises Frederick the Great, 166
Merriam, Charles E., Hutchins Commission, 8
Merriam Co., G. & C., 46
Metropolitan Opera, repertory comment, 171
Metropolitan Museum of Art, 184
Miami, convention city, 168
Miaskowsky, tempo of symphony, 193
Michigan Journalist, deletion from text, 99
Michigan, University of, a lecture, 99
Michaud, a French editor, 171
Mikkleson, Paul, AP executive, 163
Million Dollar Club, 168
Milwaukee, travelers to, 239
Minneapolis, urban uniformity, 74
Minneapolis Symphony, 167
Missouri School of Journalism, 251
Monopoly: Americans oppose it, 114; its economic power, 115; license and monopoly, 129
Monteverdi, his operas unperformed, 196
Montgomery, Harry, reader service, 145
"Moonlight Sonata," critic's competence, 169
Moore, B. V., 222
Morrell, Gov., aids W. A. White, 81
Morse, Charles J., publications manager, 239
Morro Castle, follow-up on disaster, 31
Mowrer, Edgar Ansell, foreign correspondent, 164
Mowrer, Paul Scott, foreign correspondent, 164
Mozart: the G Minor Symphony, 214; music composed for salon, 196; music known to masses, 148

Munsey, Frank, editorial on his death, 82
Murphy, Francis S.: local autonomy ends, 97; stays on for Gannett, 91
Musical Quarterly, 193

Napoleon and Grouchy, 26
Nashville, School News Service, 33
National Conference of Editorial Writers, 37; origin and purpose, 63
Neal, Jack C., in student survey, 267
News, Ann Arbor, 267; analysis of content, 269
News, Lima, Ohio, 128
News, Macon: analysis of content, 269; in student survey, 267
New England Society of Newspaper Editors, 100
"New Frontiers of Freedom," 160
New England, town bulletin board, 18
News & Observer, Raleigh: editor and AP, 15; in rebuttal to Hutchins, 44
Newsroom: clock and the deadline, 22; cost pressures, 24; news gathering day shortens, 23
New York and Long Beach, 106
New York Central, PR man speaks, 212
New Yorker magazine, 178; John Hersey's story, 219
Niebuhr, Reinhold, Hutchins Commission, 8
Ninth Symphony, what new to say, 195
Northcliffe, Lord, on expenditures, 86
Nutcracker Suite and the critic, 169

Objectivity, "the bitch goddess," 62
Ochs, Adolph S., heirs of, 103
Ohio State Journal, Columbus, 145
Oistrakh violinist acclaimed, 164
Oklahoman, Oklahoma City, 54
Omar, pot to the potter, 38
Ontario Hydro *News,* house organ, 239
Oregonian, Portland, 206
Outlook, critical article, 42

Paganini, a tour de force, 193
Palmer House, cabs waiting, 85
Paris conference table, 153
Parker, H. T., Boston critic, 167
Parsons, Margaret, Worcester critic, 183

Pasternack, cold war position, 165
Pastoral Symphony, program music, 192
Patriot-Ledger, Quincy, 156
Patten, David, and objectivity, 62
Payne, Stanley L., on asking questions, 220
Pentagon, AP classification, 132
Peoples' Gas Light, manager writes, 239
Pett, Saul, news analyst, 143
Philadelphia convention, Gannett candidate, 97
Phil *News,* house organ, 239
Pictures, in content analysis, 275
The Pit and the Pendulum, 22
Plain Dealer, Cleveland: cost of texts, 144; editor answers critics, 42
Plum, Senator, loan to W. A. White, 81
Poe, Edgar Alan, 22
Pogo, comic strip, 136
Politics reporting: city manager system, 231; depth of interest, 230
Pope, election of, 17
Post, Houston, publishing of texts, 145
Post, Washington: on book reviewing, 179; texts wanted, needed, 145
Post-Dispatch, St. Louis, 44: on book reviewing, 179; former executive writes, 222; on interviewing, 223; Q. and A. is dull, 146
Post-Gazette, Pittsburgh, 119; public relations comment, 241
Post Office Department, 50
Potomac, Langley's crash, 28
Prager, Karsten: on content analysis, 269; student survey, 267
Praxiteles, historical perspective, 197
Press, Houston, reviewer praised, 177
Prince, Albert I., on paper sale, 88
Proceedings of ASNE, 50
Productivity supervision, 204
Prudential, quoted by UP, 205; denial by company, 206
Pulitzer and personal journalism, 70

Queeg, *Caine Mutiny Court-Martial,* 159
Quill, article on house organs, 239
Quotidien, a Parisian daily, 171

Rachmaninoff, Sergei, provincial criticism, 169
Ragan, Sam, predicts fewer papers, 15

Raphael, critic and sincerity, 170
Reader guides, content analysis, 276
Red Badge of Courage, 27
Record & Journal, Meriden, 106
Redfield, Robert, Hutchins Commission, 8
Reese, Ben, interviewing technique, 222
Register & Tribune, Des Moines, 119: content analysis, 268; publisher warns, 147; in student survey, 267
Research in mechanical processes, 108
Religious News Service, 159
Reviewers of books, 176: Book-of-the-Month Club editor comments, 181; in national publications, 178; "in the provinces," 183; publishers' returns, 179; reporters assigned, 177; unfavorable review, 180; victims in rebuttal, 182
Reviewers of drama, 175
Reviewers of movies, 173
Reviewers of music, 172; question of competence, 173
Reynolds, Roy, student in survey, 267; content analysis, 268
Revenue-Related Reading Matter, 273
Richard III, 192
Ridder, Bernard H., communities differ, 106
Ridder brothers, 105
Right to know, 52
Right of privacy, 48; too little recognized, 49
Rinehart & Co., publishes follow-up, 31
Ripley, Arthur, 175
Robinson, Frederick B., 172
Rochester, N. Y., force of suggestions, 93; view of financing, 99
Roosevelt or Gannett?, 97
Rowse, Arthur E., 102
Russia and science reporting, 65
Ruml, Beardsley, Hutchins Commission, 8
Ryan, William, a news analyst, 143

Sampson, old-time editor, 79
Sandburg, Carl, delivers Lincoln tribute, 15
Santa Claus, editorial by F. P. Church, 60
Saturday Evening Post: its fiction, 17; journalistic report on Marlands, 31
Saturday Review: its book reviewing, 178; editor on movie review, 194; its newspaper origin, 180
Schlesinger, Arthur M., Hutchins Commission, 8
Schliemann, Dr., Troy excavations, 30
School of Business Administration, 251
Schmetterlingschlacht, 166
Schumann, Robert, composer as critic, 193
"Scoop," hopeless battle of the, 19
Seitz, Don, criticism of the press, 42
Senate, U. S., paper company investigation, 96
Sensationalism, geographical measure of, 232
Shaw, Bernard, as a critic, 193
Sheppard case and its headlines, 203
Shedd, Fred Fuller, asks ASNE vote, 56
Sherman, Clifton L.: announces paper sale, 89; resigns from the *Courant,* 95; stipulates democratic policy, 92; tests "local autonomy," 91
Sheehan, Vincent, foreign correspondent, 164
Shuster, George N., Hutchins Commission, 8
Shopping column, content analysis, 276
Sigma Delta Chi; "journalese" definition, 46; journalism graduates, 240; on public relations, 237
Slichter, Sumner H.: on competition, 123; on public's judgment, 124
Smith, Blanche Hixon, at London round-table, 106
Smith Act and Bar Association, 15
Sockman, Dr. Ralph W., before ASNE, 43
Sodom, bargaining for the righteous, 61
Sorcerer's Apprentice, 192
Southern School News Reporting Service, 33
South America, coverage by wire services, 133
Soviet Russia: beachhead of confidence, 60; uniformity of the press, 117
Spock, Dr. Benjamin, criticizes headline, 202
Springfield Museum of Fine Arts, 172
Sputnik: boosts science news coverage, 64; education made scapegoat, 229; hysteria caused by, 254; press unprepared for, 228

Spilman, Charles H., flood coverage, 217
Star, Kansas City, W. A. White worked there, 82
Star, Indianapolis, editor in Hazen case, 139
Star, St. Louis, woman reporter, 223
Star & Tribune, Minneapolis, 119: editor in rebuttal, 44; sponsors high school seminars, 157
State Journal, Lansing: content analysis, 267; news-advertising ratio, 268
St. Louis, urban uniformity, 74
St. Patrick's Day, page feature, 146
Sterling, Donald J., ASNE origin, 44
Steven, William, in ASNE debate, 44
Stevenson, Robert Louis, on volcano, 160
Stoneman, William, foreign correspondent, 164
Stowe, Leland, foreign correspondent, 164
Stratton, Lloyd, reads AP report, 140
Strauss, Richard, program music, 192
Strike, publication suspensions, 52
Sudermann, play in Davenport, 166
Sulzberger, Arthur Hays, on Chattanooga, 103
Sun, Baltimore, on criticism, 191
Sun, Binghamton, research report, 206
Sun-Times, Chicago, book reviews cited, 179
Supreme Court of U.S. and Bar Association, 15: in AP news reports, 133; lawyers critical, 150; Smith Act experience, 149
Sutherland, Halliday, on prejudice, 194
Swift *News*, a house organ, 239

Telephone *News*, house organ, 239
Times, Bay City: content analysis, 268; surveyed, 267
Times, Chattanooga, editorial policy, 103
Times, Geneva, New York, 110; foreign news policy, 156
Times, Hartford, and the AP, 144
Times, London, and its "leaders," 106
Times, Louisville, its editor at APME, 139
Times, New York: in foreign field, 133; full text of ABA, 151; its own wire service, 164; report on ABA meeting, 150
Times, Shreveport, the Hazen case, 138
Times, Trenton, texts of speeches, 144
Times-Herald, Port Huron, 267
Tokyo bureau, AP staff, 157
Toledo, monopoly situation, 119
Transit *News*, house organ, 239
Tripp letter in E. & P., 101
Tschaikowsky, symphonies known to all, 148
Tyerman, Donald, in the London *Times*, 106

"Uncle Joe," image of, 162
Union, San Diego, and foreign news, 156
Union-Leader, Manchester, N.H., 125
Union Theological Seminary, 8
United Press: in Haverhill, Mass., 100; its merger with INS, 130; on social research report, 205; story not supported, 206; takes over Acme, 97
United Press-International, 131: on ABA meeting, 149; comprehensive service, 132; meets extra requests, 133
United States leadership, 20; and the sputnik, 65
University of Chicago, 8
University of Michigan, 102: critical press, 206; Macdonald lecture, 147; productivity research, 204; talent scouts on campus, 251
University of Pennsylvania, 8
Unruh killings in N.J., 134

Van Cliburn, his success in Russia, 164
Vanguard service of AP, 163
Vieuxtemps' *Polonaise* recorded, 167
Virginian Pilot, Norfolk, 28
Voss, German city editor, 166

Wagner, Richard, as a critic, 193
Waldorf Astoria, AP annual meeting, 140
Wallace, Tom, urges ethics resolution, 54
Wall Street Journal, eastern editors, 14
War and Peace reviewed, 194
Warner, Mrs. Charles Dudley, 168
Warren, Chief Justice, resigns ABA, 150

Washington, ASNE meets, 38
Waterloo, Napoleon and Blücher, 26
Watson, Carrie, in Chicago, 85
"The Wayward Press," 38
Webster's, on "journalese," 245
Wellington at Waterloo, 26
Wells, Thomas B., editor of *Harper's*, 42
Wethersfield prison, 86
Whig, A. E. Burr asked to become, 93
White, William Allen, 81
Williams, George B.: on foreign news, 156; "forget color," 110

Wilson, Blake, sums up the press, 45
Wright, first powered flight, 28
World, New York, 42; FPA and "Conning Tower," 187
World-Telegram & Sun, New York, 177

Yale University, 8
Yellow Kid, earliest comic, 108
Yost, Caspar S., an ASNE founder, 44
Young, Leslie, news editor, 89